FIRST STEPS

A Guide to
Social
Research

MICHAEL DEL BALSO

ALAN D. LEWIS

Dawson College

I(T)P® International Thomson Publishing

The ITP logo is a trademark under licence

Published in 1997 by

I(T)P® Nelson

A division of Thomson Canada Limited
1120 Birchmount Road
Scarborough, Ontario M1K 5G4

Visit our Web site at http://www.nelson.com/nelson.html

Canadian Cataloguing in Publication Data
Del Balso, Michael, 1953-

   First steps : a guide to social research

Includes bibliographical references and index.
ISBN 0-17-604882-0

   1. Social sciences — Research.   I. Lewis,
Alan D. (Alan David), 1943-   II. Title.

H62.D44 1996   300'.72   C96-990107-0

Publisher and Team Leader	Michael Young
Acquisitions Editor	Charlotte Forbes
Production Editor	Marcia Miron
Project Editor	Evan Turner
Production Coordinator	Brad Horning
Art Director	Sylvia Vander Schee
Interior and Cover Design	Sylvia Vander Schee
Composition	Elaine Andrews, Zenaida Diores
Input Operator	June Reynolds

Printed and bound in Canada
   3 4 BG 00 99 98

Contents

Preface

Our interest in writing this book comes after several years of teaching college and university students in different social science disciplines and interdisciplinary programs (most recently at Dawson College and McGill University). We have found that the mere mention of "research methods" sets up negative expectations. Students expect to be bored or intimidated by the subject matter even before the course has begun. They see research methods as having to do with a lot of abstract concepts and possibly a lot of statistics. They expect research itself to be a rigid and mechanical application of rules and tools carried out by others, but which is of little interest or importance to them. Despite being generally interested in the results of social science research, students are less enthusiastic about learning how these results are obtained.

To overcome these problems

- we have written the book in a nontechnical and conversational style that encourages students to become actively involved in learning research methods rather than to see themselves as passive onlookers;
- we have used newspaper articles to illustrate concrete examples of the importance of social research. These readings, together with the boxes and exhibits, also serve to sustain the readers' interest;
- we have focused on contemporary Canadian examples wherever possible to emphasize the relevance and accessibility of the research that social scientists do;
- we have covered the major types of research methods used in all the social sciences, without focusing exclusively on any one discipline or discipline-based approach to research; and
- we begin each chapter with a social condition that arouses the readers' interest to find out how social research is relevant to their everyday life situations and helps them to understand the social world.

Many students correctly assume that they may never carry out social scientific research beyond the requirement of a course. However, they are likely to read about social research studies in the popular media, often in connection with issues that will affect their lives. Hence, the book is designed to show both that research is the reason why social sciences are so interesting and that it is important for all of us to learn about research methods so that we are at least critical consumers of research.

INSTRUCTOR'S MANUAL

We have prepared an Instructor's Manual (ISBN: 17-604923-1) to assist in the preparation of lectures, class discussions, and exams. The text and the manual reflect the view that learning about research should be an active process. Research methods make more sense for students when placed in the context of issues, debates, and concerns that lead to research. The manual includes

- hands-on exercises that give students a taste of the excitement of social research and in the process help them learn the concepts and techniques of social research;
- exercises that are focused on the newspaper articles, which can serve as class discussions and introduce the purpose and methods of social research;
- multiple choice questions that may be used as the basis for quizzes, exams, or class discussions;
- learning objectives that identify what the students should understand or be able to do after completing the chapter; and
- additional material that can be used in class lectures and discussions.

ACKNOWLEDGMENTS

The extent to which we have succeeded in any of our aims is due in no small part to the efforts of others who have encouraged our work along the way. First, thanks to our acquisitions editor, Charlotte Forbes, for recognizing the need for such a book, for encouraging us at various stages, and for providing helpful advice when most needed. To Fay Rogers we owe special thanks for so carefully and conscientiously reading different drafts of the entire book. We were very much encouraged and helped by our reviewers, Hans Bakker (University of Guelph), Susan H. Nelson (Malaspina University-College), Gary Parkinson (Douglas College), Sandra Ward (Champlain Regional College), and Jan Warnke (Champlain Regional College), and by our colleagues Susan Caldwell, Adele Carrier, and David Muhlstock, who read specific sections. Thanks also to Patrick Bolland (Montmorency College), who was involved in an earlier part of this project and helped shape the direction of the book. We are also grateful to Michael Rosenberg for his encouragement and for his practical suggestions. To our colleagues in the Dawson Social Science Program we extend our gratitude for their contributions to the stimulating collegial atmosphere that sustains us daily. We especially owe an enormous debt to our students, who have been remarkably patient with us over the years. A special thanks to Evan Turner and Heather Martin for making certain that the book was properly reviewed and organized. We are indebted to Tracy Bordian, Marcia Miron, and Chelsea Donaldson, as well as to the rest of the "team" at ITP Nelson for their contributions to the realization of this book. Finally, we dedicate this book to our families and thank them for their patience and for their constant reminders that there is more to life than what is on the computer screen.

Michael Del Balso
Alan D. Lewis
Dawson College

Why Know About Social Science Research?

WHAT YOU WILL LEARN

- what is particular about social research
- why carry out social research
- the rise of the social science disciplines
- the basic steps in carrying out social research

INTRODUCTION

Relaxing at an outside café on a warm sunny day your two friends, Robert and Jane, are each drinking their favourite brand of cola while you drink a glass of orange juice. At one point you embark on a discussion about the influence of television. You argue that people generally take the influence of television for granted. In support of your argument you point out that each friend is drinking a different brand of cola. "What does that have to do with the impact of television?" Robert asks. Jane adds, "I drink this brand because it tastes better." To this Robert answers that the brand he drinks tastes better. This leads you to ask whether they can actually distinguish between the taste of the two brands. They are amazed that you would even ask such a question. Both are convinced they can tell the difference. (Are they right? How can you find out?)

Robert notes that most workers at the café are students. He comments that student workers are usually less committed to their jobs than older, nonstudent workers. "What makes you say that?" you ask. He quickly points to an exchange between a student worker and a customer and notes that the student is neither friendly nor helpful. Jane quickly points to an exchange between another student worker and customer and notes that the exchange seems quite friendly. You point out that it is hard to tell whether they are students and note if they are students they probably give their job little importance. "After all they do not plan on doing this work all their lives." (Who is right? How can you find out who is or is not a student worker and whether the service given by workers of different backgrounds varies?)

Jane agrees and remarks that although students who work part time expect to find better jobs when they graduate, they perform poorly in their studies. She states, "Students who work part time have lower grades than those who do not work part time." You point out that you have held a part-time job for a long time and that it has not interfered with your studies. She answers that you may be the exception. You argue that most of the students you know who work part time pass their courses. There seems no end to the argument. (Who is right? How can you compare the academic performance of students who work part time with those who do not work part time?)

Robert adds that maybe it is best that students work part time. "They will at least have a job when they graduate." He wonders whether nowadays it is worth getting a university degree "with so many graduates looking for work." You argue that a university degree opens up more job opportunities. "Then why are so many university graduates having a hard time finding a decent job?" he responds. Jane notes that she read a newspaper article that claimed in the long run a university degree is worth the time and effort. She argues, "University graduates have better paying jobs, face lower unemployment rates, and do generally less physically demanding work. Robert disagrees. "Tell that to the university graduates who can find only hamburger-flipping jobs." (Who is right? How can you find out about the relationship between education and jobs?)

Throughout life we are confronted with questions about human nature and the social world. Is it worthwhile to get a university degree? Can we really distinguish between the taste of two different brands of cola? Are we influenced by television advertisements? Does holding a part-time job affect a student's academic performance? We attempt to answer our questions in various ways. Some questions seem trivial and we attribute little importance to the answers. Other questions concern our well-being, or hold a special interest for us, so we attribute particular importance to the answers.

To find answers we may consult an authority such as a parent, teacher, or someone we believe knows the answer. Or we may rely on sources such as books, newspapers, or television. Should we simply accept these answers? What should we do when two authorities disagree? What if there are no authorities to answer our questions?

Questions about human beings and their social world have been raised since antiquity. However, for countless generations the answers were based on superstition, intuition, and speculation. This has changed in the last two centuries or so with the development of a more systematic mode of inquiry. Intuition and speculation have given way increasingly to a scientific way of collecting verifiable facts. The result has been a remarkable expansion of our knowledge about ourselves and our social world that could never have been achieved through intuition and speculation. With the development of a scientific mode of inquiry there gradually emerged separated disciplines focused on studying human beings and their social world. Together these disciplines— anthropology, economics, history, political science, psychology, and sociology—make up the social sciences. They all rely on a logical, systematic approach to social research.

The social science disciplines are based on understanding the social world using the methods of science. This is not to say that "common-sense" explanations are entirely useless, but if we rely only on common sense we have no way of knowing whether or not our assumptions are correct. For centuries people believed it was "common sense" that the earth was flat or that the earth was the centre of the universe. Only when individuals raised questions about these cherished beliefs and started looking for verifiable evidence were these views eventually dismissed.

As in the past, today we often rely on common-sense knowledge in our everyday life. Common sense might tell us that people can distinguish between the taste of two brands of cola, or that students who work part time have lower grades than those who do not work part time, or that university graduates can find only "hamburger-flipping jobs." But science encourages us to look for verifiable evidence. It is not enough to depend on our common-sense notions. Instead, social research challenges us to scientifically study various aspects of human behaviour. Can people distinguish between the taste of two brands of cola? Do students who work part time have lower grades than those who do not? Are university graduates finding only low-paying, dead-end jobs? The social science disciplines have developed various methods to find answers to our questions. Social science encourages us to question our assumptions, look for evidence, and interpret and reinterpret the evidence.

Social science research—and scientific research in general—have become part of our daily life. The mass media are full of reports and debates about scientific research. Have crime rates increased in the

Youth Violence Exaggerated, Expert Says

ST. CATHARINES, ONT.— School violence is an urban myth fed by the media, politicians and, in some cases, teachers, says a University of Regina education professor who has studied youth crime statistics.

"Kids haven't gone to hell and schools are not unsafe," Rod Dolmage told a session of the Canadian Society for Studies in Education annual conference yesterday. "We need to be a great deal more critical about how we interpret what we see about reporting on youth crime." The session was part of the Learned Societies Congress, held at Brock University.

He cited Statistics Canada reports on youth crime, which show a 5-per-cent decrease in the number of incidents from 1993–94 to 1994–95, while the number of violent episodes dropped 2 per cent over the same period.

He also argued that statistics on youth crime can be used to convey different pictures of young people. For example, he said that the number of those aged 12 to 17 accused of murder rose

63 per cent from 1987 to 1992, but dropped 55 per cent if measured from 1975 to 1993, by Statistics Canada.

The contradictory statistics, he concluded, do not support a view of schools as hotbeds of violent activity.

"Violence is a problem in schools and we need to deal with it," he conceded. "But we should know what the facts are."

The media hype on school violence, he said, has encouraged a "safe-school industry" that leaves parents and students unjustifiably fearful. A spokesman for the Canadian Association for Safe Schools, a group founded by teacher unions and school trustees, could not be reached for comment.

Mr. Dolmage, an associate professor of education, said teachers also feed the myth of increased violence in schools because many are unhappy that they have to deal with students with behavioural problems who, increasingly, are integrated into the regular classroom. In the past, they were kept in segregated classes.

"It [the school violence issue] doesn't hurt teachers at negotiation time," Mr. Dolmage said.

But he also directed his criticism at politicians, who have adopted so-called zero tolerance as a high-profile, get-tough response that fails to address the source of students' violent behaviour. In recent years, school boards in Ontario and other jurisdictions have adopted policies that require acts of violence, even minor issues, to be reported to the police. In some cases, under zero-tolerance policies, students as young as 13 have been expelled from school.

"Zero-tolerance policies can produce results which would be laughable, if they were not so tragically foolish," he said, citing a 1995 incident in which a 13-year-old student with the York Region Board of Education in the Toronto area was suspended for five days. He had a paring knife to slice open a bagel that his mother had not thawed.

Mr. Dolmage said the solution to school violence lies in

early intervention for troubled youth and families by social service agencies, not schools. However, he noted that preventive measures are among the first to be cut by deficit-conscious provincial governments.

Irene MacDonald, another speaker at the session, said schools and teachers have to rethink their approach so that students understand there are consequences for physical and verbal incidents.

Ms. MacDonald, a doctoral student at the University of Alberta, cited research that she and colleague Jose da Costa conducted at five Alberta junior high schools that showed a "perception gap" between students and teachers on how schools deal with physical and verbal incidents.

In the survey, one third of students said they would never report violent behaviour, citing fear of reprisal, lack of teacher awareness and ineffective responses from the schools.

In this reading two researchers question some widespread views about schools and youth violence. What do they find wrong with the "urban myth" about violence in schools?

Source: Jennifer Levington, "Youth Violence Exaggerated, Expert Says," *The Globe and Mail* (5 June 1996) pp. A1, A5. Reprinted with permission.

past year? Is there a rise in the rate of high-school dropouts? Has the income gap between males and females narrowed in the past decade? Is the family falling apart? Despite the media exposure of the social sciences, and the close connection between social science research and our everyday concerns, social science does not seem to have the prestige of the physical and natural sciences (see Box 1.1). More importantly, what goes on behind the headlines—the research process itself—is not well known and understood.

Popular culture in the form of soap operas, films, comics, and books have shaped our image and understanding of science. We generally associate science and scientific research with the natural and physical sciences. The many Hollywood versions of *Frankenstein* give us an image of the scientist as an obsessive, driven person, whose only concern is to dominate and manipulate the forces of nature regardless of the consequences. Television and movie hospital dramas often present doctors as cold, unfeeling people who treat their patients impersonally and ignore the emotional and psychological experiences of their illnesses. Comics often present scientists as crazy or psychologically abnormal. Alongside these images of the scientist are depictions of test tubes, Bunsen burners, sparking electromagnetic devices, robots, and, of course, the computer.

Do any of these media images capture anything real about science? To some extent, yes, they do. The best reports on scientific research give us some sense of the kinds of questions that are of interest in various

BOX 1.1

Personal Judgment or Social Science?

The popular image of the social scientist is neither so impressive nor as clear as that of the natural scientist. The social sciences deal with the stuff of everyday life. Anyone can comment on, for example, teenage violence, health care, marital relationships, immigration, population growth, and the deficit. Not everyone can comment on why the sky is blue or what causes earthquakes. Perhaps, then, the emphasis is usually placed on the "social" with little regard to the "science." Thus, popular culture sees the social scientist as less of a scientist than, say, the chemist or physicist.

Have crime rates increased in Canada? Why is there a disparity in the average income of Canadian males and females? Are Canadians taking better care of their health today than a decade ago? We can all provide "answers" to these questions. But how do we know what we know? Our answers are likely to be opinions influenced by our values and our exposure to the media. We often know little about the methods of social science inquiry that check the influence of values and provide more reliable and valid data than journalism. Because we lack this knowledge we often expect too much from social scientists and are frustrated by their apparent inability to solve pressing social problems. In our frustration we may conclude that they do not know much more than we do. We hope that this book will lead you to the realization that this conclusion is wrong!

sciences, and some of the discoveries or "facts" that are presently known. These reports may also highlight debates about the facts; consequently we come to realize that facts are open to interpretation, and that current interpretations may be challenged by new factual discoveries.

Even the caricatures and stereotypes in the entertainment media have a kernel of truth: scientific thought and activity are different from the viewpoint of ordinary life and common-sense thought. Scientists are trained to downplay their emotions and to be logical, impersonal, and sceptical or critical in what they assume or believe. Scientists do use complicated technical tools that help them to observe systematically; to measure precisely; and to see, hear, and record what their unaided senses cannot reach.

However, what we do not see in these media images is how scientific research proceeds. We may not fully grasp why it is necessary to be logical and critical and the circumstance in which certain research instruments are appropriate. We may also wonder how it is possible that there are arguments over scientific discoveries or ideas when science is supposed to get at the "truth."

Along with the media images of science outlined so far we are also often told that scientific information has overwhelmed us. We are told that we live in the "age of information" or that we are in the midst of a "knowledge explosion" and that our feelings of confusion and uncertainty are due to *too much* information. But this popular perspective completely ignores *the quality* of the information we receive.

The purpose of this book is to show you how certain types of high-quality information are possible as a result of social science research. We also try to give you a way of critically evaluating social science information by considering the research process that went into producing that information. But why do we need this high quality information? What is wrong with common-sense or nonscientific information? To answer these questions we need to look at information generally and explore its varieties and qualities.

FACTUAL INFORMATION AND CASUAL RESEARCH

In our everyday lives we accumulate a lot of information. We need to make sense of or be informed about our surroundings in order to act in them. We need to know what is going on and why, and what people expect us to do. We often refer to this information or knowledge as our beliefs, opinions, and values. In certain areas we think we know the "facts" because we have read a magazine or newspaper article, or seen a documentary. Or we may have looked up information in an encyclopedia or read one or two books on a subject. As we grow older this knowledge increases, we gain experience, and we may trust our insights and intuitions more. It may come as a great shock to learn that all this "knowledge" that we base our lives on is seen as almost worthless by science! For people engaging in scientific research, all of the socially acceptable ways of knowing in everyday life are deeply flawed.

Where does this conventional information come from? Much of it comes from parents, teachers, and other **moral authorities**. This information is *traditional* or *customary*—it is the right way to proceed because it has always been right. Questioning or criticizing it is blasphemous or deeply disrespectful. In earlier times this kind of information would be almost all that was available. However, we are now

Canadian Girls Suffer Stress, Study Says

They Smoke, Diet, Drink to Cope

Stress is causing Canadian girls to suffer more headaches, stomach aches, backaches and insomnia than their counterparts in 23 other countries, a new study has found.

The World Health Organization study highlights the price Canadian girls aged 11, 13 and 15 are paying as a result of peer pressures and stresses at home and at school.

In addition to the health problems, the study found that Canadian girls are trying to deal with their stress with high-risk behaviour, such as smoking, drinking and dieting, said study author Alan King, director of Queen's University Social Program Evaluation Group.

"They are expected to do even more than they used to," he said in an interview last night. "It's only in the last few years that that's been internalized by girls who feel they have to be thin and beautiful."

He said the stress will lessen as the girls get older.

"It's pretty bad for girls in particular through those middle teen years. But then there's a kind of stabilization as they come out of it with a little better sense of who they are and where they're going."

The report, entitled *The Health of Youth, A Cross-National Survey*, was based on surveys of more than 100,000 children aged 11, 13 and 15 in 24 countries conducted in the 1993–94 school year. It is the fourth such study since 1982 …

Countries participating were: Austria, Belgium, Canada, Czech Republic, Denmark, Estonia, Finland, France, Germany, Greenland, Hungary, Israel, Latvia, Lithuania, Northern Ireland, Norway, Poland, Russia, Scotland, Slovakia, Spain, Sweden, Switzerland and Wales.

The survey included questions on risk behaviours, physical activity, diet, physical ailments and medication use, relationships with parents and peers, psychosocial adjustment and school experience.

The study found that 75 per cent of Canadian 15-year-old girls would like to change something about their body. Only 58 per cent of boys are unhappy about their appearance. And twice as many girls as boys have either been on a diet or want to be thinner.

Sixty-one per cent of Canadian 13-year-old girls have taken headache medication in the month prior to the survey—the highest reported by any of the participating countries. In comparison, 41 per cent of Canadian 13-year-old boys took medication during the same period.

Mr. King said that many girls deal with stress by taking up smoking and hanging out at school with fellow smokers.

"They know smoking is bad and yet they take it up. It only makes sense as a kind of response to pressure. It's a chance for groups to get together to share common feelings."

Mr. King said that part of the reason Canadian girls are under greater stress than those in the other countries surveyed can be attributed to a school system that provides little for those who are not going on to university.

"When you look at the response of Canadian kids in response to aspirations you get more that count on going to university than ever will go," Mr. King said. "In other countries there's a better idea of who's going and who's not and what the others are going to do."

Canadian schools tend to pay more attention to the approximate 28 per cent who are university-bound, he said. And since fewer girls go on to university than boys, girls who are not furthering their education are under greater strain, he said.

Mr. King said the Canadian findings are important because "for the first time we've been able to look at the relationship between schools and the health of kids. It's clear that how you run your school, how you relate to kids affects their mental health."

But not all the news was bad for Canada. For example, Canadian boys and girls reported that they like how their teachers relate to their students. In comparison, students in Finland are the most unhappy with their teachers and the authoritative manner in which their schools are run.

Canadian youngsters also said they find it easy to talk with their mothers. However, they ranked the lowest in being able to talk with their fathers.

Mr. King said he wants Canada to look at its policies and programs, especially in regard to health programs in schools and the role schools play in the mental health of students.

In modern society we are surrounded by many inconsistent moral guidelines and ideals. What guidelines and ideals seem to create especially high levels of stress among Canadian teenage girls?

Source: Gay Abbate, "Canadian Girls Suffer Stress, Study Says," *The Globe and Mail* (12 June 1996), p. A6. Reprinted with permission.

exposed to television, radio, newspapers, magazines, and books. When we go to school we find teachers have different ideas from our parents and our schoolmates have still other ideas. We soon discover that different people or information sources present different ideas of what is real, appropriate, or good.

How do we choose when there are conflicting or alternative ideas? Most of us become very good at interpreting what rules apply to a particular situation, and adjust our behaviour and attitudes accordingly. When we are with our friends and intimates we are relaxed and follow different codes of behaviour than we would in, say, a classroom or a work setting. In other words, we use social information *practically*, to cope with life. We do not think too deeply about the information itself, whether or not it is logically consistent, whether or not it is really "true."

What is this social information like? What are its characteristics? Essentially, this information consists of **faith** and **folkways,** or stereotyped rules of thumb. Faith means that something is unquestionably right, and that it is simply wrong to disbelieve or criticize, or to try to explore and evaluate a belief or action. Folkways are working assumptions about ways of doing things and thinking about things, based on social routines and habits. These assumptions stabilize our experience and give it meaning and organization, whether or not reality actually works in accordance with the stereotypes. Prejudices are an extreme form of stereotyped rules; they identify a particular group or institution in a generalized way and define how an individual or community should relate to that group. If someone does not fit the stereotype she becomes the "exception which proves the rule," not a reason for re-examining the stereotype. In ordinary, everyday living we use a lot of unquestioned information that *shapes our observations* rather than being *shaped by observations.*

Nowadays we also live in a world which values *factual information,* and we get much of this from media sources such as television and radio news documentaries, as well as newspapers and magazines. You are aware, no doubt, that this information has its limitations too. Newspapers and news magazines tend to have political biases that may colour the way news stories are written. Furthermore, the most successful media do not present much detail because that would reduce their ability to provide a variety of news items and might reduce audience interest. Instead of analyzing and going into the specific reasons why things happen, media news briefly describes what happens, presents only the most dramatic aspects of a news event, and tries to focus on a particular personality connected with the event. There is little follow up on previous news stories, so we do not get the context, which might help us to understand more about what is happening and why. Thus, "news" tends to become entertainment; only the highlights of the moment are presented, and these quickly disappear when another story emerges. It requires a lot of effort on our part to put together a coherent and meaningful story from this continuous stream of unrelated bits and pieces. Most of us do not have the time or the tools to do this. As well, we are missing essential information that would allow us to do so.

We have already identified some problems with various forms of everyday knowledge: faith cannot be questioned or analyzed; stereotyped routines shape our observations; and most news is fragmented and superficial. But what about factual knowledge drawn from the "serious" media or from encyclopedias and books? These sources do at least delve more deeply into particular subjects and are less superficial than ordinary news. Most of us treat news magazines, in-depth reporting, and nonfiction books with a special kind of respect. We assume

BOX 1.2

Why It Helps to Know About Social Research

Although we may not realize it, the findings of social research receive much attention in the popular media. The reported findings influence our lives in far more ways than we may be aware of.

For one thing, consider how social research helps shape some of our opinions and behaviour. Suppose this morning's paper reports that the unemployment rate last month sharply increased. In addition, another article cites a study which shows workers are generally pessimistic about their future employment. Worse still, those who hold the very occupation you were hoping to have in the future are the most concerned. These articles, which would all likely be based on social research, will undoubtedly have an impact on what you think about the state of the economy and whether you should pursue a particular career. But are you able to critically assess the reported findings?

Peruse any major newspaper or magazine and you are bound to find articles that cite findings generated by social research. Some findings are even headline news. This is particularly true of the latest information on Canada's unemployment rate, the gross domestic product, the consumer price index, and much more. Sometimes the media themselves fund the social research study whose results are then given prominent attention. Such is the case with many opinion polls. Or consider *Maclean's* annual ranking of universities; it too is a product of social research. Should you accept the rankings at face value? Are there limitations with the study?

Much of what we are told in the popular media may also be mistaken as "scientific evidence." It is common for television reporters to interview a few people "in the street" and then leave the impression that their opinions reflect those of a larger population. But do they? Whose opinions do the people "in the street" reflect?

Further, politicians who design social policies that have a profound impact on our lives will often defend these policies by citing findings from social research studies. This, it would seem, gives scientific justification for the policies. But what were the purposes of the cited studies? What were the conclusions and weaknesses of those studies?

Private organizations use the findings of social research to assist them in various business and managerial decisions. But they also use the findings of social research to determine ways to influence consumers to buy their products. Advertisements and commercials tell us that tests show one product is better than another, or that a survey shows consumers prefer one product to another. What is wrong with these "tests" or "surveys"?

Thus, it is in our own best interest to understand the benefits and limitations of social science research.

these sources are written by *experts* who know what they are talking about and who are telling us the "truth." We do not normally ask ourselves exactly how the information was obtained, or whether the right people were interviewed. We assume that the reporters and writers have done their research properly and are presenting the facts correctly. But this means we are taking these reports *on faith*, unquestioningly.

This approach to factual information—taking the work of experts at face value—is the way most of us deal with experts in our lives. We believe our doctors, bank managers, etc., without much questioning or cross-examining or looking around for second opinions. When we do "research," for example, to buy a new car or stereo system, we tend to do very quick checks using the most accessible sources of information. This way of proceeding might be called "casual" or lay research. How is it different from scientific research?

Scientific Research

Science differs from other ways of knowing and doing research because of its aims and the procedures it uses to pursue those aims. Faith, folkways (i.e., the working assumptions and rules of thumb guiding our behaviour), and everyday factual information give us moral and social guidelines for solving immediate, practical problems in our lives. Science aims at objective or disinterested knowledge—that is, knowledge that is not tied to immediate personal or practical problems, but is sought for its own sake.

In order to understand the procedures science uses it is necessary to understand a little about its history. Scientific research is a very recent development in human history. Ideas associated with science such as experimentation, precise measurement, and the application of mathematics to description and explanation, developed in the period between 1600 and 1800 in Western Europe. For most of human history science simply did not exist.

When science first developed, scientists were quickly challenged by the church and other authorities who argued that scientific claims were fraudulent, or worse, blasphemous. Scientists found that there were two very strong ways to defend themselves. The first was to persuade their critics to look at the evidence for themselves and to show how this evidence was obtained. If cardinals and bishops looked through the telescope they, too, could see mountains on the moon; it was not just a subjective claim by the scientists. Scientists quickly found that the more open they were about their findings and the ways these findings had been achieved, the more likely they were to be believed.

The second strong defence against their critics was to present their findings clearly and logically. Using closely reasoned logical arguments to justify their interpretations of their discoveries made it harder for traditional religious and moral objections to stand up. Logic could be used both to defend scientists' explanations of what they had found and to criticize those who argued against scientific reasoning. These two ways of defending science from attacks by nonscientific authorities soon became a basic part of the **scientific method.** For research to be acceptable to scientists, it had to be logically reasoned, follow explicit procedures, and be open to inspection by others, even to the point of being repeatable by other researchers.

Above all, science became distinguished from other areas of human activity as **systematic empirical research.** To be systematic means to use specially developed procedures for gathering information and to use these procedures carefully and thoroughly. The aim of systematic empirical research is to observe, describe, explain, and predict in order to improve our understanding of reality. This is in contrast to casual research, which quickly gathers the most convenient and accessible information, often in a haphazard way, in order to solve a pressing problem. To be empirical means that you do not assume that you already know the answers; your research is not shaped by moral convictions or other traditional cultural assumptions that operate elsewhere in your life. On the contrary, you have to set these assumptions aside, be open-minded, and operate according to the special assumptions of scientific research.

THE SOCIAL SCIENCES

Just as there is no single "science of nature" but several different natural sciences specializing in the study of different aspects of nature (physics, astronomy, chemistry, botany, etc.), so there are several different social sciences. Each social science focuses on one particular

Immigrants Healthier than Canadians, Study Says

TORONTO—Immigrants tend to be healthier than people born in Canada, but the longer immigrants live here the more likely they are to develop chronic health problems, according to a survey by Statistics Canada released yesterday.

People who immigrate tend to be "the healthier part of the population" in their home countries, said Russell Wilkins, a senior analyst in the agency's health-statistics division. "It's not as if you're randomly selecting people from those countries."

Employability, income and education—factors that are rated highly by Canadian immigration policy—are also indicators of good health, the Statscan report says. Canada also screens potential immigrants for health problems.

Immigrants, both recent arrivals and those who have lived in Canada for more than 10 years, are also less likely than their Canadian-born counterparts to smoke, another known factor in preventing serious illness, Mr. Wilkins said.

Canada is not unique in observing that immigrants are healthier than the rest of the population. Similar effects have been observed in Australia and the United States.

The data were derived from the 1994–95 National Population Health Survey, which examined the health of 41,045 people, of whom 6,379 were immigrants. About 4,000 of the immigrants were European and the overwhelming majority of them had lived in Canada for more than 10 years. The non-European immigrants were about evenly divided between those who had been in Canada less than 10 years and those who had lived here longer.

The survey differentiated between European immigrants (including people born in Europe, the United States, Australia and New Zealand) and non-European immigrants because migration patterns have shifted dramatically in the past 30 years.

In 1994–95, immigrants represented about 21 per cent of the Canadian population. And while European immigrants accounted for 58 per cent of the general immigrant population, the recent immigrant population was 74 per cent non-European.

Immigrants are generally younger than the general population, but even when the data were adjusted for age immigrants were less likely to suffer from 12 chronic conditions such as joint problems, allergies, hypertension and headaches.

Nearly 57 per cent of the Canadian-born population suffered from chronic conditions, compared with 50 per cent of all immigrants.

The healthiest immigrants were those from non-European countries who have arrived in the past 10 years. Only 37 per cent of that group suffered from chronic conditions.

Immigrants were also less likely to have smoked. About half of all immigrants had never smoked, compared with about one-third of the Canadian-born population.

European immigrants who had lived in Canada for more than a decade had a similar rate of having never smoked as did Canadians. Three-quarters of non-European recent immigrants had never smoked.

Non-European immigrants, whether recent arrivals or long-term residents, were more likely to be physically inactive during their leisure time than the Canadian-born population or European immigrants: The figures were 67 per cent for non-European immigrants, 57 for the Canadian-born population and 52 for European immigrants.

The longer immigrants live in Canada, the more likely they are to develop health problems. In part, this is due simply to the process of aging, Mr. Wilkins said. Researchers also speculate that as immigrants spend longer in Canada they may adopt a diet and lifestyle similar to the Canadian-born population.

The findings of this research may well surprise many Canadians. What would their "common sense" tell them about the health of immigrants? What do the facts clearly show?

Source: Lila Sarick, "Immigrants Healthier than Canadians, Study Says," *The Globe and Mail* (2 April 1996), p. A6. Reprinted with permission.

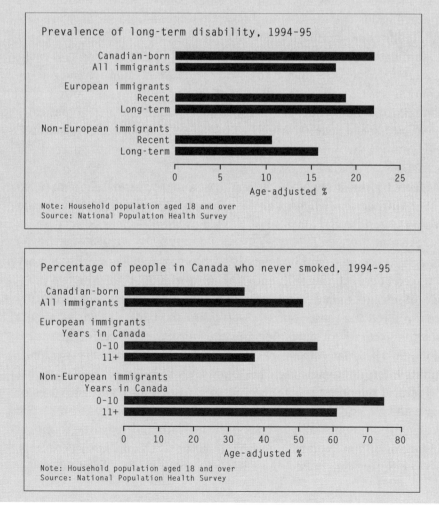

Prevalence of long-term disability, 1994-95

Canadian-born
All immigrants

European immigrants
Recent
Long-term

Non-European immigrants
Recent
Long-term

Age-adjusted %

Note: Household population aged 18 and over
Source: National Population Health Survey

Percentage of people in Canada who never smoked, 1994-95

Canadian-born
All immigrants

European immigrants
Years in Canada
0-10
11+

Non-European immigrants
Years in Canada
0-10
11+

Age-adjusted %

Note: Household population aged 18 and over
Source: National Population Health Survey

CHAPTER 1 *Why Know About Social Science Research?* 15

aspect of human life, develops its own theories in a language of its own making, and often uses certain **research methods** more than other social sciences do.

Anthropology studies the origin and varieties of human beings and their societies. It emerged as an independent discipline in the 18th century when Europeans were beginning to apply scientific reasoning to social life. Two centuries of European exploration had led to the discovery of societies of vastly different character and of peoples who differed in appearance and custom from Europeans. The two main branches of anthropology are physical anthropology and cultural anthropology. The former focuses on human evolution and variation and is closely tied to genetics and other life sciences. Cultural anthropology focuses on ways of life and varieties of belief, customs, language, and artifacts. Field research, where the social scientist lives with and participates in the life of the people studied, is a major research technique used in cultural anthropology.

Economics studies how human beings allocate scarce resources to produce goods and services, and how these goods and services are distributed for consumption. Economics also emerged in the 18th century, stimulated by the rise of markets and industry. It too has two main branches: macroeconomics is the study of entire economies and microeconomics is the study of individual firms, consumers, and other economic actors. Economics is the most quantitative and mathematically developed social science. Much of its research is based on economic and demographic information available from government sources such as Statistics Canada.

History is the study of the human past and, appropriately, is the oldest of the social sciences. The first scientific study of history in the Western world was Thucydides' history of the Peloponnesian Wars in the 5th century B.C. This work is considered to be exceptional for its time in its accuracy and its objectivity. Modern social scientific history is traced largely to the 18th and 19th centuries. At that time the practice of using original records, documents, and letters, and carefully cross-referencing these sources to establish the truth of facts or events and the accuracy of dates became the normal practice for historical research. Historians stress the importance of documentary evidence and its interpretation as their basic research technique.

Political science studies the processes, institutions, and activities of governments and groups reacting to and involved in these processes. While the study of politics dates back to Plato and Aristotle, political science again emerged as a discipline in the 18th and 19th centuries, when scholars such as Montesquieu attempted to classify the varieties of government and explain why these varieties existed. With the growth of democracy emerged the analysis of elections and voting patterns. Consequently, much political science research involves the use of polls and other survey research techniques.

Psychology is the study of human thought processes, focusing on what is common to all human beings rather than on group, cultural, or social variation. Psychologists do research on such areas as perceptions, memory, problem solving, learning and using language, adjusting to the physical and social environment, and normal and abnormal development of these processes from infancy to old age. The two most widely used techniques for studying behaviour are observations of the behaviour of humans and animals, and experimental studies on the effects of environmental changes on behaviour.

Sociology developed in the 19th century as the study of all aspects of social life in industrial or modern societies. It is a very broad discipline with many subdivisions and many overlaps with all the other social sciences. Because of its breadth and variety it does not lean towards any one research technique.

The emergence of the social sciences was stimulated by the dramatic changes in European societies from the Renaissance onwards: the discoveries of sea routes to Asia and the Americas, the Protestant Reformation, the scientific, commercial, and industrial revolutions, and others. However, the social sciences first developed as a set of philosophical ideas and only later involved systematic empirical research. (See Box 1.3 on the rise of the social sciences in Canada.)

While the social sciences share the basic perspective and approach of the natural sciences, some features are unique to the social sciences. Where natural scientists study inanimate objects—chemicals, physical forces, stars, etcetera—or animate but nonhuman beings, social scientists study human beings with whom they can communicate. This gives social scientists special advantages in devising methods of research. Natural scientists may carefully and systematically observe and experiment but they cannot communicate with what they study. Social scientists can do interviews, conduct survey research, read documents and letters written by long-dead individuals, and learn about cultures by participating in their lives and experiences. Social scientists, then, have a broader variety of research techniques available to them than do natural scientists.

However, the social sciences differ from the natural sciences in other less advantageous ways. The possibility of communication between social scientists and their subject matter brings up the danger that the research may be coloured by emotions, political concerns, and other

BOX 1.3

Origins of the Social Sciences in Canada

The emergence of the social sciences as research-based, empirical disciplines has several stages. One is the separation of a discipline from predecessors such as philosophy, or from nonacademic fields such as art or journalism. A second stage is the development of the discipline in its own right, with a focus of study and an approach to its field that is distinct from other disciplines. Associated with these developments is the emergence of institutions that reinforce the practice of research as an open, shared process based on common interests and standards. Professional associations, journals where research can be published, and universities where researchers can be trained and research sustained are the most important of these institutions. In Canada, social science institutions have developed relatively recently. In the 1940s there were ten social science associations with seven journals; by the 1990s, there were thirty-seven associations publishing thirty-two journals. These aspects in the development of the social sciences in Canada are also complicated by the distinctness of the French and English intellectual traditions.

Anthropology in Canada can trace its predecessors to the missionaries of New France and the explorers and travellers who opened up the West and Northwest in the 18th and 19th centuries. In 1910 a federal government department of anthropology was set up as part of its land survey organization. The famous American linguistic anthropologist Edward Sapir was appointed head and he proceeded to recruit Canadians who had studied with British cultural anthropologist Edward Tylor. This group published several major ethnographies of the native peoples of the Northwest coast and Western Arctic Inuit. One of these pioneers was responsible for establishing the first centre for ethnography at Université Laval which has specialized in the study of Quebec rural life. The first university department was established in 1925 at the University of Toronto.

Economics in 19th century Canada was closely associated with amateur writing on policy issues by government officials and business people. At that time economics was known as "political economy," reflecting its close association with politics. In anglophone universities professors of political economy were appointed to Queen's University and the University of Toronto in the 1880s, although much of their writing was historical and political. In 1918 the Dominion Bureau of Statistics (Statistic Canada's predecessor) was founded and provided standardized, national and provincial statistics for economic analysis. University departments were established during the 1920s and the Canadian Political Science Association, with a membership that included both economists and political scientists, was established in 1929. The association published the *Canadian Journal of Economics and Political Science* from 1935 to 1967. Two separate associations were formed in 1967 with economists setting up the Canadian Economics Association. Since 1968 it has published the *Canadian Journal of Economics*. For many years economic research among francophone academics was concentrated at the *École des hautes études commerciales* (HEC), today part of Université de Montréal. HEC was founded in 1907 and began to publish the journal *L'actualité economique* in 1925.

During the 19th century *history* was closely associated with classical studies, literature, and political lobbying. Much historical writing was semifictional romantic or moralistic storytelling. The creation of the *Public Archives of Canada* in 1872 contributed to the idea of compiling an objective record and common sources for historical analysis. In the 1880s political economists at Queen's University and the University of Toronto turned to the writing of systematic, empirically based, economic history. In the next decade chairs of history were established at these universities. In 1922 the Canadian Historical Association was founded, along with its own professional journal, the *Canadian Historical Review*. In francophone universities departments of history were set up at Université Laval and Université de Montréal after World War II. An influential and controversial figure who did much to promote the study of history in Quebec was Father Lionel Groulx. In 1915 he set up a chair in Canadian history at the Montreal campus of Université Laval. (The Montreal campus later became part of Université de Montréal, which became a full-fledged university in 1920.) He helped create in 1947 *l'Institut d'histoire d'Amerique française*, which publishes the journal *Revue d'histoire de l'Amerique française*.

In anglophone universities *political science* was dominated by economics or "political economy" until after World War II. Prior to the 1950s political analysis was largely focused on economic issues, with some smaller attention devoted to constitutional matters. The Canadian Political Science Association and its journal the *Canadian*

Journal of Economics and Political Science were primarily devoted to economics. In 1967, when the economists formed their own association, the Canadian Political Science Association founded the *Canadian Journal of Political Science.* The development of political science in francophone universities followed a different path. In part, the rise of political science coincided with the rapid social and political changes in Quebec in the 1950s and 1960s. The first political science department in a francophone university was set up in 1954 at Université Laval. Political science expanded along with the various francophone universities in later years. A francophone association of political scientists was set up in the early 1960s which is today known as the *Société québécoise de science politique* and publishes the journal *Politique.*

Psychology was seen as a subdivision of philosophy until the end of the 19th century. The first experimental laboratory was set up in 1889 by James Mark Baldwin, who taught in the University of Toronto philosophy department. The first university departments in English Canada were established during the 1920s. Canadian psychologists had no professional association of their own until the Canadian Psychology Association was established in 1939. The association also published its own journal, the *Canadian Journal of Psychology,* from 1939 on. Prior to this date Canadian psychologists joined the American Psychological Association, which was founded in 1892 as a transcontinental organization. Separate departments of psychology in francophone universities were established in the early 1940s and were dominated by a Roman Catholic philosophical orientation. However, by the late 1950s the focus turned to basic research, and today psychology departments are well established in all of the francophone universities.

Sociology was very much a late developer despite the establishment of departments at McGill University and the University of Toronto in the 1920s and 1930s respectively. In 1941 the prominent University of Toronto economist Harold Innis described it as "the Cinderella of the social sciences." However, in both anglophone and francophone universities sociology began to emerge as an independent discipline in the 1940s, spurred on by S.D. Clark at the University of Toronto, Everett Hughes (an American) at McGill University, and Father Georges-Henri Lévesque, who set up the social science faculty at Université Laval. Each of these scholars promoted systematic empirical research. No separate professional association or journal existed for sociologists in Canada until the 1960s. Instead, they joined the Canadian Political Science Association and published their works in its journal or in American and European journals. In 1966 sociologists and anthropologists founded the Canadian Sociology and Anthropology Association, which publishes *The Canadian Review of Sociology and Anthropology*. In francophone universities sociology was at first under the influence of the Roman Catholic church and was associated with the rise of a political reform movement, *Action Catholique*. The church influence diminished over the years with some, particularly Father Georges-Henri Lévesque, calling for a secularized view of sociology. As in anglophone universities, sociology expanded in francophone universities in the 1960s and new journals were started, including *Sociologie et Société*, which began in 1968.

sources of bias. Social reality appears to be a much more difficult matter to investigate and about which to produce strong, firm conclusions and explanations. Experimentation is much harder, so a researcher often cannot pin down exactly how one thing affects another. It is also much harder to identify clearly measurable qualities and characteristics in social life than it is in the natural world. Apart from economics, social phenomena tend to be qualitative—describable in words but not so clearly and easily represented by numbers.

It is difficult to pin down beginnings and endings of social phenomena. When did the "Quiet Revolution" in Quebec start? When did it end? You cannot identify these points with any great precision. Social life is also continuously and rapidly changing. Where it takes billions of years for solar systems to evolve and millions of years for biological systems to evolve, societies now change within decades or less. The speed of social change makes it difficult for social scientists to keep up with and accurately describe, let alone interpret and explain, the changes. These complications mean that the social sciences are less able to produce small numbers of powerful explanations or general theories that apply to a large number of different phenomena. Instead, generalizations and explanations in social science apply to a small range of times and places, seem to have many exceptions, and are often argued over more intensely than is the case in the natural sciences.

Social Science Research

We have said that the scientific method involves following procedures which are acceptable to other scientific researchers. This book introduces you to these procedures so that you can understand how social science research takes place. With this understanding you can become an informed and critical reader of social science literature, and you can begin to learn how to do your own research.

Social research that is acceptable to other social scientists follows certain steps, which are presented in Exhibit 1.1 and elaborated on in following chapters. Briefly let us note that research is a process made up of a series of sequential steps. However, researchers develop their own styles of how they go through each step. We have chosen a certain way of describing the research process that we believe will inform you of the necessary steps. We are not suggesting, however, that this is the only way of describing the process. Here we provide an overview of the research process and in Chapter 2 we elaborate on the process and introduce more terminology.

EXHIBIT 1.1

The Research Process

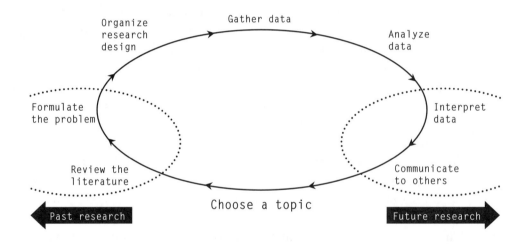

Social research requires careful preparation. The research process begins when we *choose a topic* from our knowledge base—that is, the general knowledge we have about an area. For example, you might decide to carry out a study on the images of women in the mass media because you have a personal interest in the topic. Therefore, you would already have some knowledge about the topic; perhaps you are familiar with some debates on sexual stereotyping of women in the media, and you may have ideas on the topic based on your own observations and readings.

Your next goal is to be more precise about the issue you want to examine. To help you in this effort you concentrate on relevant background information, including scholarly studies on the topic. In other words, you *review the literature*. In the process, you become aware of what specific issues other researchers have examined, what techniques they used to collect facts, how they defined certain terms, such as "sexual stereotyping," and much more. The review of other studies and discussions on the topic will help you carefully *formulate the problem* that you intend to research. The stated problem has to be a clear, focused statement that will guide your search for evidence. For example, after a review of the literature, you may want to concentrate on how women are portrayed in television advertisements. Let us suppose you surmise that women are more likely to be portrayed in homemaker roles in television advertisements shown during daytime soap operas than in those shown during prime-time (evening) family sitcoms. What you are saying is that there is a relationship between how women are portrayed on the television advertisements and the time of day the advertisements are presented. This speculative statement can be put to the test, and that is the goal of your research.

But before doing so you will have to further clarify what you are examining. For example, what do you mean by "homemaker roles"? People will have different ideas of what homemaker roles are. Thus, it is important that you provide a clear definition of what you mean, a definition that is used for the length of your study.

Next, which programs does your study concern? There are many daytime soap operas and prime-time sitcoms. Which programs will you actually study? How will you select them? What procedures and techniques will you use to collect the data? In other words, you need to *organize the research design*. This is a key step in the research process and the focus of much of this book. For example, you may decide to focus only on soap operas and sitcoms that have been on the air for at least five years and deal with family situations. From these you may choose to examine a certain number shown on particular days and times of the week. It is *your* study and therefore you must decide how to select—and how to examine—the programs and the advertisements. However, you should be able to justify the design you choose.

The next step is to *gather the data*, as you spelled it out in your research design. After you have collected and recorded the information, you need to *analyze the data*. The data have to be sorted, organized, and analyzed in order for you to interpret the data. *Are* women more likely to be portrayed in homemaker roles in television advertisements shown during daytime soap operas than during prime-time (evening) family sitcoms? In other words, do the results confirm or reject what you had expected to find? What have you concluded? What can you say about the general issue of the portrayal of women in television advertisements?

Finally, you will want to *communicate to others* your data and conclusions. This is usually done in a research report that traces each step of the research process. In other words, you should explain how the topic was chosen and developed, how you conducted the research, what you found, and your interpretations of the data, and then draw up a conclusion. In addition, you would want to point to the limitations of your study and make suggestions for future research.

Thus, social research is a process. It begins with a general question, usually one in which we have a personal interest, that we then make more specific in order to be able to search for an answer. We gather and evaluate data to answer the specific question and thereby shed light on our general question. Research contributes to our accumulation of knowledge about the issue and suggests further avenues to research. Consequently, research never really ends. As one study comes to a close another begins and continues the process of expanding our knowledge about ourselves and our social world.

In Table 1.1 we indicate which chapters of this book deal with the various steps of the research process. Throughout, we present the steps in a simplified way, but comprehensively enough for you to carry out your own research or to assess the research of others. Although the book provides a guided tour of the social research process, no book can capture the excitement that comes from doing your own social research.

TABLE 1.1

STEPS IN THE RESEARCH PROCESS

1. Overview of the research process	Chapter 2: What is Social Research?
2. Choose a topic and review the literature.	Chapter 3: Finding a Topic
3. Choose whom or what to study.	Chapter 4: Choosing Whom or What to Study
4. Gather the data.	Chapter 5: Social Survey
	Chapter 6: Experimental Research
	Chapter 7: Field Research
	Chapter 8: Indirect or Nonreactive Methods
5. Analyze and interpret the data.	Chapter 9: What are the Results?
6. Communicate to others.	Chapter 10: The Research Report

Tallying Where None Has Gone Before

They've listened to the advice about travelling in twos and leaving purses at home, but when the training session turns to what to do if they get stabbed with a needle, the intensity at the tableful of census-takers moves up a notch.

Don't touch the plunger is the first ironclad rule. Just pull the syringe out and make the puncture bleed. Go to the hospital at once if you're injected, and take the needle so whatever was in it can be tested. A consoling thought: A dose of the anti-AIDS drug AZT within two hours can be remarkably effective in forestalling full-blown infection from the virus.

Call it urban-guerrilla training for the last census of the century. The dozen or so people gathered around this table are part of a nimble experiment designed to help enumerate the residents of 14,000 homes in Vancouver's notorious downtown east side. The project aims to tally the virtually uncountable, but it also risks putting the enumerators face to face with danger.

"It's different from the traditional view of census-taking, going around from nice little house, with a white picket fence, to nice little house," said Ellen Gee, chairwoman of sociology and anthropology at Simon Fraser University in Burnaby.

The project was developed here in Vancouver by Statistics Canada two censuses ago and has proved so successful that it was exported to Calgary and Edmonton for the last census. On May 14, census day, it will be tested for the first time in the urban cores of Winnipeg, Toronto and Montreal.

It's a small slice of the massive census machine that even now is being cranked up for next month's count.

The ritual takes place every five years in Canada and has been conducted at various intervals since the first census in the colony of New France in 1666.

In all, this year's census effort will involve 50,000 workers (many, like the Vancouver crew, are hired for just a few weeks) and cost $347.4 million over the eight-year cycle of development, collection, analysis and publication.

But the census staff sitting around this table aren't doing the count the way it is done in most other parts of the country. They are trying to get information about people in Canada's poorest neighbourhood, an inner core that has more than its fair share of drugs, prostitution, homelessness, mental illness and illiteracy in several languages.

In other words, filling out the census form is not at the top of the list for many residents. But in an era when provinces are clamouring for accurate counts of every single marginalized group (scarce federal dollars depend on official numbers), what's a census-taker to do?

The solution: Instead of simply dropping off the census form with an admonition that it's a contravention of the Statistics Act not to fill it out, which would be the least of many residents' legal problems, the census-takers returned to the old-fashioned method of enumeration. They tried going door to door, face to face, and just asking the questions and ticking off the answers, confidentiality assured.

Getting the data in person has reduced costs tremendously, said Gail Fentiman, the second-in-command of the census for the Pacific region and one of the people who came up with the idea. Community leaders say the accuracy of the numbers has improved, too.

But the process means that this group of enumerators is in contact with members of the public for far longer than their counterparts who just drop off the forms. And while every enumerator across Canada gets safety training, the face-to-face interviewers in this program get extra.

In Vancouver, some of the safety problems have intensified even since the 1991 census, partly because volatile cocaine is replacing sleepy heroin as the drug of choice, police tell the census staff.

A map pinned to the wall above the table where the census staff are being trained outlines the area, which is divided into portions coloured pink, green, blue and red. Near the centre is the toughest area of all, coloured black. This is where several thousand men live in the

so-called "hotels" along East Hastings Street, in rooms about 10 feet square with just a hotplate and no bathroom.

Constable Dave Dickson, who runs a storefront safety office in the area, warns the census staff that the pairs of enumerators may have trouble capturing the attention of some of these men for the 15 to 30 minutes it will take to fill out the long form of the census, which has 54 questions and must be given to every fifth household. (The short form takes only a few minutes.)

He says the census takers will have to convince residents that they are not undercover police officers and advises them to conduct the questioning in the hall if possible.

"I don't know if I'd want to go in," he says. "Some of the rooms are moving. The door will open and you'll get this waft of odour. It's not a very nice job. Some of those hotels are pretty grungy."

Somebody asks about the wisdom of carrying a whistle to call for help.

"People aren't going to listen to it down there," Constable Dickson says. "There are screamers going off all the time down there and people don't pay any attention."

Barb Daniel, executive director of the Downtown Eastside Residents Association advises census staff to steer clear of the communal bathrooms in the "hotels," where residents often inject drugs. They're sometimes spattered with excrement and blood, she notes.

"You can talk about it all you want, but when you really get into it, you can freak out," Ms. Daniel tells the group.

There are other pieces of advice, some of it from the staff of the needle exchange, the second-largest exchange in North America behind New York City. Never sit on chairs (a prime hiding place for used needles). Never touch the walls (drug users will often spray the final contents of a syringe on them). Consider carrying a plastic toothbrush holder, the perfect size for an abandoned needle.

Get out of the way if someone coughs, because the incidence of highly contagious tuberculosis is great in some parts of the neighbourhood. And forget trying to enumerate on "cheque day," which is the day the welfare cheques arrive, or on the day after.

The staff assembled here are supervisors. They will hire

roughly 200 others for $9.50 an hour to do the door-to-door interviews for a couple of weeks starting on census day. Most of the supervisors, and the people they will eventually hire and train in these safety measures, live in the area and are fiercely proud of it. They are unshock-able and will hire people who are too. It's one of the keys to the program's success.

"The job qualification, basically, is grinding poverty," Ms. Daniel from the residents association tells the census staff. "Class tells. It does, I'm sorry."

The enumerators have the backing of the street-wise community associations in the area. In fact, the major community players, who know the value of a census statistic when they see one, have become intensely involved in persuading people who live there to participate.

For some, the efforts to include marginalized groups in the census are proof that they are no longer being ignored by authorities.

"What Census Canada does is validate that these people exist," said Carole Brown, co-ordinator of the Ray-Cam Co-operative Centre on East Hastings Street.

It was not always so, of course. George Emery, a his-torian of demography at the University of Western Ontario in London, noted that censuses of the last cen-tury tended to miss counting groups such as racial minori-ties or the poor, much less get detailed information about them. Even several decades ago, there was less emphasis on counting everyone.

"The people at the bottom end of the social scale have a better chance of being left out than others," he said.

Today, that politic has changed, partly because the provinces and Ottawa are in such pitched battles over who pays for the poor's programs.

In the United States, this very issue has become a nasty political and legal fight because the census in 1990 missed about 1.6 per cent of the population, many of them from minority groups and urban cores. Because so much federal money rode on the count, and because many of those missed were big users of federal aid programs, the issue landed before the Supreme Court.

But one of the legacies of the failure to count well in the inner core is that the United States will begin counting only 90 per cent of the population in the 2000 census, and then mathemati-cally estimate the rest. In an admission of the difficulty of enumerating these groups, U.S. statisticians reckon this will actually improve accura-cy, as well as shave the better part of $1 billion off the cen-sus tab.

The idea is anathema here, where the adamant goal next month is to count every sin-gle resident.

"I guess as an organization, we pride ourselves in our professionalism and the qual-ity of the information we gather," said Jim Selley, the top Statscan official in the Pacific region.

At first sight the steps in the research process may seem obvious and perhaps dull and technical. Yet carrying out research is often quite an adventure and even involves personal risks. Can you imag-ine other areas of social research which might require the kinds of special training illustrated in this reading?

Source: Alanna Mitchell, "Tallying Where None Has Gone Before," *The Globe and Mail* (5 April 1996) pp. A1, A6. Reprinted with permission.

WHAT YOU HAVE LEARNED

- There are some important differences between faith, folkways, and casual knowledge, on the one hand, and scientific knowledge, on the other.

- Science is concerned with systematic empirical observation and logical analysis in order to understand and interpret observations.

- Several distinct social sciences have developed, applying a variety of empirical research techniques to different aspects of human life.

- Social sciences share characteristics of the natural sciences and have certain characteristics that are uniquely their own.

- Research generally proceeds in a patterned series of steps and stages.

KEY WORDS

sceptical	anthropology
moral authorities	economics
faith	history
folkways	political science
scientific method	psychology
systematic empirical research	sociology
research methods	

REVIEW QUESTIONS

1. Identify the ways scientific thinking differs from nonscientific thinking.
2. Identify some belief that you feel is true. Examine the grounds for your confidence in the truth of this belief. Can you identify and sort out these assumptions in terms of their basis in authority, intuition, personal experience, or fact? Does this exercise change your belief or your confidence in this belief in any way?
3. Follow a major news story through the reports on radio, television, and one newspaper for two weeks. Identify the ways that you can tell that the story is a major one. How does its presentation shift over the course of two weeks?

4. Identify a social issue about which you believe you have some knowledge or strong opinion. For example, "Why do students drop out of high school?" or "What are the characteristics of drug addicts?" With the help of your instructor or a librarian, try to find some social scientific research on the topic. Compare the ideas and findings of the researchers with your own knowledge or opinion. What have you learned in doing this?

RECOMMENDED READINGS

Babbie, E. (1986). *Observing ourselves: Essays on social research.* Belmont, CA: Wadsworth.

A book of lively essays in the field of social science research written mainly for the layperson. The author, widely known for his textbooks on social research, encourages the reader to think critically and raise questions about the social world.

Hunt, M. (1985). *Profiles of social research: The scientific study of human interactions.* New York: Russell Sage Foundation.

An engaging book written in nontechnical language about the work of social science researchers. It provides an inside look at the drama and excitement that went into various widely known and influential research projects. It is also a useful introduction to the importance of social research.

CHAPTER 2

What Is Social Science Research?

WHAT YOU WILL LEARN

- how research begins
- the sceptical or critical values of research
- the "scientific" and the "humanistic" approaches to research
- basic steps in the research process and their pitfalls

INTRODUCTION

Imagine you met a foreign student from a country with a different language and culture from your own. Before coming to Canada the student learned some English, read up on the history and politics of Canada, and became quite informed about the climate. Yet in his first week in Canada he feels disoriented, lost in the crowd, unsure what to expect. He is particularly puzzled about a gesture that he has witnessed on a few occasions. At times when two people approach each other, they partly extend their right arms, open their hands, take each other's hand and shake it. He is baffled by this gesture, especially since someone tried to do it with him and he was at a loss what to do. Fortunately, he has become your friend and feels at ease to turn to you for help. He asks, "What is that gesture?" Perhaps you are shocked that someone would have to ask and so you answer, "It's a handshake." But your friend is still at a loss. He now asks, "How do you do it? When do you do it? Why do you do it?" You try your best to answer his questions, but it seems that every answer elicits more questions: "How far should I extend my arm? How strong should my grip be? Should I do the same with males and females? Should I do the same with different age groups? Should I ..." You are stunned by the complications your friend sees in what to you, until now at least, was such a simple common gesture. (How would you answer these questions? What other questions do you think he might ask?)

Now imagine yourself in a foreign country with different customs and language from your own. Suppose you, too, read up on the country and learned some of the language. But nothing prepared you for the first encounter with your host in the new country. Before you even have time to greet him with a handshake, he sticks out his tongue at you. Fortunately, he seems to mean well. You quickly offer him your hand but he turns around. You are baffled by his behaviour, so you turn to him for help. His immediate response is to say, "It's an extended tongue." But you are still at a loss, and ask: "What is that? How do you do it? Why do you do it?" (Consider other questions you would want to ask your host. For example, how far should the tongue be extended?)

None of us have taken Handshake 101 and yet we know what it is, when to do it, and why we do it. But it can be quite bewildering for someone who is unfamiliar with the custom. Likewise, if we had to move to another country, we would want to know more about the people and their customs. We would want to be able to communicate with them and so we would learn the language. However, we would also note many activities that they generally take for granted. We would have many questions about these activities, and would want to learn how, when, why, and so on.

Social scientific research is full of the same curiosity; we want to know more and try not to take things for granted about ourselves and our social world. Social scientific research is logical and applies systematic approaches to gathering and analyzing information. As one question is answered many others arise. Further, social researchers use various words in a technical way in order to clearly communicate among themselves, regardless of their discipline.

At first, social scientific research may seem as baffling as trying to adapt to the ways of a new country. But with time the logic and use of social research concepts will become routine, like greeting someone with a handshake.

As with the foreign student who already knew something about Canada, but was unfamiliar with the handshake, you already know something about social research, but are not yet acquainted with certain aspects of the topic. You have heard of polls in the media, you have used the library, and probably you have discussed theories in courses. You have even carried out casual research, such as informing yourself about various colleges and universities before deciding where to apply. But, as you may have realized from reading Chapter 1, these activities are not scientific research. As we noted there, science is a way of knowing things that is distinguishable from other socially acceptable ways of knowing. Therefore, social scientific research is different from casual research. But how different?

To answer this question, let us consider two basic questions about the research process. How do ideas for research begin or emerge? What are the aims and rules of scientific research? After answering these questions we will elaborate on the steps in the research process.

Because we emphasize those aspects of scientific thinking that are different from common sense, you may find parts of this chapter challenging. Think of the ideas discussed here as a different language or a new place to visit. Take time to become aware of the differences between what you know and the new language or place you do not know. As you become more familiar with a new language or place you begin to feel more at home. As you read beyond this chapter you should find that it makes even more sense. A simple "map" of some key differences between science and common sense is provided for your guidance in Table 2.1.

In this chapter we shall look at three aspects of the **research process**:

1. How ideas for research begin or emerge in the first place;
2. The norms and outlook of scientific research;
3. The steps in the research process.

HOW RESEARCH BEGINS

"How did they think of that?" "Where did they get the idea to do *that* research?" These are common reactions when people read about scientific research in the media. It is often hard to imagine how the researchers thought of doing the research in the first place. The popular image of scientists suggests that their research begins with a brilliant flash of insight—that they suddenly have an idea that nobody else has thought of. This image of research is misleading; it suggests that all you need for research to begin is for someone to come up with a brilliant new idea. If this were the case there would be far less research than there is because brilliant ideas are always in extremely short supply.

It is true that research begins with an idea or question that concerns the people willing to do research. But this idea is likely to have

TABLE 2.1

SCIENCE AND COMMON SENSE

	Common sense	**Science**
Basic foundation	Faith in unquestioned and unchanging truths	Working assumption of order in the universe
Examples	"Violent images in the media are always bad."	"Media images and audience responses are complex; so are the relations between them."
Community rules	Folkways—commonly accepted ways of believing and behaving that are taken for granted	Objectivity, empirical verification, open and clear communication, which are subject to critical examination
Examples	"We should ban violence in the media."	"We need to do research on: 1. the variety of media images: cartoons, horror, psychological thrillers, etc.; 2. circumstances in which people view these different images; 3. the range of responses of different groups and individuals."
Searching for knowledge	Casual research—what is needed to make a specific decision or solve a particular problem	Systematic research— conscious attention to rules of description and explanation
Examples	"My children were so upset when they saw that movie. I'm never going to let them see another one like it."	Experiments exposing groups of children in controlled ways to media images and then observing behaviour.

complicated origins in the way the researcher's background, current social circumstances, and ideas in the social sciences themselves come together.

Personal experience can play an important role in shaping people's research interests. Refugees from Nazi Germany in the 1930s played a prominent part in performing social scientific and historical research into totalitarianism and dictatorship in the 1940s and 1950s. Feminist ideas for social research emerged in the 1970s after an ever-increasing number of women had begun to graduate from universities.

Current social phenomena and social problems are likely to be of interest to many researchers even if they themselves are not directly affected. For example, since the arrival of the personal computer, there has been a very rapid growth of social science research into the impact of computer technology on work, leisure, education, and so on. Slow economic growth in the nineties has led to a renewed interest in economic explanations of depression and poverty.

Much, perhaps most, research is stimulated by the research of others. From the point of view of the individual researcher this is intellectual stimulation—a game of ideas that may not connect directly to personal experience, a major social problem, or a contemporary event, but which is nevertheless interesting and worth exploring further. Much historical research is like this. What was life like for the early settlers of Canada? Who supported Louis Riel and why? These are interesting questions in themselves, even though they may have no direct relationship to contemporary issues and problems.

Other people's research can be a stimulus to further research in various ways. The research may have gaps or omissions. For example, there is a lot of research on the nursing profession as a "feminized" occupation—as one that has been primarily identified as a female occupation. Much of the research focuses on the way nurses are subordinated to the traditionally male role of doctors and surgeons. However, there are a growing number of male nurses and female doctors. This suggests that doctor-nurse relations may well be changing as the gender compositions of the two occupations shift.

Research may be marked by controversy and disagreement. For example, there is much research into the relationship between media violence and aggressive behaviour, but a great deal of disagreement exists about what the data show or prove. Researchers often discover new information that is surprising but not explainable. The statisticians at Statistics Canada recently discovered that, with the exception of youth crimes, police reports indicate a decline in crime rates over the

Alzheimer's May Begin Early in Life, Study Suggests

Low Linguistic Ability in 20s Tied to Higher Risk, Researchers Say

CHICAGO—Alzheimer's disease may stalk its victims early in life, decades before it destroys the mind, suggests a study of nuns who are donating their brains to science.

Alzheimer's may be like hardening of the arteries, resulting from a life-long biological deterioration that becomes apparent only when people are older, authors of the study say.

The study analyzed nuns' youthful writings and found that those who showed low linguistic ability when they were in their 20s had a much higher risk of Alzheimer's when they were elderly.

The findings could indicate Alzheimer's impairs language ability when people are young, the researchers said. On the other hand, greater linguistic ability early in life might indicate a healthy brain resistant to Alzheimer's later on.

"It's a chicken-or-egg thing at this point," said the lead researcher, David Snowdon,

an associate professor of preventive medicine at the University of Kentucky.

The findings are published in today's issue of The Journal of the American Medical Association.

The researchers studied the autobiographies of 104 nuns from the School Sisters of Notre Dame. The order's 678 nuns have agreed to donate their brains for research.

The women wrote one-page accounts of their lives for the order's archives just before taking their vows, at an average age of 22.

Scientists performed autopsies on the brains to 25 nuns who died, 10 of whom had Alzheimer's. Those who had low linguistic ability when young had abundant neurofibrillary tangles—the lesions of Alzheimer's disease—when they were old.

Nine of the 10 nuns who developed Alzheimer's disease (90 per cent) showed a low linguistic ability in their autobiographies, compared

with 13 per cent among those who did not have Alzheimer's, the study says.

"That's what's most incredible about it—this relationship between what they wrote in their 20s and what their brains looked like 60 years later," Dr. Snowdon said. "It's a disease process that's underlying this."

He said he has no reason to believe the findings would be different in men.

A scientist at the national Institute on Aging, which financed the study, said it is an important contribution to understanding the progression of Alzheimer's, but he also urged caution in interpreting the results.

It may be that inherited differences in thinking ability affect the way Alzheimer's develops in a person, said Neil Buckholz, acting associate director for the institute's Neuroscience and Neuropsychology of Aging Program.

Many previous studies have linked higher education

to a lower risk of Alzheimer's disease, but it appears that some component related to education, such as language aptitude, rather than education itself is key, Dr. Snowdon said.

"These findings are not due to education," he said. "When we look at a subgroup who were lifetime teachers with at least a bachelor's degree, the findings were just as strong."

The greatest differences in brain lesions among subjects with Alzheimer's and those without it were in the temporal lobe, the primary language centre of the brain, Dr. Snowdon said.

In the study, linguistic ability was measured by two traits—grammatical complexity and idea density, or the number of ideas per number of words.

For example, a nun who died of Alzheimer's wrote, "I prefer teaching to any other profession." Another nun, alive and mentally healthy when the study was prepared, wrote: "Now I am wandering about in 'Dove's Lane' waiting, yet only three more weeks, to follow in the footprints of my Spouse, bound to Him by the Holy Vows of poverty, Chastity and Obedience."

The first sample had a complexity of five on a scale from one to seven and an idea density of five per 10 words, researchers said. The second had a complexity of seven and a density of nine per 10 words.

Measuring sentence complexity is the next best thing to IQ tests, which weren't available for this study because they weren't given before the Second World War, Dr. Snowdon said.

The cause of Alzheimer's is unknown, and there is no cure or reliable treatment. It slowly robs victims of memory, reasoning powers and ability to function.

Research into Alzheimer's is a growing area of social and medical research. What has contributed to the rise of interest in this disease?

Source: Brenda Coleman, "Alzheimer's May Begin Early in Life, Study Suggests," *The Globe and Mail* (21 February 1996), p. A11.

last several years. Apart from contradicting "common-sense" assumptions and the impression created by the media, these statistics were presented as bare facts without any explanation or interpretation. This lack of interpretation provides an opportunity for other researchers to develop satisfactory analyses and explanations.

What we are suggesting here is that the very beginnings of research are quite complicated. All of the factors we mention—personal experience, current social issues or problems, the stimulus of other people's research—often combine to pull people into undertaking social science research. What events or experiences in your own life could be beginning points of research? Can you think of current events that might even connect with your life or that interest you in some way? If you can say yes to any of these questions then you have taken the first step on the road of social research.

The next step is to narrow down your topic. For the research to get anywhere it has to become focused, explicit, and developed enough to make it clear, communicable, and acceptable to a community of researchers, as well as to others who may be concerned with the practical results of your research. A clear and focused topic allows you to better communicate your research to others who may provide useful resources, inspiration, and aid.

THE AIMS AND RULES OF SCIENTIFIC RESEARCH

Having become interested in an issue or topic, your next problem is how to follow it up. Becoming interested in an issue could lead you into different ways of expressing and exploring this interest. If your interest is in poverty, you could develop a political platform to reform society; you could try your hand at a journalistic exposé of the issue; or you might try writing a novel or directing a documentary video about the experience of poverty. Each of these activities has its own aims and rules or procedures. Here we shall look at the aims and procedures of a social scientific research approach.

If you have ever tried to read an article in a social science journal, you no doubt found it hard going. Even though the subject matter sounds interesting the writing style and the terminology seem strange and abstract. This is partly because each social science has developed special terms to express its ideas. As well, scientific researchers have developed rules and procedures to avoid the limitations and problems with intuition, experience, common sense, tradition, and authority. The terminology and the abstraction serve as reminders to the researchers themselves to be scientific in their outlook.

Since the articles are written for fellow professionals the basic assumptions of scientific research are not spelled out. Hence, unless you already know the assumptions, the language of research seems very strange and difficult to comprehend. We are going to identify these assumptions and introduce the jargon associated with them.

Underlying the rules and procedures of social research are four basic values commonly held by researchers in all fields of science.

1. Researchers are committed to **objectivity** in their research work. That is, whatever their personal biases, researchers are committed to using the appropriate procedures for gathering and interpreting data, and to presenting their discoveries honestly, even if they go against cherished personal beliefs and values.
2. Scientific researchers aim for **empirical verification** of their ideas. That is, since scientific knowledge is based on observation in the

world, scientific ideas must at some point be connected to observations to see if researchers' theories or speculations are in line with the facts. Researchers do not depend upon experience, intuition, faith in authority, or tradition to provide answers to their questions.

3. Consequently, scientific research should be designed to add to those discoveries by making a contribution to and building on other scientific knowledge. Research is viewed as a cooperative or collective endeavour; it builds on past research and lays the foundations for future research.

4. Finally, researchers can only make a contribution if they communicate their research clearly and honestly. This must be done in enough detail so that other researchers can fully understand how the research was carried out and how the data were interpreted.

These basic values or aims can be summed up as scepticism. The value system of research leads researchers to disbelieve any statement that cannot be "proved" or supported by empirical evidence that has been discovered by following the accepted ways of doing research. In order to survive this disbelieving or doubting attitude researchers have developed procedures to ensure that their ideas are clearly and logically developed from previous research; that these ideas can become the basis of research plans that ensure empirical evidence is systematically gathered; and that the evidence is carefully analyzed and interpreted according to accepted rules and not according to the personal whims and beliefs of the researcher. These procedures will be outlined in the next section.

Scepticism could be called the negative or critical side of scientific enquiry. But research is also founded on some positive assumptions as well. The first assumption is that the universe is orderly or, as Einstein once put it, "God is not a madman." If there are regularities and patterns—events or processes which happen over and over again in nature and society—we should be able to discover them. This idea originated in the West with the ancient Greeks. It distinguished them from their neighbours, who believed that nature was ruled by the whims and passions of gods, goddesses, spirits, and demons, and that the only way to cope with the resulting chaos was by following religious and magical rituals. The universe was seen as a disorderly place ruled by mysterious forces; it was not possible to understand how and why those forces worked the way they did, so magic was the key to survival.

The ancient Greeks also saw that if the universe is orderly human thinking needs to reflect and express that order. They developed philosophical and mathematical ideas as the basis of rules for describing the orderliness of the universe. The Greeks emphasized the importance of **deductive reasoning**—that is, drawing particular conclusions from more general assumptions. For them illogical thought and vague, unclear language were the main obstacles to scientific knowledge. Much later, during the Scientific Revolution in 17th-century Europe, other thinkers stressed the importance of empirical observations and **inductive reasoning,** which begins with particular observations and infers general patterns or principles from them. For these thinkers purely logical ideas that had no reference to observation, or that did not help to steer observation, had no part in science. Scientific research is now understood to involve both types of reasoning.

Table 2.2 indicates how both types of logic fit with the research process. Deductive logic—thinking in terms of the relationships between ideas—is used when we change the ideas of a theory from a broad focus to a narrow focus and then further refine the theory into a hypothesis. Inductive logic, by contrast, refers to thinking which organizes, summarizes, and interprets factual information and tries to draw out implications or conclusions from observations. We use this kind of logic when we look for patterns in the data we have gathered. Both kinds of logic, then, are essential to the research process.

Another assumption, related to the idea of orderliness in nature and logic in thought, is the idea that order in nature can be explained. If you can clearly describe *how* things are the way they are, you should be able to develop ideas which explain *why* things are that way. The ultimate aim of research is to provide explanations, and the group of systematic, logically connected ideas that explain a factual discovery is called a **theory**. Theories explain why things happen by linking **effects** to their **causes**; they specify the circumstances or conditions under which things happen; they permit us to **predict** events because we can look for those circumstances and conditions in advance of the outcome suggested by the theory.

Theories are ideas that provide us with coherent, systematic syntheses of how we understand particular areas of reality. Yet scientific theories, unlike faith, are flexible. They are organized so that they are open to modification and development based on new empirical information arising from research. Such organization allows for the logical drawing out of **hypotheses** from theory. Hypotheses are statements that express cause-and-effect relationships in a special language that indicates that they are not yet as supported by data as are theories. Testing hypotheses through research extends the theory to new circumstances, conditions, and events. Without the process of hypothesis development and

TABLE 2.2

LOGIC, THEORY, AND RESEARCH

Theory		What are the general ideas, arguments, and puzzles in a particular area? How do they relate to each other? What kinds of research topics do they suggest?
	Deductive Logic	
Hypotheses		How can these ideas and debates be translated into cause-and-effect statements? What kind of evidence is needed to test the resulting hypotheses? What range of techniques is needed to gather such evidence?
Independent and Dependent Variables		What kinds of evidence will demonstrate changes in the variables and their relationships? What tools will be used to measure or identify such changes?
Data Gathering Data Analysis	*Inductive Logic*	Do the data indicate any grouping or pattern? Are there any qualitative or quantitative distinctions to help group the data? What ideas do these patterns or groupings suggest?
Revising the Theory	*Deductive and Inductive Logic*	What are the implications of the analysis for the theory or theories we began with? How do the findings or patterns fit with the patterns arrived at by previous research? What changes are needed in the initial theoretical ideas? What do these changes suggest for further research?

BOX 2.1

Causal Analysis

The idea of cause is a difficult and controversial one which has long been debated by philosophers. Simply put there are two basic positions in these debates. One side sees causality as a real, objective characteristic of the universe, and the task of researchers is to find evidence of this reality. The other side argues that cause is simply an idea; a logical principle that is a convenient way of organizing or interpreting our information or discoveries. In this view we do not find cause in reality, we impose it on our findings.

Wherever their sympathies may lie in this debate, researchers tend to agree that four conditions need to be met in order to accept a causal interpretation of data:

1. TEMPORAL ORDER

A cause must come before an effect. This sounds obvious and in many research situations it is. However, in social science research there are often chicken-and-egg puzzles in which this sequence is not so easily determined. For example, the "differential association" theory of juvenile delinquency argues that delinquency is a result of joining the wrong crowd. Yet it could just as easily be argued that the wrong crowd will attract a certain kind of individual. Being recruited into the wrong crowd is not a cause of delinquency but is itself an intervening (in between) variable. Further, one could argue, perhaps, that wrong crowds and problem personalities attracted to them are products of certain kinds of environments—i.e., they are both effects of a common cause. Sorting out sequences of causes and effects, then, is not always an easy task.

2. ASSOCIATION OR CORRELATION

The researcher must show that the two variables change together in a consistent way. For example, one might find that the greater the extent of poverty in a region, the more health problems are experienced by the inhabitants (a positive correlation). Or one might find that the higher the level of family income, the fewer the number of children per family (a negative correlation). If there is no consistent pattern of association, it is unlikely that there is a causal connection. Association or correlation may not be perfect; you will find healthy people in poor regions, and rich families with many children. Thus, the degree of association necessary to accept a causal interpretation requires careful assessment and often involves statistical analysis. Finding an association by itself does not mean that a causal relationship exists and the other conditions outlined here must be satisfied.

3. ELIMINATING ALTERNATIVE CAUSAL INFLUENCES

Causal or explanatory research requires the control of alternative causal factors so that clear conclusions can be drawn about the cause actually at work. Different research techniques use different means to establish such controls. The laboratory experiment is the most effective technique for eliminating alternative causal factors, but its use is often limited in social research. Consequently, other means, such as systematic comparison and statistical analysis, have been developed to perform this control function. These techniques, however, are much weaker than experimental controls. Hence, social science research is dogged by many disputes over causal explanations.

4. THEORETICAL CONSISTENCY

Finally, the discovery or interpretation of causal linkages should make sense or be acceptable in terms of the researchers' theoretical framework or assumptions. This is a difficult issue because the researchers cannot be so attached to their theories that they "explain away" results that do not fit. Such results or anomalies may be very valuable in provoking the development of more adequate theories to replace the existing ones. However, much research consolidates and extends existing theoretical understanding rather than overthrowing it. Assessing the theoretical significance of research data—for example, whether it is an extension or an anomaly—can be very difficult.

hypothesis testing, scientific theories would become closed, dogmatic, and unaffected by new research.

Hypotheses are ideas put forward to be tested; they are designed to direct our attention to the "facts." Instead of speaking in terms of causes and effects, hypotheses refer to variables. Variables are parts or aspects of reality that can be seen to change or vary. Temperature, speed, and volume are variables in the physical world; social class, nationality, standard of living, and sexism are variables in the social world. Hypotheses usually take the form of "if ... then" statements such as "if the temperature of water decreases to the freezing point, its volume will increase," or "if income increases then the amount spent on entertainment will increase."

In these hypotheses temperature and income are called **independent variables.** They are identified as changing but the causes of those changes are not specified; they just change by themselves—*independently* of other factors. Volume and spending on entertainment are called **dependent variables** because their changes are linked to, or depend upon, the changes in the independent variables. Thus, the hypotheses assume that if there are no changes in the independent variables, there will be no changes in the dependent variables.

How do we tell whether or not there have been changes in any variable? We know this by setting up ways of measuring or identifying changes. Setting up systems of **measurement** or identification of change is called **operationalizing.** Essentially, operationalizing means clearly laying out the rules for establishing changes in variables. In the physical sciences the rules have developed with instruments of measurement: temperature is measured by thermometers, speed by accelerometers, etc. In the social sciences our instruments tend to be such things as sets of questions specially designed to establish how religious we are, or how socially involved, or how satisfied with our work; or psychological tests designed to measure how intelligent, creative, depressed, or addicted, etc. we are. Other measures are developed from available statistical data to develop measures of unemployment, crime rates, the cost of living, etc.

All the measures identified so far have one thing in common: whether you are dealing with temperature, speed, IQ, work satisfaction, or the suicide rate, you can measure in precise **quantitative** terms. For example, an IQ of 115, a temperature of 21 degrees Celsius, a work satisfaction rating of 7 out of 10, and a suicide rate of 3.5 per 100 000. But such quantitative precision is not possible with many social characteristics that are treated as variables: religious differences, nationality, or sexual orientation, for example. These kinds of variations are

BOX 2.2

Theory and Research: Hypothesis Development

FROM THEORY TO HYPOTHESIS

Research is never simply an accumulation of facts. Facts are important and meaningful only in relation to questions and ideas. The general ideas that give meaning to facts are called theories. Theories summarize and interrelate empirical data by explaining how and why things happen, and by suggesting logical extensions and implications of these explanations.

For example, sociological theories of stratification or social class argue that economically based inequalities shape or determine political power and ideas, cultural patterns, family relationships, and so on. Such theories are very broad, general interpretations, not easy to test in relation to empirical evidence. For them to be useful in guiding research, two things have to be done. First, we have to break the theory down into a more narrowly focused set of ideas; second, we reformulate these ideas into data-oriented, empirically testable hypotheses. Thus:

Step 1:

General theory   =   Economically based inequalities determine or shape the major features of social life.

Specific theory   =   Economically based inequalities shape the lifestyle (tastes, cultural expression, and consumption patterns) of individuals and groups.

Step 2:

General hypothesis   =   Economic inequality determines consumption patterns.

Specific hypothesis =   As income increases, the level of spending on entertainment increases. (Therefore, income is the independent variable and spending on entertainment is the dependent variable. In other words, spending on entertainment "depends" on the level of income.)

FROM HYPOTHESIS TO RESEARCH

Our hypothesis is now in the form of an "if ... then" statement connecting variables. We must now clarify what we mean by "increase in income" and "spending on entertainment." Thus:

Step 3:

Operational

  definition   =   a. By income we mean ... (What do you mean by "income?" The definition must hold for the duration of your study and must resolve issues such as pre-tax or net income figures, earnings only or other income and wealth, individual or family incomes, the time period involved, etc.)

                     b. By spending on entertainment we mean ... (What do you mean by "spending on entertainment?" The definition must hold for the duration of your study and must resolve such issues as: do we include spending on tobacco and alcohol? How do we distinguish between "luxury clothing" worn at parties and regular or necessary clothing? Is eating out a necessity or a luxury/entertainment item? and so on.)

classifiable as different and one can describe the differences, but one cannot numerically *measure* or rate such differences. Social scientists often deal with **qualitative variables** as well as quantitative, measurable ones. This means that our hypotheses are often less precise than those in the natural sciences. (This difference in the measurability of variables is taken up in Chapter 9.)

Statements linking independent and dependent variables translate abstract theoretical ideas into specific, empirically focused ones. They do so by focusing on a small number of key factors (variables) and forcing the researchers into developing their ideas in terms of observation or data gathering (operationalizing). Thinking in terms of hypotheses requires you to identify how variables change—this can only be done by identifying *what you will see* as variables change.

Such hypotheses are like pieces of a jigsaw puzzle. As hypotheses are tested, and assuming they survive the tests of observation and data gathering, they begin to accumulate and interconnect into a bigger picture covering more and more factors, events and processes. This big picture is interpreted and described through theories that represent an overall understanding and explanation of the causes at work.

It should be pointed out that many social scientists do not entirely share this view of social science research; for them it is a mistake to follow natural science assumptions so closely. Many social scientists argue that social research is at least as **humanistic** as scientific. For these researchers the task of social research is to bring out the uniquely human qualities of psychological and social reality. This does not involve abandoning the assumption of an orderly universe or violating rules of logic; nor does it mean that social researchers should not care about empirical evidence. Rather, these researchers argue, social research should be devoted to careful description to bring out the richness and complexity of social and psychological life; and attention should be paid to the unique and the singular, not just to what can be generalized. Furthermore, social and psychological explanations have to be framed in terms of human motives and meanings, and not the impersonal, mechanical causality favoured by natural science.

Because this approach emphasizes description, variation, and meaningful explanation, there is little emphasis on hypothesis development, operationalizing, and measurement. Hypotheses are often viewed as rigid, inflexible tools, which would distort the researchers' sense of what they are investigating. Precise measurement is also less valued than precise description and trying to present the viewpoints of the people studied. We discuss qualitative research in depth in Chapter 7.

Every social science is divided, to some extent, between the "scientific" and "humanistic" approaches and there appears to be no end in sight to this division. Rather than take sides we would like to point out that, as far as social research is concerned, both approaches are thoroughly empirical and their work is generally *complementary* and not mutually exclusive. Valuable information and discoveries have been and continue to be contributed by both approaches.

STEPS IN THE RESEARCH PROCESS

Essentially, doing research involves: first, defining a topic in such a way that it is meaningful, significant, and researchable; second, developing an organized, systematic plan for researching the topic with reference to empirical data, and then following through on this plan; third, analyzing the data gathered and, finally, communicating the results of the research in full—i.e., including the definition of the topic, the research plan, the way this plan was implemented, the results, and your interpretation of the results.

In this section we will look at this process step-by-step (in fact, it is more complicated than this, with lots of two-steps-forward-one-step-back movements) to give you a sense of how to proceed. Lest we give you the wrong impression, scientific research is never problem free. Researchers are human after all; they make mistakes, they misinterpret their results, things often do not work out in the expected way, and all sorts of confusion may occur. Different kinds of things can go wrong at different stages of the research process, so along with identifying the steps themselves we shall also discuss the mistakes and problems that may occur at each step.

Step 1: Defining the Topic

As we have already stated, a researchable topic is not just a smart idea no one else has thought of. If you think you have an original idea you first have to see whether it is really so original. As a basis for research your idea also has to connect with empirical information. Consequently, the first step is to explore other people's research in order to find out what other people have thought and discovered, and to see how your ideas relate or connect to these thoughts and discoveries. In this process you will be able to clarify your initial idea, to rework it so that it takes advantage of and builds upon other people's research. By fitting in with previous research your ideas do not lose their originality or significance; rather, they become *more* important by becoming part of an ongoing set of discoveries and debates. The process of developing a research topic through examining other people's research is discussed in detail in Chapter 3.

Of course, things can go wrong even at this early stage. The area you are interested in may be very controversial, such as the effects of violence in the media on children's behaviour. You may have strong ideas on the subject and you want your research to support those ideas. Since the research on this topic is inconclusive it is open to interpretation and selective reading. In most areas of social science controversies are plentiful, so you will have to learn to be open minded and fair in your reading. Any conclusions you draw should be made on the basis of the logical and empirical strengths and weaknesses of the research and not arise from your biases. Consequently, this initial step also involves identifying your own biases on the topic.

Misinterpretation of others' research may also occur through illogical reasoning, hasty reading, and the omission of important or up-to-date information. These errors will undermine your research by introducing biases, one-sided interpretations, and mistaken interpretations, which will lessen the value of the entire research project. It is essential, then, that the research be launched properly, through a careful, critical examination of your initial ideas and the way they relate to the ideas and discoveries of other researchers in your chosen field of interest.

Step 2: Designing the Research Plan

Let us suppose that you have heard recent media reports about "punks" with squeegees who clean motorists' windshields when they are waiting at traffic lights. Perhaps you have heard about the Saturday night riot in Montreal, which was supposedly provoked by the police crackdown on these activities. Some radio interviews indicated that most of these people are young high-school drop-outs. Over the past few years you are aware that the media have reported periodically on high unemployment among high-school dropouts or young people between the ages of 16 and 24. But now you have questions which these reports do not answer. How widespread is the problem? Has it grown worse in the past couple of years? Is it expected to grow worse in the future? Are there certain social groups whose teenagers are disproportionately poor? Why is it a problem? What are its causes?

After reviewing the literature perhaps you find that there are some useful statistics available from Statistics Canada that give you a sense that the problem of teenage poverty has been growing steadily. However, very little has been written about it even though a lot has been written about poverty in general. What kind of study you should plan on doing depends on the kinds of questions you wish to pursue. In turn, the nature of your study determines the kinds of research methods you will be using.

First, the general approach: is your study to be exploratory, descriptive, or explanatory? You may conclude from your reading of others' research that there is so little information that what is needed is a "probe" into society to see what the reality is. Alternatively, you may find that there is some information on teenage poverty but that it is incomplete in certain ways. For example, where other research provides clear profiles of poverty-stricken groups such as the elderly or single-parent families, there is much less detail on poor teenagers. This would suggest that you design your study to provide a clear, detailed description of the characteristics of this group. Alternatively, you may be satisfied with the descriptions of poverty-stricken teenagers but feel there are no satisfactory explanations of why the phenomenon exists and why it has grown recently.

An **exploratory study** is designed to find out what things are like in situations where there is little firm information. "Is teenage poverty real or is it a media myth?" is the kind of question asked in such a study. An exploratory study is designed to seek out as much information as possible from, say, the teenage poor and other people who may have information concerning them.

Such a study could be qualitative or quantitative, or could combine both types of information. An example of the former would be a **field study** (see Chapter 7) where you do volunteer work at a drop-in centre, or community clinic, or other organization helping the poor, the homeless, etc., in order to make contact with teenagers living on the streets. As you make contacts and build up trust, you can find out about their lives, how they came to be in their current situation, and get leads to others in similar circumstances. In addition you may be able to talk to (interview) fellow volunteers and community-work professionals and find out what they know about the problem of teen poverty. They too may pass you on to other experts or professionals, such as social workers or teachers. From these diverse sources you could put together a picture of teen poverty combining both information on the experiences and lives of teenagers themselves, and various perspectives from people close to and informed about the problem.

The distinction between an exploratory and a **descriptive study** is not a clear or rigid one. However, it is logical to think of detailed description as something that follows from exploration. Once you have discovered the existence of a phenomenon like teenage poverty, the next step is to describe it clearly in all its variations. It is possible that the task of detailed and extensive description, then, is a project that follows from the initial exploratory research. Thus, after demonstrating the existence of teenage poverty, one could go on to do detailed studies of males versus females, differences between runaways and dropouts living at home, differences in types and levels of poverty in different regions, and so on. Such studies would probably attempt to use different data-gathering techniques from those used in the initial, exploratory research. The latter might use field research, case studies, expert testimony, documentary, and available data. The former would be more likely to use surveys by distributing questionnaires to community volunteers and professionals to distribute to their clients as well as to survey volunteers and professionals themselves. Documentary research might be extended to cover a longer time period or to extend the range and detail by moving from the study of federal government statistics to those of provincial governments.

An **explanatory study** attempts to go beyond description by collecting data to show *why* things are the way they are. In our example, such a study would try to explain why youth poverty has increased over a certain time period, or increased more in some areas than in others; why youths with certain background characteristics seem to be more vulnerable to poverty than others; or what the specific conditions and circumstances are that seem to occur commonly among poverty-stricken teens. Explanatory studies tend to be more quantitative in their approach, to use probability samples to select their informants (see Chapter 4 on sampling), and to use systematic, questionnaire-based interviews or survey techniques and even occasionally experimental procedures. These procedures allow researchers to draw conclusions more reliably than qualitative approaches do. However, explanatory research often includes exploratory, descriptive, and qualitative material to illustrate and support the arguments made on the basis of quantitative methods. Consequently, deciding on whether your research approach is going to be exploratory-descriptive or explanatory will lead you to rely on different methods of observation or data gathering and will also tend to determine the relative balance between qualitative and quantitative analysis in your research.

Step 3: Following the Research Plan (Data Gathering)

Once you have developed your research plan and have decided on the aim of the research (exploratory-descriptive or explanatory) and the procedures you will be using to gather your data, you have to follow through on it. The bulk of this textbook (Chapters 5–8) discusses these procedures in detail. Here we should just alert you to two important problems: sampling and errors in data gathering.

Most research involves sampling—that is, you will study only a small part of the reality you are interested in. You cannot track down and interview all poor teenagers; you will not have time to visit all drop-in centres or to talk to all experts; the government may have useful statistics since 1971 but not before, etc.

For various reasons, then, any factual study is restricted to a **sample** or a part of what the researcher is concerned with. How that sample is made available or chosen for study is an important issue, as we shall see in Chapter 4. The major issue with respect to sampling is how confident you can be that the sample you have studied is representative of the whole. Without reasonable grounds for assuming your sample is representative, your study can be criticized as potentially biased and providing a distorted, selective view of reality.

The second problem is that all research procedures have the potential for creating **errors.** Questionnaires asking people to tick off an appropriate box provide *opportunities* for people to accidentally check off the wrong box, or to skip the question, or to deliberately give the wrong reply. Experimenters cannot stop people from trying to guess the purpose of the experiment and altering their behaviour to help or hinder the experimenter achieve the assumed purpose. Even the best participant observers may slightly alter the behaviour of the people they are observing. All these methods are necessary to gather data but they also have the potential of producing erroneous information. Since these methods are the only ways we have of gathering data, the best we can do is to try to be aware of their problems and limitations and try to minimize their sources of error.

Step 4: Analyzing and Interpreting the Data

Facts rarely if ever speak for themselves. The facts or data that are collected in the course of research always need organizing and analyzing before their patterns and implications can be seen or understood. Notes on fieldwork have to be read and reread before you can see what values, interests, and perceptions people share; the answers to dozens or even hundreds of questionnaires have to be coded and counted before you can identify patterns of opinions and connect these patterns with characteristics of people with different opinions; statistics from government documents have to be sifted through and reorganized in order to discover trends or other patterns. These processes of analysis, interpretation, reorganization, and sifting and sorting make up the stage of **data analysis,** where you find out what data you have gathered and what sense can be made of it. As we shall see in Chapter 9, data analysis takes different forms in quantitative and qualitative styles of social research.

Organizing the data badly can give unclear and misleading impressions. Two major problems encountered at this stage of research are drawing improper conclusions and "fudging" unexpected or surprising discoveries. We are often tempted to overgeneralize and make strong claims on the basis of too few or not very strong examples. Our tendency to want to fit observations into clear and distinct patterns may lead us to oversimplify and force evidence into logical groupings. With respect to the second problem, unexpected findings break through the logical groupings expressed in our hypotheses and research questions and leave us with the problem of how to account for these surprising facts. In our concern to explain all of our data we improvise new explanations to fit the facts without fully thinking through how these explanations fit with our initial ideas.

Step 5: Writing the Research Report

Research is meaningless if it remains known only by the original researcher. The entire point of research is to add to existing knowledge and, in the case of applied research, to improve our ability to do things effectively—to cure mental illness, reduce poverty, or improve job satisfaction. If no one else knows what you have found out, past mistakes go uncorrected, new conditions are not understood, and attempts to improve or cope with social problems are less effective than they might otherwise be.

Hence, the final step in the research process is writing up and circulating a research report. This may take the form of an essay for your teacher; a paper written for publication in a journal; or a report submitted to a client or organization. Regardless of who you write the report for, it has to communicate clearly why you selected your problem; what your research design was and how you carried it out; and what the results were and how you interpreted them. Each of these points has to be presented with sufficient detail and clarity so that, in principle, other researchers could **replicate** or repeat your research if they so wished. The point of this is that other researchers may not be entirely convinced of your findings and they should be able to try their hand at the same kind of research. If others come up with similar results, your research will be accepted as valid and as a foundation for others to develop. Of course, your research may be sufficiently convincing not to need repeating. In either case, at this point it is no longer *your* research. In a sense, it now belongs to all researchers; it has become "what everybody knows."

CONSTRAINTS OF THE RESEARCH PROCESS

So far we have presented social science research as an almost entirely intellectual process. This is only part of the story. Research requires resources of all kinds and part of the researcher's time, energy, and skills is spent in trying to obtain and manage the needed resources. In addition, research is a human activity—the researcher brings to it a variety of social and personal assumptions and perspectives. Those who are being researched are not always passive subjects opening up their lives for scientific inspection. A variety of social circumstances influence how research issues become important and how they are thought about and researched.

Resources

Doing research requires time, money, and other resources, all of which are in limited supply. Can you finish your report by the deadline? Can you afford to mail out questionnaires to a large enough sample? Will you be allowed to interview residents in an institution? People who undertake research for the first time are shocked to discover that so much of their time and energy is taken up with organizing these resources so that the research can actually get done. You need to assess the amounts of time, money, and other resources you are going to need prior to setting out to do the research. These considerations have to be part of the development of the research plan, the second step in the research process. A *researchable* topic is one that is not only feasible in terms of its meaning and significance in relation to other research, but is also practical in terms of the resources that the researcher has access to.

Elusive Targets: Problems with Human Data

Social researchers also face a variety of constraints arising from their subject matter—other human beings. The most important of these constraints involves **ethics:** what are the responsibilities of researchers to the people they do research on? Experiments on human subjects are obviously limited by basic obligations to treat others with decency and dignity. But almost all social research methods raise ethical questions concerning how much stress the research should be permitted to impose, how much information should be extracted, and how much people's right to privacy should be protected. All professional social science associations have developed ethical guidelines for their researchers. Institutions such as universities and governments that support research routinely monitor studies by applying these guidelines. Ethical issues will be discussed as part of the presentation of each major research method in subsequent chapters.

Human beings can be troublesome to researchers for a variety of other reasons. People may be unwilling to be interviewed or to allow others to observe their activities; only a minority of people will return mail questionnaires; people in power—and deviants—tend to be secretive about their actions and resist studies of their lives; some people are inarticulate and unable to express their feelings and perceptions clearly; and historians often find it difficult to get at the lives of the humble majority who do not leave written documents and monuments behind as evidence of their actions. Social researchers, then, have to be extremely aware of the many ways human beings can hide and be hidden, deceive, and limit our access to their lives and thoughts.

The Social Context and the Personal Equation

Another set of constraints or pressures arises from the social and personal circumstances surrounding research. Social research looks at a fast-changing and controversial part of reality: society, human relations, and human psychological characteristics. Not long ago spousal abuse was not a prominent topic for social research. In the 1970s Canadian social scientists debated and did research on the American domination of the Canadian economy; in the 1990s many of these same social scientists are now doing research on the impact of the "global economy" on Canada. Shifts like these arise from changing social conditions, which contribute to altering definitions of what are important issues, ideas, and phenomena in society. This, in turn, encourages researchers to turn their attention to new areas and to lessen their interest in others.

Addicts in HIV Study Won't Be Treated

Vancouver Research Project Involving 1,200 Intravenous Drug Users Is Unethical, Doctor Charges

A study of whether intravenous drug users will contract the AIDS virus is unethical because it doesn't offer them treatment with methadone, which can help keep them from catching the virus, says a Vancouver doctor who treats addicts.

Stanley de Vlaming said he finds it intolerable that researchers are prepared to sit by and watch a group of more than a thousand injection-drug users, waiting to see whether they contract the AIDS virus, when treating them with the heroin substitute would very likely save some of them from catching the disease.

"It's a beautiful study from an epidemiological point of view," he said of the Vancouver Injection Drug Use Study, just being launched by several prominent AIDS physicians. "But from the humanistic side, I think it is lacking."

Medical ethics demand that effective treatments be offered if they exist, Dr. de Vlaming, who provides methadone treatment for 75 heroin addicts at his Gastown Medical Clinic, said in an interview. In a letter addressed to one of the researchers on the study and obtained by the Globe and Mail, Dr. de Vlaming protested vigorously against the study.

"There already exists a large body of medical evidence which indicates that the rate of HIV infection can be reduced by treatments aimed at the primary illness of addiction," he wrote. "Methadone treatment, coupled with counselling, is an example of a minimum standard. To withhold treatment, or not to offer a treatment which has proven efficacy, is unethical."

However, two ethics committees have con-cluded that the research-ers should not have to bear the brunt of society's failure to offer adequate treatment to intravenous drug users, and they have given the study the go-ahead.

"Quite honestly, I don't feel right about it. I feel correct, but I don't feel right about it inside," said Jim Kennedy, who chaired the research review committee at St. Paul's Hospital, which approved the study after some debate.

"Morally I am really on Stan's side, but ethically, our hands are kind of tied," Dr. Kennedy said. "We felt we couldn't say it was [the researchers'] responsibility to provide that treatment because society has deemed it not important enough to provide that treatment."

The researchers have started to interview people who will be among the 1,200 injection-drug users to be studied over three years. They will be interviewed, counselled and tested for AIDS and tuberculosis exposure at six-month intervals. The study will cost $300,000 a year and will be funded by provincial and federal governments.

Methadone, which is chemically similar to heroin, is given to addicts once a day, mixed in orange juice. People on methadone are still addicts but don't use needles (the source of most AIDS-virus transmission in intravenous drug users) or crave heroin. They are thus enabled to lead more normal lives.

The ethics committees for St. Paul's and the University of British Columbia (which also had to approve the project) decided that since funds for methadone treatment and physicians willing to administer it are in short supply, the researchers are free to study intravenous drug use without offering methadone.

Dr. de Vlaming said some of the money for the study should be going into methadone treatment.

"These are individuals that could be treated," he said. "It's not like treatment doesn't exist, or is prohibitively

expensive or impossible to administer."

Dr. de Vlaming is also concerned that the addicts are to be paid $25 every six months when they come in to participate in the study. "That's just about the cost of a hit of cocaine."

Dr. Kennedy said the issue of payment was of great concern for several members of both ethics committees. However, they were persuaded that it would be discriminatory and condescending not to follow the normal practice of paying people for participating in a research study because there were doubts about how addicts might spend their honorariums.

Researcher Steffanie Strathdee said the study may, in the long run, improve treatment for addicts as well as helping to control the spread of the human immunodeficiency virus, because what is learned about their behaviour will help develop treatments.

The first stage of the study showed that incidence of HIV infection among intravenous-drug users rose to 6 per cent from 2 per cent in about 18 months. "If we knew what would stop HIV

transmission in this group, we would be doing it already," she said.

As well, she and fellow researcher David Patrick said it was unlikely that methadone treatment would do much to keep the intravenous-drug users in the study from contracting HIV. That is because the highest incidence of HIV transmission is among people who inject cocaine, not heroin, and methadone does not work to control cocaine addiction. Dr. Strathdee said they expect cocaine to be the drug of choice for most people involved in the study.

However, Dr. de Vlaming said there are few pure cocaine addicts: Most intravenous-drug users inject both heroin and cocaine or a combination of the two, known as a speedball.

"These people are polyaddicted to heroin as well as cocaine, and research has shown that if you put those people on methadone you can often reduce or eliminate cocaine use as well," he said.

He said he has found it possible to reduce infection of cocaine by his patients by refusing methadone to people who are not prepared to give up cocaine. Regular

Source: Jane Coutts, "Addicts in HIV Study Won't Be Treated," *The Globe and Mail* (4 June 1996), p. A8. Reprinted with permission.

In addition, social research can use a diverse range of designs and methods: laboratory experiments, surveys, fieldwork, analysis of documents, statistical analysis, etc. There are many different *styles* of social research ranging from the hard scientific style of experimentation and statistical analysis, to the humanistic style of oral history and of many field studies. Each researcher develops an interest in specific issues and a taste for a certain style of research because each of us brings our individual concerns, outlook, and skills to research. Some may enjoy working with historical documents or personal letters and trying to recreate the lives and times of individuals and groups in a humanistic style. Others will enjoy the challenge of designing experiments or developing statistical interpretations of economic and demographic data.

As you come to learn the different approaches to research, you too will develop a leaning towards particular approaches, and become better at using these approaches than others you are less interested in. This is not a problem as long as you are aware of the limitations of *all* research methods and do not convince yourself that your way is the only way of doing research. Each design and procedure has advantages and limitations; often the strengths of one method compensate for the weaknesses of others. The different research methods are each equally valuable and can often be used in a complementary way. Combining different methods in the same research design is often essential, as is remaining open minded about all the available methods for obtaining empirical evidence.

WHAT YOU HAVE LEARNED

- Research may begin with questions or issues arising from personal issues or social issues or from the puzzles and questions posed by previous research.

- The initial issue or question needs to be developed and focused by relating it to what is already known and thought in a broader area of social science.

- All research follows basic guidelines requiring objectivity, empirical verification, and openness to inspection and analysis by others.

- These guidelines rest on certain assumptions that emphasize the orderliness of reality and the need for logical thinking.

- Much social science research is developed through testing hypotheses which extend theories by focusing on a small number of variables that are assumed to be causally connected.

- Variables are defined in terms of the evidence required to show how they change—an approach called operationalization.

- Some social scientists de-emphasize hypothesis testing and approach social research in a humanistic manner, stressing description over explanation.

- Research is a complicated process involving several steps: defining the topic appropriately; developing a research design and following it through; analyzing the data; and communicating the results.

- Research is affected by nonscientific factors such as the scarcity of resources, ethical considerations, the social context, and the personal character of the researchers.

KEY WORDS

research process	independent variable
objectivity	dependent variable
empirical verification	measurement
deductive reasoning	operationalizing
inductive reasoning	quantitative/qualitative variables
theory	humanistic
cause and effect	exploratory study
prediction	field study
hypothesis	descriptive study

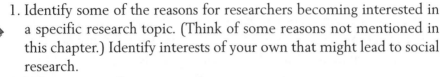

explanatory study	data analysis
sample	replication
errors	ethics

REVIEW QUESTIONS

1. Identify some of the reasons for researchers becoming interested in a specific research topic. (Think of some reasons not mentioned in this chapter.) Identify interests of your own that might lead to social research.
2. What is scientific scepticism?
3. What are the basic assumptions of scientific enquiry?
4. What is explanatory research and when is it used?
5. What are the differences between the scientific and the humanistic approaches to social science research?
6. What is the relationship between theory and hypothesis?
7. What are the steps in the research process? Can you identify reasons why these steps are flexible and not rigid?

RECOMMENDED READINGS

Hyman, H. H. (Ed.). (1991). *Taking society's measure: A personal history of survey research.* New York: Russell Sage Foundation.

A behind-the-scenes, personal account of the early development of survey research in North America.

Lewis, G. H. (Ed.). (1975). *Fist-fights in the kitchen: Manners and methods in social research.* Pacific Palisades, CA: Goodyear.

An offbeat collection of lively pieces on ethical, political, and other problems associated with social research.

Shaffir, W. B., & Stebbins, R. A. (Eds.). (1991). *Experiencing fieldwork: An inside view of qualitative research.* Newbury Park, CA: Sage.

Researchers recount their experiences in studying a great variety of social situations.

CHAPTER 3

Finding a Topic

WHAT YOU WILL LEARN

- how to select a topic for research
- how to use a library
- how to expand the number of sources of information
- how to plan and organize the literature review

INTRODUCTION

Jane finally saved enough money to buy her own car. What would you advise her? Should she simply buy the first affordable car she sees, or should she become more informed about the cost, quality, and diversity of cars available in her price range? Ali wants to buy a computer, but knows very little about computers. What would you advise him? Should he simply buy any computer or should he become more informed about the cost, quality, and diversity of computers available? And how can they become more informed? You would probably advise them to collect some background information, that is, find out what is already known about those products. They can read magazine articles and reviews of the products and ask friends and acquaintances for more information. The more informed they become, the more discerning they will be about which product to buy.

Scientific research follows a somewhat similar procedure; it too takes into account what previous researchers have found about an issue. But, of course, scientific research is far more complex and challenging than everyday inquiries, and it can also be far more rewarding.

In the preceding two chapters we have argued that there are important differences between scientific and everyday, common-sense thinking. A scientific approach is based on two elements: an attention to the structure of the reasoning and ideas used in thinking about an issue; and the use of systematic procedures designed to get at the facts of the matter at issue.

When you come to college or university after high school, the difference between common sense and science begins to appear in your classroom experience. In high school teachers generally encourage students to discuss topics whether they really know much about them or not. The emphasis in classroom discussions tends to be on participation. Teachers encourage you to give your opinions, to state these opinions as clearly and reasonably as you can, and perhaps to debate and modify your opinions in response to those of others.

At college and university your opinions are no longer so highly valued. Instructors challenge you to be logical and reasonable, to take account of ideas that are accepted in a particular discipline, and to provide evidence to support your arguments. This forces you to become familiar with the concepts, theories, arguments, methods, and data of entire groups of social science researchers.

At first you may be shocked that your ideas alone are not good enough to be accepted as the basis for class discussions and assignments. In high school you could write essays combining clever ideas from off the top of your head with "data" or "information" from an encyclopedia or a single library book. At college or university you are expected to go beyond this and organize your thoughts in terms of the accepted ways of thinking in sociology, anthropology, political science, economics, psychology, or history. Your instructors may set essays in which you will be asked primarily to summarize the ideas of specific areas of social science research. An important part of the research process is to discover, summarize, and critically assess previous research on the issue or topic of your concern.

By directing our attention to what has been done we eliminate wasteful efforts and needless rediscoveries of what is already known. Previous research suggests ideas that may be developed, methods that may be applied, and puzzles that are still unexplained, and provides data that may be reanalyzed or added to. Even if you have a completely original idea, looking at past research is likely to show that it connects with other ideas and information; and these connections indicate just how relevant or important an idea or discovery may be. Scientific research is a cooperative process (although it also involves much competition between individuals or teams of researchers) and it is also a cumulative process in which each piece of research builds on previous knowledge and leads towards new research.

At the moment you may be a long way from thinking of yourself as a social scientist or researcher. However, you are likely sometime to need to find out more information about a social issue or phenomenon. Perhaps you want to know more about income inequality in Canada. You may simply want to know the extent of income inequalities. But such descriptive information is insufficient to explain income inequality. You will also need to be informed about the discussions of the phenomenon by others. What works exist on the subject? How do they define and measure income inequality? What are the main causes of income inequality? What are its social effects?

How would you obtain information on these issues so that these various questions could be answered? This chapter takes you through the process of becoming knowledgeable about a topic or field associated with social science knowledge. There are three basic aspects to this process:

1. How do you find out about what has been done (thought about, discussed, and discovered) on a particular topic?
2. How do you organize a review of your knowledge of what has been done?
3. What contribution would such a review make to the research process?

FINDING OUT WHAT HAS BEEN DONE

Selecting a Research Topic

The starting point in research is selecting a topic. Whether the topic is assigned by the instructor, proposed by you, or selected from an instructor's list, it is essential that the research is achievable. You would certainly want to take into account the time you have available to do the project, as well as other constraints, including costs. Thus, no matter how interesting the topic you need to be sure that you can carry out the research given the time and other resources you have available.

There is no one best strategy in selecting and narrowing the topic for research. No matter where the topic idea came from (it may have been sparked by curiosity, a magazine article, a class discussion, and so on), one way to begin is to write down the research issue as a complete phrase. Say you have read that there are an increasing number of college dropouts, and that most are males. Do not simply write down "dropouts." Remember you want to narrow the topic to formulate a clear statement of the issue to research. You might therefore write down:

    More male students are dropping out of college
    than female students.

You will now want to narrow down this issue. One way to clarify and limit the issue is to write down questions about the statement. You might begin with the concepts.

    What is meant by dropout?

    What is meant by college students?

Next ask yourself what information you want to find out about the issue. For example:

    Are they completely breaking their ties with the
    college?

    Did they hold part-time employment before dropping
    out of college?

Continue to ask whatever questions help make the issue clearer. A key one to ask is:

    Why are more male students dropping out of college
    than female students?

Write down the possible explanations. For example:

    Females have higher academic aspirations than
    males.

    Females invest more time and effort in their
    studies.

    Females are less likely to find full-time employ-
    ment than males.

Each of these explanations suggests another research topic. For example: Do female college students have higher academic aspirations than male college students? What are the academic aspirations of college students? Why do college students have certain aspirations? And so on. As you raise questions about the issue, you are also coming up with factors that contribute to the explanation. Take the earlier explanations as an example. Each point to the following factors:

- academic aspiration;
- amount of time spent on studies; and
- employment opportunities.

The more questions you ask, the more likely you are to come up with a topic that interests you. Your next step is to concentrate on one or two specific questions you want to research. To begin you would want to find out what others have written about the issue. That can help you narrow your topic further.

Becoming More Informed About the Topic

In finding out what others have written about the topic, begin with what you already have. Media reports often identify sources of information, such as Statistics Canada or the name of the researcher and their place of research.

Note that although you may get some ideas and even data from the mass media, you should not treat these items as scholarly sources. Newspaper or magazine articles may provide you with some leads to begin with, but your research project has to be grounded in first-hand knowledge of social science research, not second-hand, journalistic accounts of this research. However, you can collect newspaper clippings, or make notes on TV and radio news reports as a way to begin collecting ideas and information.

Class readings or texts will have references, footnotes, bibliographies, or "further readings" mentioning relevant books, articles, etc. It is easy to make notes on your class texts and handouts and begin to develop a list of sources of information for your topic. If your textbook deals with the topic in some depth, be sure to read the appropriate section carefully, and check the index for other references to the topic. Textbooks are useful starting points because they present material in a straightforward, easily understood way. They are also continually revised and updated so that the sources of information they contain are quite current.

Another easily accessible and familiar beginning point is a multi-volume encyclopedia, such as the *Encyclopedia Britannica*, found in most college and university libraries. You will have used these in high school and they are now readily available in CD-ROM format. They too have the advantage of being written for the general reader so you can obtain a clearly written overview of a topic, perhaps accompanied by a brief bibliography or list of related topic entries elsewhere in the encyclopedia. You should be aware, however, that general encyclopedias lack depth and detail and should be considered an initial source only. Another disadvantage is that encyclopedias take a long time to be prepared before publication and will not provide up-to-date information.

The textbook and general reference encyclopedia should overlap to some degree in their presentation of key ideas, most important findings and researchers, etc. Both sources may have footnotes, references, or a bibliography identifying the most important or up-to-date books and articles on the general topic.

It is useful, even when you are new to social science research, to develop a critical approach to what you read and to continually review your critical assessments. Even though these assessments are likely to change over time, you will be working with a purpose, rather than aimlessly collecting mountains of references.

What will you get out of this initial search for information? First, you will have obtained some basic information on a topic. Are there recurring major definitions, concepts, and ideas? What are the names of major researchers or research traditions associated with those ideas? What types of empirical data are often noted?

Second, at this early stage in the literature search you can begin to assess the basic information in terms of your own assumptions and interests. Do the ideas and data confirm or challenge your assumptions? Do the ideas and data arouse your interests? Do they puzzle you? Do you see gaps or other aspects of the information with which you are dissatisfied in some way?

Third, you now have a first list of sources of information to take to the library. In the process of making your list, you have also become more informed about the topic that interests you and possibly narrowed it down further. The next step is to examine the sources and find out what other researchers have done. For that there is no better place to start than the library.

Using the Library

The fastest and easiest way of learning how best to use a college or university library is to go on the "library tour" put on at the beginning of the term. You will learn what services the library has to offer (if you can have access to interlibrary loans, or computer searches, for example), the location of the various books, catalogues, reference materials, etc., and the basics of how to use the library. If you need help at any time in finding information in the library, never hesitate to ask one of the reference librarians; their job is to help people gain access to information and they are experts at that job!

Most libraries in North America use the **Library of Congress Classification System.** There are twenty classes in the Library of Congress Classification System, each of which is then divided into subclasses. The categories are made more specific with the addition of other letters and numbers. Here are the main classifications:

```
A       General works
B       Philosophy, psychology, and religion
C-F     History
G       Geography, anthropology, recreation
H       Social science
J       Political science
K       Law
L       Education
M       Music
N       Fine Arts
P       Language and literature
Q       Science
R       Medicine
S       Agriculture
T       Technology
U       Military science
V       Naval science
Z       Bibliography and library science
```

Each of these classifications is extremely broad, and searching for books in a large library under any of these headings would result in an extensive list, one too long to work with. The classifications are further divided into more specific subclasses. The broad category H, social science, is broken into subclasses by adding another letter. For example, from HB to HJ are books on economics and business, while from HM to HX are books classified as sociology. Each of these areas is further subclassified.

Today, computers are the principal means of searching for books, periodicals, and documents in a library. While libraries use an array of computer programs to set up their collections, they all basically allow you to search by author, title, or subject, and inform you if the book is available in the library or checked out. As well, the information that appears on the screen may suggest other places to search. It is well worth the time to familiarize yourself with how to do searches at your college or university library.

Typically, the following information on a book will appear on the screen:

```
┌─────────────────────────────────────────────────────────────────────┐
│                                                                     │
│   Author:           Lipset, Seymour Martin                          │
│   Title:            Continental divide: the values and              │
│                     institutions of the United States              │
│                     and Canada/Seymour Martin Lipset               │
│   Publisher:        New York: Routledge, 1990                       │
│   Description:      xviii, 337 p.; 23 cm.                            │
│   LC Subjects:      United States—Civilization                     │
│                     Canada—Civilization                            │
│   Call Number:      E 169.1 L545 1990                               │
│   Status:           Item is in the library                          │
│                     (or, Out to user, followed by due              │
│                     date.)                                          │
│                                                                     │
└─────────────────────────────────────────────────────────────────────┘
```

Begin by finding out if the work is in the library. Usually, if the item is out, the due date is provided. Even if the work is checked out, you can still make good use of the call number. Given the way the LC system is set up, there may be other useful works located in the general vicinity of the one you are searching for. Thus, a suggestion is to go to the stacks where the work would be located and browse through the nearby works.

Also helpful are the LC subjects under which the work was classified. Take the above example. The work is classified under the broad subject category "United States," and subclassified under "Civilization." In other words, if you do a subject search for "United States," you will find the subclass "Civilization," in which the work by Lipset is classified. Other works will also be listed under the same classifications, and these may be useful to you.

Broadening and Deepening Your Knowledge

Armed with your preliminary list of names, references, and key concepts or ideas, you are now in a position to begin to look into your topic in some depth, using more specialized literature and data sources. The breadth and depth of this stage of the literature search will depend upon the purpose of your review and the time you can spend on it.

The computerization of library card catalogues has made searching for information a much easier and faster process. The Internet makes it possible to browse through the catalogues of libraries and research centres worldwide. The negative side of this technological change is that you can be easily overwhelmed by the amount of published material available on any topic. You have to continually ask yourself, "What is the purpose of my literature search?" By having or developing a clear purpose, and reviewing that purpose throughout the course of the literature search, you will save effort by focusing your attention on relevant materials, which will in turn contribute to a clear-minded and well-organized end product.

The literature search and review will involve continuous note taking—not just listing sources, but annotating, summarizing, and critically reviewing material. For this effort to pay off you need to be extremely efficient at finding the appropriate sources. Box 3.1 provides an overview of the major sources useful in the social sciences. It is not an exhaustive list; that would be impossible. We have organized our review of the sources below to follow the outline of Box 3.1.

Searching for Sources

A.1 Books

Not all libraries are computerized and many do not computer catalogue older books, so you may need to use the traditional card catalogue to find out if the library has a book and where it is located. In the card catalogue each book is described on three separate file cards, arranged alphabetically in three different files. One set of cards is filed by author, a second by title, and the third by subject matter. This arrangement permits you to find any book in the library in three ways: by author, by title, or, if you only have a general subject reference, by subject.

Computer catalogues are faster and easier to use than card catalogues once you have mastered the simple commands. In addition to the three ways of filing used in card catalogues, computer catalogues allow you to search for titles according to key words. Using a key word will bring up a list of titles in which the word appears. This increases the number of books you can locate that might be of interest to you. Library computers are now increasingly linked so that it is possible to browse through the catalogues of neighbouring libraries (or even those further afield) without having to visit those libraries in person.

As noted earlier, most academic libraries identify and arrange their books using the Library of Congress Classification System. Given its wide usage, part of the Library of Congress information is also available on the copyright page of books. In the United States books have a heading entitled "Library of Congress Cataloguing-in-Publication Data." Books published in Canada, including this one, have "Canadian Cataloguing in Publication Data" (CIP). The information given is to help librarians index the book in their libraries. But this information can also be useful to you. It includes the Library of Congress (LC)

BOX 3.1

Major Reference Sources for Social Sciences

A. SEARCHING FOR BOOKS

A.1 **Book Listings**
Library catalogues
Books in Print
Canadian Books in Print
Cumulative Book Index
Forthcoming Books

A.2 **Bibliographies**
Bibliographia Canadia
Bibliography Index
London Bibliography of Social Sciences
International Bibliography of Sociology

A.3 **Book Reviews**
Book Review Digest
Book Review Index
Book Review Index to Social Science Periodicals
Canadian Book Review Annual

B. ENCYCLOPEDIAS, ETC.

General: e.g., *Encyclopedia Britannica, The Canadian Encyclopedia*
Special: e.g., *International Encyclopedia of the Social Sciences*
Atlases: e.g., *Atlas of Ancient Archeology*
Almanacs: e.g., *The Canadian Global Almanac*
Yearbooks: e.g., *Urban History Yearbook*
Annual Reviews: e.g., *Annual Review of Psychology*

C. JOURNAL ARTICLES

C.1 **Indexes to Journals**

The Serials Directory
The Standard Periodicals Directory
Ulrich's International Periodicals Directory

C.2 **Indexes to Articles**
Current Contents: Social and Behavioural Sciences
Humanities Index
Reader's Guide to Periodical Literature
Social Sciences Index

C.3 **Abstracts**
Abstracts of Native Studies
Crime and Delinquency Abstracts
Human Resources Abstracts
Psychological Abstracts
Sociological Abstracts

C.4 **Citation Indexes**
Arts and Humanities Citations Index
Social Science Citations Index

D. DISSERTATIONS

Canadian Theses
Dissertations Abstracts International
Index to Theses with Abstracts

E. GOVERNMENT DOCUMENTS

C.I.S. Index (United States)
Government of Canada Publications Catalogue
HMSO Monthly Catalogue (United Kingdom)
UNDOC: Current Index (United Nations)

F. OTHER SOURCES

Canadian News Index
Canadian Index
Facts on File
Keesing's Record of World Events
New York Times Index

number and appropriate subject headings in order of importance. The following is an example of the information included on a copyright page.

```
Canadian Cataloguing in Publication Data
[Author]      Reitz, Jeffrey G.
[Title]       The illusion of difference: realities
              of ethnicity in Canada and the United
              States

              (Observation, ISBN 0826-9947; no. 37)
              Includes bibliographical references.
              ISBN 0-88806-342-3

[Possible     1. Ethnicity—Canada. 2. Ethnicity—
subject       United States. 3. Canada—Ethnic rela-
headings]     tions. 4. United States—Ethnic
              Relations. 5. Multiculturalism—
              Canada. 6. Assimilation (Sociology).
              I. Breton, Raymond, 1931—. II. C.D.
              Howe Institute. III. Title. IV.
              Series: Observation (C.D. Howe
              Institute); no. 37.

[LC Number]   FC104.R45 1994 305.8'00971
              C94-931368-8
              F1035.A1R45 1994
```

The CIP information can help you find other works on the same subject by providing subject headings that you can use as the basis for a computer or card catalogue search. For example, you could check to find out what works exist under the main subject heading "Ethnicity" in the subclass "Canada."

The LC number (known as the call number or stack number) is useful even if you already have the work and the library does not have a copy. Recall that the LC system places works in the stacks according to subject. Thus, you may want to go to where the work is located in the library (or where it would be located if the library does not have a copy) and browse to see whether there are other relevant works for your research.

A.2 Bibliographies

In searching for more sources, find out if your library has bibliographies on the topic or a related topic that you are interested in. **Bibliographies** are works listing books and articles on particular topics. (They are generally kept in the reference section of the library.) They are very useful because someone else has done the hard work of searching for sources. However, you will still have to look up the sources, and your library may not necessarily have them.

Bibliographies may also vary considerably in scope, ranging from those that cover broad topics, say unemployment, to those with narrowly focused listings, say youth unemployment in Alberta. Some bibliographies are annotated, and provide brief notes that explain the content of the book or article. Many just list the article or books and give essential information: author, title, and date and place of publication.

A.3 Book Reviews

Using card or computer catalogues and bibliographies will quickly produce a long list of material to read: possibly far too long for the time you have. You may also feel that you are not yet experienced enough to determine which books are worth your time and which should be ignored or given a lower priority. Two basic rules of thumb are useful guides in prioritizing: books published by major academic and commercial presses (a librarian can help you identify these) are generally more reliable than those published by obscure, unknown publishers; and the more recent an edition or publication, the more current the information. You can use recent books or articles to track down important earlier material, but obviously you cannot use dated material to get to more recent publications.

Book reviews are very useful not only in summarizing a book but also in critically assessing the work, giving us a sense of how reliable it is. Reviews also place the book in context, providing more background information on the researcher(s) or topic and relating the book to other research, debates, and discoveries in the field. Book reviews, then, help to make your literature review more manageable, by showing that some of your titles are not as relevant as they appeared. They can also steer you to other pertinent material and can be a source of additional information and ideas on your topic. Book reviews vary in length, ranging from very brief and basic summaries of the book's contents, to long articles that go into considerable depth. Reading book reviews is useful, finally, as a guide to showing you how to prepare a book report for your own course assignments.

An example of a publication dedicated solely to book reviews is the *Canadian Book Review Annual*, which covers an array of subjects, including the social sciences. There also exist specialized book review publications in the various disciplines. Three major ones are *Contemporary Psychology*, *Contemporary Sociology*, and the *Journal of Economic Literature*.

B. Atlases, Encyclopedias, and Handbooks

We have already mentioned general encyclopedias such as *Encyclopedia Britannica*. A number of other general reference works provide overviews and summaries of specific areas of knowledge, including *The Canadian Encyclopedia*, also available on CD-ROM as *The 1996 Canadian Encyclopedia Plus*. Specialized encyclopedias, such as *The International Encyclopedia of the Social Sciences*, cover an issue in greater depth than do general encyclopedias. Although specialized encyclopedias may be dated, they provide basic information about major concepts, findings, events, etc., and provide you with a useful introduction to a topic, as well as a sense of its broader context.

Another special category of general works are *annuals*, which review the progress of research in specific subject areas. Three notable social science examples are the *Annual Review of Psychology*, the *Annual Review of Sociology*, and the *Annual Review of Anthropology*. Each annual edition contains review essays on various topics. The bibliographies of the essays are also helpful in providing a long list of the latest works on the topic.

C. Journal Articles

Academic journals are publications for professionals or specialists in which fellow experts present and discuss their latest ideas and discoveries (see Box 3.2). Articles are reviewed by a panel of experts in the same field as the author or authors before being accepted for publication. Journal articles are very important sources of information because they are more up-to-date, more focused, and more specific than books. The longest article is also generally much shorter than a book. Current, unbound journal issues are usually located in a special, "current periodicals" area of the library. Past issues of journals are bound in annual hard cover volumes and are located either in the area where books of the same discipline are located or in a special area of their own. Browsing through unbound and bound periodicals would be very time consuming, so more efficient ways of locating articles of potential interest to researchers have been developed, namely, various types of indexes.

C.1 Indexes

Indexes are regularly published lists of articles, organized to help the researcher find relevant material. Depending on the particular index, the entries may be organized by author, title, or subject matter. Subject matter is classified according to each index's listing. A guide to this listing and to using the index is generally found in the front pages of each index. Box 3.1 lists the most useful general and social science indexes.

C.2 Abstracts

Abstracts are indexes that provide additional information through a brief summary of each article listed. Abstracts are very useful in helping you to decide whether or not an article is really relevant, or how high a priority you should give it. They are organized alphabetically by author, title, or subject matter to help you quickly and easily obtain the information you need.

C.3 Citation Indexes

Citation indexes show how social science research is a cooperative and a cumulative process. Essentially, a citation index lists the appearance of an article in other articles, or where it has been mentioned in the writings of others. Citation indexes are organized like other indexes so that you can use author, title, or subject to trace a source in the index. What you will find is a list of articles that mention the article you have in hand. Using this index allows you to trace responses to a particular piece of research and to gather together references that relate to a common issue or topic. Many abstracts and indexes are now available online or in the highly convenient CD-ROM format; you should check this with your reference librarian.

D. Dissertations

Social science students writing doctoral **dissertations** (the research projects that qualify them for a Ph.D.) are expected to do original research and to carefully document their sources and research methods. Such works are often very useful, because they usually contain an extensive review of the literature and a large bibliography on the topic. In addition, the research design and the methods used are usually clearly spelled out and justified. Indeed, both the description of methods and the literature review will be far longer and more detailed than would be found in a book or article. For these reasons alone dissertations are well worth checking out. They are normally very limited in scope so it is unlikely you will need to look at many of them. However, unless the dissertation is written at a nearby university and is directly accessible, ordering them through an interlibrary loan or direct computer access can be very expensive.

E. Government Documents

Most college and university libraries have a special area set apart for **government documents.** Here you will find Statistics Canada publications, such as the Census and the monthly Labour Force Survey, and information on health and the economy. There will also be documents and publications, including policy papers and special studies, from the

BOX 3.2

Social Science Journal Articles

Many of your sources are likely to be articles in academic social science journals that report on empirical research. These articles are basically written for experts, but you should not simply ignore them. There is much of interest that you can learn from them. As you become more familiar with research methods and an area of your discipline, you will gain more confidence and find these articles easier to understand.

For now, even if you never conduct empirical research beyond your college or university research project, you can benefit greatly from learning about research someone else has carried out. It can help you with your own project as a source of information about a topic and as an example of how to carry out social scientific research.

A typical social science article that reports on empirical research is organized in four or five standard sections usually indicated by headings: abstract or summary, introduction, method, results, and discussion.

1. ABSTRACT OR SUMMARY

Most academic journals require the authors to provide either an abstract (a one-paragraph outline placed at the beginning of the article) or a summary placed at the end of the article. You should read these sections first. They give you an overview of the article and you can quickly decide whether it is relevant to your research project. In these sections the authors usually briefly state the main purpose of the research, the methods, the main results, and the general conclusion.

Thus, the abstract or summary quickly answers the following questions:

What is the purpose of the research?

What is the main method used to collect the data?

What is the main finding of the research?

What is the author's main conclusion?

2. INTRODUCTION

Once you have concluded from the abstract that the article is worth reading, begin with the introduction. (It will not necessarily be labelled as such, but is generally quite obvious.) The introduction will provide some information about the general question examined in the article, report on what previous research has found, state what the particular study attempts to find out, and in the case of many articles end with the hypothesis to be examined.

Note that the introduction was probably written for individuals who have some familiarity with the research topic. Therefore, the authors are likely to cover certain issues only briefly; for example, they may not fully explain a theory, or they may cite sources without elaborating on their content. Nevertheless, this section contains essential information that can help you increase your understanding the topic. You will become aware of the major issues raised and of the concepts that have been recognized as important. Moreover, the cited studies can serve two purposes: you can look them up to see if they are relevant sources for your research project, and you can read these articles to gain more background information on the topic.

The introduction is likely to answer the following questions:

What is the particular research about?

Why is the particular research relevant?

What is the main hypothesis (if any) or research question?

3. RESEARCH METHOD

Next, read the methods section to find out how the study was carried out and the data collected. This section is generally quite detailed; it usually provides enough information for the reader to be able to replicate the study. It provides information on the research method used to collect the data (for example, the type of social survey, experiment, field research, and so on); how the method was used to collect the data (Were interviewers used? How were the respondents contacted? And so on.); the population considered for the study and the sampling procedure used (Who or what were they mainly interested in studying? What procedure was used to select the sample—the participants or material for the study—from the population?); and the dependent and independent variables and the operational definitions (What do the authors expect to be cause and effect? How are the concepts defined and measured?)

Although at this time you may not be familiar with some of the terminology used in these articles, you should still gain a general understanding of these issues:

```
What method was used to collect the data?

What are the independent and dependent variables?

What are their operational definitions?
```

4. RESULTS

The main findings of the research are contained in this section. In many articles, this section can be especially intimidating for a beginning student in research methods and for the nonmathematical reader. It will likely contain statistical notations and technical language that summarize the data. Don't despair. The authors will more than likely explain their main findings. However, the reader with little background in statistics will simply have to accept that the appropriate statistical analysis was carried out.

The main findings, remember, were briefly stated in the abstract or summary, but the results section is more detailed. Thus, you may have to disregard some of the explanations of the analyses carried out and limit yourself to the main findings.

Whatever your knowledge of statistics, you should be able to determine the following:

```
What are the major findings?
```

5. DISCUSSION

The discussion section (at times combined with the results section) is where the authors state their conclusions and the implications of their study for future research. The authors will also offer possible explanations of why they had certain results, and point to similarities or differences between their results and those of other studies.

This section will help you answer these questions:

```
What is the major finding?
```

> What have the authors concluded about their finding?
>
> What should be the direction of future research?

The above is a limited introduction to reading social science journal articles that are based on empirical research. While you may never carry out a research project, after graduating you are likely to read such articles often as you become more specialized in a specific discipline. But you are also likely to concentrate on articles covering research issues with which you are familiar. The knowledge acquired over time in a discipline, together with your increasing understanding of research methods and possibly statistics, will lead you eventually to make more critical evaluations of such articles.

various ministries of the federal and provincial governments. This section of the library is also likely to contain some major publications from international agencies such as the United Nations, as well as from other countries, such as the United States.

The publications in the government section of the library are generally classified differently from those in the rest of the library. For example, Statistics Canada publications are usually classified according to their catalogue number. Say your research was on youth employment and one of the sources you wanted to examine was the Statistics Canada publication *Labour Force Annual Averages, 1989–1994*. Its catalogue number is 71-529. The government section is likely to contain an area with only Statistics Canada publications, classified in numerical order according to the first two catalogue numbers. To find your source you would first go to where publications starting with number 71 are located and then look for the one subclassed as 529. Again, whenever in doubt about how to find a source in the government section, it is best to ask the assistance of the reference librarian.

F. Other Sources

The more you use the library the more you will discover just how many varieties of information and information guides, directories, and lists there are. At this stage the most important "other sources" are sources of current-event information. Most libraries have a selection of major Canadian newspapers and magazines. There are also likely to be foreign newspapers and magazines, such as *The New York Times* and the magazine *The Economist*. Increasingly, back issues of magazines and certain newspapers are stored on CD-ROM. For a fee, some magazines and newspapers provide access to back issues over the Internet. If you need to examine back issues, it is best first to find out from the reference librarian what is available. If you need to know in which issue an article appeared or what articles exist on a particular topic, there are various indexes that you can use. Again, it is best to find out from the reference librarian which sources are available in the library.

There are, of course, other documentary sources that are not found in libraries. Businesses, educational institutions, voluntary associations, political organizations, community groups, and individuals in public life often produce and maintain a large volume of printed documentation of their activities for their own use. These may be invaluable to some types of research. However, because they are not public, they are harder to track down and usually involve personal contact and negotiation with representatives of the group in order to gain access to them.

ORGANIZING THE LITERATURE REVIEW

Planning the Literature Review

Now that you have a sense of the range of information available to you, we turn to the actual process of writing up the literature review. This process may vary according to the purpose of the review—and this may alter as you proceed with your research. At the outset you may not have a very clear idea of what you are looking for, beyond a very general area of interest. As you work your way from initial, general sources—such as textbooks or encyclopedias—to card or computer catalogues, bibliographies, indexes, and abstracts, two things will probably happen. First, the sheer amount of information on the general area will seem overwhelming. Second, you will begin to see that there are particular lines of research that have been advanced, some areas of controversy, some puzzling findings, and perhaps even some (you think) obvious areas of research that need to be done.

At this point you need to sit down and use pen and paper (or computer) to review where you have been and where, precisely, you need to go. First you have to summarize what you have learned about the field. What seem to be the agreed upon perspectives, theories, or concepts? What ideas are in dispute? Who are the major researchers in the field? What are their positions and what do they believe the evidence shows? What kinds of data, research designs, and procedures are most used in studies in this field? Where does the research seem to

BOX 3.3

The Internet

The Internet is a "network of networks" of computers that are inter-linked throughout the world. It allows for electronic mail, the ability to retrieve and transmit documents, and more. One popular means of accessing documents, pictures, sound, and even animations over the Internet is the World Wide Web (WWW, W3, or simply the Web). Documents prepared for the Web are in "hypertext," which means you can simply point and click your mouse on a marked part of the document and quickly access either another related part of the document, another linked document at the same site, or a linked document at another site. The result is a complex web of connections among documents that may be spread out at different sites around the globe.

Although there is much information available on the Internet, it is not a replacement for your college or university library. Instead, consider the Internet as an extension of the library's resources. You should first examine the information available in the library and then, if necessary, search for other information on the Internet. Unless you know where to look for the information, the Internet can be time consuming and costly. You will also want to be extra cautious about the quality of the information retrieved, since you may not be able to verify its authenticity. We suggest you concentrate on the information available from established organizations such as university and government departments and research institutes.

Below are the addresses of a few Web sites. The first set lists addresses of some key sites that have links to information on Canadian society, history, politics, economy, and more. The second set includes for each of the social science disciplines, one discipline-related address and two general sites with resources on the social sciences.

CANADA

Canadian Government Information on the Internet
http://library.uwaterloo.ca/discipline/Government/CanGuide/

This is an excellent annotated bibliography prepared by Anita Cannon, Reference/Public Service Librarian at Mount Allison University. Hundreds of sites are listed, with a brief description of the type of information available at each. Unlike text-based bibliographies which list sources but do not provide access to them, this one allows the user to access many sources directly by simply pointing and clicking on a listed address. For example, if you are looking for information on aboriginal peoples, you could point and click your mouse on the listed site of the Ministry of Indian and Northern Affairs. There you would find the texts of various publications, as well as maps and Indian treaties from pre-Confederation to 1923.

The Canadian Resource Page
http://www.cs.cmu.edu/Web/Unofficial/Canadiana/README.html
This site was set up by a Canadian student at Carnegic Mellon University. It has a long list of links to sites in Canada, including newspapers, museums, archives, sites on history, politics, and more. It is well worth a visit when searching for information on Canada.

Government of Canada
http://canada.gc.ca
This is the home page of the Government of Canada with links to federal government departments and agencies and to provincial and municipal government sites. Of particular interest is its keyword-searchable feature.

National Library of Canada
http://www.nlc-bnc.ca/
This site provides a virtual tour of the National Library of Canada, links to Canadian libraries, as well as a section on access to Canadian information on the Internet.

SOCIAL SCIENCE GUIDES

Numerous sites exist with information relevant to specific disciplines. Here we list one site for each discipline, at which you can obtain a guide to resources on the Internet in that discipline. Each site allows you to point and click to access the linked site or document. However, much of the information at these sites is of American origin. If you need information on Canada we suggest you first examine the Canadian sites listed above.

Anthropology
http://www.nitehawk.com/alleycat/anth-faq.html
The site contains the "Anthropology Resources on the Internet," a long list of links on sources of anthropological relevance throughout the world.

Economics
http://econwpa.wustl.edu/EconFaq/EconFaq.html
This gives you direct access to the guide "Resources for Economists on the Internet," an annotated list of hundreds of sites of special interest to economists compiled by the economist Bill Goffe. Most sites are based in the United States and deal with American economic issues, with a few sites from Canada, other countries, and international organizations.

History
http://history.cc.ukans.edu/history/
The site is called the "Index of Resources for Historians" and contains more than 1700 connections arranged alphabetically by subject and name. However, only a few sites are listed under Canada.

Political Science
http://www.trincoll.edu/pols/home.html
This site contains the "Political Scientist's Guide to the Internet," which provides much information of political relevance, but mainly on U.S. politics.

Psychology
http://maple.lemoyne.edu/-hevern/psychref.html
This site is known as the "Resources in Psychology on the Internet" and has links to sites and documents of specific and general relevance in psychology. The site is divided into three sets of Web pages: general resources; teaching and research; and topical research.

Sociology
http://www.socioweb.com/-markbl/socioweb/
The "Sociological Resource Centre," as this site is called, contains links to numerous sites of interest to sociologists, on topics such as the family, criminology, and world affairs.

```
Social Science (general)
Research Engines for the Social Sciences
http://www.carleton.ca/-cmckie/research.html
```
This is the home page of Professor Craig McKie in the department of Sociology and Anthropology at Carleton University. It provides a remarkable list of links to hundreds of sites of interest to the different social science disciplines.

```
WWW Virtual Library: Social Sciences
http://coombs.anu.edu.au/WWWVL-SocSci.html
```
This site is maintained at the Australian National University and is updated almost daily. It contains numerous links to sites that provide information in the different social science disciplines.

be headed? Do there seem to be gaps, puzzles, omissions, or other significant limitations?

At this stage your review of these questions does not have to be detailed or formal: it is an outline to help you move along in your own research. Looking over this review, do you find aspects or issues that intrigue you or connect with your interests or life experiences? Remember that research is demanding and that unless you have some interest in the topic it will tend to become pure drudgery. Consequently, any area you find personally interesting is one you would do well to consider seriously as the area to follow.

Having identified aspects of the field that interest you, you must next consider what kinds of research seem to be acceptable and needed given the state of the field. Are there obvious gaps where no one seems to have done any research? For example, perhaps no one has looked in detail at the growing number of teenagers suffering from stress. A descriptive study filling in this gap is required. Or perhaps some studies have been done but circumstances have changed so that the same kinds of studies need to be repeated (a procedure called *replication*) to produce more up-to-date information. Possibly some studies have been done but they do not satisfy you in other ways: experiments have been done where you think a survey is more appropriate, or a survey has been used where you believe a qualitative field study would be better.

As you sharpen your focus onto a more specific topic within a field your interest will move from a vague, general concern, to a series of questions about what is known, how it is known, and what needs to be discovered. That is, you will begin to develop a series of questions that relate to the research that has been done before (its achievements, its limitations, its gaps). It is quite likely that you will return to the library several times in the course of this process. You will be reviewing some of the literature you have already discovered; and looking at specific sections of articles or books more closely—say, their methods sections, or perhaps their samples, or the time period of the study. You are likely to move deeper into the more specialized journals and use the citations index to trace interconnecting pieces of research, follow-up studies, critiques, and so on.

Throughout the process of reviewing the literature you need to be systematic. Be sure to copy down all details of the references as you locate them. It is best to record more than the minimum bibliographic elements needed to form a citation. See Box 3.4 for details on bibliographic references.

Before the arrival of personal computers researchers kept their references on file cards. The bibliographic information would go on the front of the card, and an abstract, brief notes, and cross-references on the rear. Now bibliographic files can be created on the computer very easily using word processing programs. It is best to do this as you gather the references, rather than leaving all that data input for the end. Putting in your references on a daily basis minimizes the tedium and fewer errors are likely to creep into your file. This file can be copied and brief notes and cross-references added to create an annotated bibliography. You can also modify your files, dropping works that turn out to be irrelevant, organizing the files in subsections according to priority or your own classification of subject matter, etc.

Remember when photocopying sections of books and articles to write down the full bibliographic information on the photocopy to identify its source. While photocopying is a great timesaver in one way, it has its drawbacks. It is expensive; it often takes a lot of time (lining up for the photocopy machine!); it creates a lot of material to keep track of in your files; because it seems easy you may end up with a great collection of photocopies that you never get around to reading; and unless you highlight carefully or take good notes (in which case why photocopy), you often end up rereading the material anyway because you remember less of it than the items you take notes on. For these reasons, it is best to use photocopying sparingly and develop your abilities to be a careful and efficient reader and note taker.

If you find that there are many studies on your topic, you will need to be more selective than in an area where there are few studies. There are several ways of being selective. You may choose only those studies that are most directly related to your own research project. That is, you

Essential Bibliographic Information

A. BOOKS

1. Author(s): Last name, first name, and initials
2. Title: Complete title including subtitle
3. Edition/Volume: note the edition (if it is not the first edition) or volume number
4. Place of publication: city, province or state, and country
5. Publisher
6. Year of publication

B. CHAPTERS IN BOOKS OR READERS

1. Author(s): Last name, first name, and initials
2. Title of chapter
3. Page numbers
4. All the information on the book as in A1 to A6 above

C. JOURNAL OR PERIODICAL ARTICLES

1. Author(s): Last name, first name, and initials
2. Title of article
3. Title of journal or periodical
4. Volume and number
5. Year of publication
6. Page numbers

look at those studies that deal with the same kinds of individuals or groups as you plan to examine; or studies that share your particular theoretical approach, research design, or methods. You could limit the time span of your general literature search and select only the most recent studies. Since scholarly books and articles provide references, you will still be able to target earlier material that appears to be relevant later on. (At this stage you may also want to find out if your instructor has, for whatever reasons, imposed certain restrictions on the type and number of sources you are to examine.) Finally, some areas of research are dominated by a few authorities, and this permits you to select only material that relates to the work of these individuals.

Organizing the Writing of the Literature Review

You have collected the works and documents you need, or know where to find them. Your next task is to summarize and evaluate the material, and to do a comparative analysis of the material. Then you need to organize and write up the literature review.

After you have completed your search of works related to your study, you need to critically assess the various works. You need to move from doing a literature search to writing a literature review. The literature review is likely to make up most of the introduction to your research project. (We will have more to say on this in Chapter 10.)

Thus, it is best if you note down early the main points of each work you examine. Below are various suggestions to serve as a general guide to help you summarize and assess the main points of a published work. For each work examined:

1. Write down the author and title of the work in a standard bibliographic form.

If you followed the earlier suggestion and wrote down the bibliographic information of the sources as you found them, then you already have the necessary information. The advantage in doing it here is that if you plan on using the source in your research report you will save time when it comes to noting the work in the citations and in the bibliography.

2. Decide what the authors are specifically trying to find out.

If they provide a hypothesis or research question, write it down word for word, place it in quotations, and note the page number. If you prefer to paraphrase, it can always be done later; at least for now you have the exact wording and know where it is situated in the work. The focus of the work is often stated as a possible fact, with phrases or terms that are probably clarified in the text.

Say you noted that the main focus of the work was to demonstrate:

Most Canadians believe that their quality of life has improved.

This in itself will raise certain questions in your mind: What do the authors mean by "quality of life has improved"? How will they measure quality of life? And so on.

If the work examined is a book, then you may want to concentrate on the sections or chapters that deal with the topic that interests you. For example, if the book is on various issues related to voting behaviour, but you are mainly concerned with voting behaviour of retirees, then you may want to concentrate on the sections or chapters that deal with age and voting behaviour. But be careful not to take the arguments put forth by the authors out of context.

Pay attention to the date and location of the publication. Is the work still useful? Are the arguments and given information outdated? Should you look for more recent publications?

Also, pay attention to the place of the study. Say the work concerns marriage and divorce in the United States. Be careful to restrict the claims made by the authors to the United States. Do not simply assume the same is true in Canada. (However, you may want to consider whether the same arguments hold for Canada.)

3. Examine how the study was carried out.

Is the work based on empirical research? If so, ask

```
What was the research method (survey, experiment,
field research, and so on)?
What was the population (people, items, or events
of interest to the author)?
What was the sample (a portion of the population
actually studied)?
Which were the important variables (e.g., quality
of life)?
Which were the operational definitions of the vari-
ables (e.g., what do the authors mean by quality
of life)?
```

If the work was not based on empirical research, then you will still want to note the main arguments of the authors and what they mean by the variables. Furthermore, note the kind of evidence provided in support of their arguments.

4. Note the findings.

In the case of a work that is based on empirical research, you will want to note the specific results. Take much care in what you write. For example, assume the main finding was that women between the ages of 35 and 45 expressed more satisfaction about their employment situation than women between the ages of 55 and 65. Do not simply write down "Younger women are happier about their jobs than older women." Instead, write down the complete information, including the level of satisfaction, and clearly note the age groups. Such information will help you when you want to compare this study to another study.

If statistical analyses were carried out, then write down such statistical information as the level of significance. Of course, how much statistical information you will want to note will also largely depend on your level of understanding of statistics. And while your knowledge and interest in statistics may be limited, you should be able to consider the findings in relation to how the study was carried out. Remember, statistics is only a tool that the researchers have used to analyze the data. The statistics are not a measure of the quality of the data collected or whether a study was properly carried out.

5. Note the conclusion.

What did the authors conclude? For example, did the authors conclude that most Canadians do indeed believe that their quality of life has improved?

6. Make critical comments.

At the end, leave space to note whatever weaknesses or strengths you believe exist with the study. You may also want to note any similarities the work has to other studies you may have read.

After you have completed the search and examined each work to your satisfaction, you will have to organize and write up the literature review, at least in draft form. You may want to organize the review around particular subsets of the issue considered. For example, in studying the concentration of economic power, you may decide first to cover what the publications have to say about the concept of power, then follow it by your critical assessment of the research methods they used to study the phenomenon. You may instead want to discuss the various works chronologically. This may be the case if you want to show that interest in a particular phenomenon varied over time and what contributions they made to the understanding of the phenomenon. For example, say your research was on spousal abuse. A literature review organized chronologically can illustrate what importance social scientists have given to this issue and how they have examined it over time.

As with all research writing, the literature review needs careful planning and clear writing. All of the rules of good writing (clear organization, appropriate paragraph structure, logical division of the paper into sections and subsections, an introduction and conclusion, etc.) apply to the literature review as to any other section of a research paper. You will probably go through several drafts before you get the literature review to fit with the other sections of your final research report. It is even possible that you may discover gaps in your review during the evolution of your research. If so, you will have to return to the library and extend your original literature review. Similarly, some original material may become less relevant and be dropped from consideration.

To write a good literature review you have to bear in mind its purpose. You will find that there are several kinds of literature review, apart from that undertaken in the course of a piece of empirical research. Journal articles and even entire books may be lengthy review essays which look at the historical development of an issue or research area over time; or review in depth the different theoretical approaches to a particular issue; or focus on the methods of research used to investigate a specific topic or the degree of agreement and accumulation of data.

Where a literature review is part of the report on a piece of empirical research, it is supposed to show how your research fits in with the research of others. This does not mean that you simply list and summarize a series of earlier researches. You have to show how the earlier research develops or ties together as a series of interconnecting and mutually supporting ideas and discoveries and how your own research will flow out of these interconnections. Usually this involves both a critical assessment and a synthesis of previous research. As we have already suggested, all research has limitations and part of the task of the literature review is to highlight these limitations and problems and suggest ways of overcoming them. This is the critical aspect of the literature review.

The synthesizing process involves clearly drawing out only the main points of previous research which are relevant for your own study. This means you extract common or complementary ideas, themes, and data and state them clearly, and draw out their implications as the context of and justification for your research. You may conclude with a clear statement of the research question or hypothesis that you intend to examine empirically.

What the Literature Review Contributes to the Research Process

The preceding sections on undertaking, organizing, and writing a literature review provide some indication of how the literature review contributes to the research process. By learning what others have done and what is known you can become an informed researcher, able to identify the purpose of your research more clearly and to make better research decisions. After surveying the literature, you can see where further research is most needed, what useful methods or procedures have been used, and what ideas are current in thinking about the issues.

As a researcher making informed decisions about your research, the quality and the importance of your research are likely to increase. Having understood an issue in depth and being able to link your research to a broader context also make you credible to other researchers. They are likely to take notice of your research should it be published or circulated. Consequently, your research will make its own independent contribution to the growth of knowledge in a particular subject area.

WHAT YOU HAVE LEARNED

- Social scientific research is cooperative and cumulative so that every new piece of research builds on previous research.

- To begin to do research you need to know what other researchers have discovered and what they think, so you can use their ideas and data to focus and develop your own research topic.

- Finding out about other people's research involves systematic use of the library, moving from general reference sources such as encyclopedias and handbooks to recent books and articles, located through reference aids such as indexes and bibliographies.

- Such a literature review is best undertaken with a clear purpose in mind. This purpose may change as you proceed and so it should be reviewed and reassessed along the way.

- The literature review should be written in such a way that it places your research project in a clear context by showing its connections with the research of others.

KEY WORDS

Library of Congress
  Classification System
bibliographies

book reviews

annuals

academic journals   citation indexes

indexes   dissertations

abstracts   government documents

REVIEW QUESTIONS

1. Why is it essential to find out what previous researchers have discovered and discussed?
2. What can you achieve in a search for information from basic sources such as class notes, textbooks, and encyclopedias?
3. What are the main advantages of computerized library catalogues?
4. Why are book reviews useful as a source of information in a literature review?
5. What is the difference between an index and a citation index?
6. How can you be selective in an area where there are very many studies on your chosen topic?
7. What does a literature review contribute to the research process?

RECOMMENDED READINGS

Cuba, L. (1993). *A short guide to writing about social science* (2nd ed.). New York: HarperCollins.

A brief book that covers various facets of writing about social science, including the literature review.

Light, R. J., & Pillemer, D. B. (1984). *Summing up: The science of reviewing research.* Cambridge, MA: Harvard University Press.

A helpful book on the importance of examining and evaluating previous research. It is filled with suggestions on what to look for in published works, as well as how to summarize and judge the findings of previous research.

Stern, P. (1979). *Evaluating social science research.* New York: Oxford University Press.

Shows how to read critically and evaluate articles in academic journals. The book includes various journal articles with examples of what to take into account in reading them.

CHAPTER 4

Choosing Whom or What to Study

- the concepts of "population" and "sample"
- why sampling is essential
- the difference between random and nonrandom sampling
- how to decide on the size of a sample

INTRODUCTION

Sampling is the most widely used technique associated with gathering information of any kind. In one sense sampling is a shortcut to information that we are already familiar with in our everyday life. If we want to know whether an instructor of a particular course is an "easy marker" we may ask a friend who took the course last semester and then judge the instructor from what our friend tells us. Our friend is the sample selected from the population of all the students who took the course. And based on what our friend tells us we generalize about whether the teacher is an easy marker or not. The basis of sampling and generalization in research follows a similar reasoning, except that much care goes into the selection of the sample.

As a fast solution to a particular everyday problem this convenience sampling is very useful, saving us much time, energy, and anxiety. But things can go wrong even with this simple sampling activity. Your friend may have become personally antagonistic to the instructor, or may underestimate how much her grades actually reflect her own skills rather than easy marking. These factors will bias or distort the report that you get. Maybe you discover that the way your friend evaluates courses is not the way you do, and that the information you get is not so useful after all.

The point we are making is that sampling, even in its everyday, casual form, is a tricky business. A sample may give you more information, but this information may be distorted or biased, or the information may not be what you are looking for. However, we can rarely avoid sampling—we have to ask some people, not all; we have to look at a few things, not everything. Because of its efficiency, it is used both in everyday life and in scientific research, although in the latter case, sampling has to be done much more carefully and systematically. It has to overcome problems of bias and often try to achieve a sample that is *representative* of the population—the shortcut to information is no longer so short!

POPULATIONS AND SAMPLES

In defining the topic of your research, you need to be clear about what it is you are interested in studying. Broadly speaking this means two things. The first is that you need to be clear about the questions and ideas framing the research and about the range of empirical observations you are going to be making when exploring or researching these questions and ideas. The second issue—choosing who or what you will study—is where sampling is of great importance.

In most areas of research we are faced with the kind of choice we discussed in the introduction: we need to get information about a group of events, people, actions, etc. by using a small proportion of this group as our source of information on the whole group. Consequently, we are faced with the problem of selecting who or what will be in the group we actually study. This selection problem is the key issue in sampling.

For example, who do you want to study? All the students at your college or university? All the clients of a community clinic? All shoppers at a mall? All women over 60 years old that live on their own in your community? The group you are interested in is known in technical terms as the **population.** Take note, however, that the meaning of the term "population" is different from its everyday usage. In research, you determine which people, or objects, make up the population about whom you want to draw conclusions.

BOX 4.1

Quebec Sovereignty Polls

The result of the Quebec independence referendum on October 30, 1995, was 50.6 percent for the No side and 49.4 percent for the Yes side. Five polls were carried out in the ten days preceding the referendum. Below are the results of the five polls. Although each poll placed the Yes side ahead among the decided voters, because of a "margin of error" of at least three both sides had about an equal possibility of winning.

There was also the question of what to do with the undecided or "refused to reply" responses. Various approaches were used to allocate the response of voters who did not state a preference. One polling agency, for example, used the age and language, as well as responses to other questions. Nonetheless, for various reasons it was widely recognized that at least 75 percent of respondents who did not state a preference would actually vote No. The table also gives the expected results including those who did not state a preference, distributed 75 percent supporting the No side and 25 percent the Yes side. Compare these results with the actual referendum results.

Polling company	Sample size	Date completed	No	Yes	Undecided or refused to reply	Breakdown of undecided or refused to reply	
						No 75%	Yes 25%
						Expected Results	
						No	Yes
Leger & Leger	1005	Oct. 20	42.2	45.8	12.0	51.2	48.8
CROP	1072	Oct. 23	42.2	44.5	13.3	52.2	47.8
Angus Reid	1029	Oct. 25	40.0	44.0	16.0	52.0	48.0
SOM	1115	Oct. 25	40.0	46.0	14.0	50.5	49.5
Leger & Leger	1003	Oct. 27	41.4	46.8	11.8	50.2	49.8
			No	Yes			
Referendum result:		Oct. 30	50.6	49.4			

Take note of the number of interviews carried out. A little over 1000 interviews! And yet pollsters were able to come within a fraction of a percentage point in estimating the voting intentions of nearly 4.7 million voters. How was that possible?

It is often difficult or impossible to study all the members of the group you are interested in; or stated differently, to study the whole population. Moreover, doing so may be unnecessary. It is often more desirable to study some individuals from within the population—that is, to select a **sample.** For example, instead of studying all the students at your college or university you could examine only a certain number of students, say 300 out of 6000 students. The manner in which you select the sample (the 300 students) will determine the extent to which you can generalize from your results to the population (the 6000 students). Which results would you be more willing to accept as reflecting the 6000 students? The study that gave all 6000 an equal chance of being selected for the sample of 300 students, or the study whose sample of 300 students was made up of students who lingered in the cafeteria?

Can we generalize from the opinion of only one student, as we did in checking out how easy a marker an instructor was? Can we generalize about 6000 students based on the opinion of 300 students who linger in the cafeteria? In both cases students who were immediately available were used, and one can only hope that their views reflect those of the population. Researchers instead aim to select a sample that reflects the population as accurately as possible.

Would you be more willing to accept the conclusions if, for example, we asked every fifth student on the class list from last semester for their opinions about a course? Would you be more willing to accept conclusions about students at your college or university if every twentieth student that registered this semester was interviewed? Needless to say, these techniques in drawing the sample from the population are more complicated than simply asking a friend or students in the cafeteria. But while these techniques are laborious and time consuming, they obtain information that more accurately reflects the views of the population. Thus, how we select the sample from the population determines the degree to which we can generalize from the results.

So far we have spoken of a sample and a population as if these terms applied only to survey research asking people questions. But almost anything can be sampled: opinions, TV programs, advertisements, historical documents, phone conversations, music on the radio, air, water, stars, rocks, volcanic eruptions, and so on. Populations, then, can be any of these things.

There are situations where sampling is not an issue (see Box 4.2). Certain studies may have a population of one, and so do not face a problem in choosing a representative group to study. Cosmologists, the physicists who study the origin and evolution of the universe, have only one case to study. Archaeologists and physical anthropologists who study ancient civilizations or the remains of early human life often have so few cases to deal with that they can study the entire population. Historians often argue that certain events or historical eras are unique and can only be studied as singular events—again a population of one. Sociologists may look at completely new phenomena, such as an emerging political movement, or a religious cult that is so small it is possible to study everyone involved. But if you plan on interviewing only some members of a larger group and want a valid picture of all the members, then you need to use a sampling procedure.

The essential problem of sampling, then, is to select a sample representative of the population from which it is drawn.

How do you select a sample? In formulating a research question or framing a hypothesis, you already in part identified a population. Suppose you want to find the most popular physical recreation activities among college students. The population would consist of college students, but you would have to be more specific about which population of college students. Do you mean college students in the whole world? in Canada? in your province? city? community? You will have to limit your population to one from which you can sample. You may decide, because of cost and time, to restrict your study to students at one college. The population would then be all the students at that particular college, and the sample would be selected from that population. Once you clearly determine your population you can decide how to select the sample. Thus, the population about which you want to generalize influences how you select your sample.

SELECTING THE SAMPLE

There are two broad types of sampling procedures: **random** (or probability) and **nonrandom** (or nonprobability). A sample will be random or non-random depending on how it was selected from the population. A random sampling procedure ensures that each member of the population has an equal (or known) chance of being selected. The procedure provides reasonable assurance that the information collected

BOX 4.2

The Census

What is the population of Canada? What are the ethnic-cultural backgrounds of people in Canada? Answers to these and many more questions are obtained by means of a unique survey, the census. The census is unique in that it attempts to collect information on the entire population of the country at a particular time. Hence, sampling is not an issue.

The first official census in Canada, and probably North America, was carried out by Jean Talon in the second half of the 17th century in what was then New France. As Intendant of Justice, Police, and Finance in the colony, Talon was responsible for encouraging the colony's economic expansion and making it self-sufficient. To help him in his effort, Talon conducted a survey, or rather a census.

The aim of the census was to collect information on the settlers and the colony. Talon was able to find out about such factors as the age, occupation, and marital status of the settlers, as well as such information as the price of lumber and number of government buildings. The data were then used by Talon to help him better administer and develop the colony.

Thanks to the census, Talon learned that the colony contained 2034 men and 1181 women of European descent. Therefore, he arranged for young single women ("filles du roi") to come from France in an effort to encourage the growth of the colony. From 1665 to 1673 nearly 900 women came. He also rewarded early marriages and large families and fined bachelors. The result was the growth of the colony's population of French descent. Meanwhile he helped set up various businesses to stimulate the economy's growth and make the colony more self-sufficient. A few years later Talon proudly noted that the number of births was on the rise and that the clothes he wore were all made in New France.

Talon and others that followed continued to turn to the census as a means of collecting information on the colony. By the time New France became a British colony nearly a century later, dozens of censuses had been carried out.

Needless to say, the information in Talon's census has become a valuable source of information for historians. Today the census continues to be the main means of collecting information on Canada's population. It is carried out by Statistics Canada (an agency of the federal government) every ten years (called the decennial census), the last of which was in 1991. Every five years, in between the decennial censuses, Statistics Canada carries out a census with a shorter list of questions, the last of which was carried out in 1996.

The census collects some information on everyone in Canada, and more detailed information on only 20 percent of the population. The purpose is to determine the number of people in Canada, their age, sex, education, income, ethnic-cultural origins, and many other details.

By comparing the census data of various years we can discern basic trends in our population, including aging, education, and occupational shifts. The information gathered is useful for governments in determining policies, for businesses in determining the consumer markets, and for researchers who need to determine a representative sample of the population of a country or region (we will have more to say on the census in Chapter 8).

reflects the population. (For simplicity's sake we will avoid discussing the statistical details of sampling.) In contrast, a nonrandom sampling procedure is used when it is impossible to give each member of the population an equal chance of being selected. The information collected cannot be generalized to the population.

Note that the term "random" in research does not mean you can select a sample any arbitrary way. For instance, suppose you were carrying out a study on the type of summer jobs held by college students. Assume your sample consisted of fifty students you met or were referred to by friends. Does this comprise a random sample? No. Persons you happened to meet, recruited through some advertisements, or were suggested by others comprise a nonrandom sample.

Random (Probability) Sampling Procedures

Random sampling procedures are designed to give everyone in the population an equal chance of being included in the sample. The aim is to avoid biasing the sample towards any group within the population. Therefore, to achieve a random sample we need a complete list of the population; in technical terms we need the **sampling frame**. A properly selected sample relies on the precision of the sampling frame for its generalizability.

Suppose you want to carry out a study on the religious behaviours of all the students at your college or university. To select a random sample you will need a list of the students. The only available list is the student directory, and you decide to select the sample from this list. The sampling frame is the student directory.

The sampling frame depends on the study. For example, it may be a list of the community clinics in a city, hockey players in a minor league, World War II veterans who are active in the Canadian Legion, or whatever. In each case the researcher must take into account any problems with the sampling frame. Is the list up-to-date? Is it complete? How was it compiled or how will it be compiled? The aim is to have a sampling frame that includes as many members of the population as possible.

But depending on the study, it may be difficult to have a sampling frame that includes the entire population. For example, not all the students are listed in the student directory, and some may have dropped out. Despite the weaknesses of the student directory, it may be the best sampling frame (list) available for the population. Thus, we have to take into account the limitations of the sampling frame in generalizing results to the population of all students. Once you have a sampling frame, you can choose a random sampling technique, of which there are four main types. (For the sake of simplicity, in the following discussion we will assume that the sampling frame includes the entire population.)

Simple Random Sample

The **simple random sample** technique ensures that everyone in the population has an equal chance of being selected. Suppose you want to study first-year students in your college or university (population) and you compiled a list of such students from the student directory. Let us assume there were 500 names. What approach would you use to select 100 students from the list that ensures that all 500 students had an equal chance of being selected?

One approach is to use a technique somewhat comparable to drawing a name out of a hat. This approach is easy but can be laborious and time consuming. The basic steps are:

1. Write each of the 500 names on separate pieces of paper of equal size and thickness that can be easily mixed. (Or you assign each student a number and draw the numbers, as in the case of provincial lotteries.)
2. Place the names in a container, mix them, and draw out a name. That student is selected for the sample.

3. To ensure that each student has an equal chance of being selected, place the name back in the container, mix the names, and draw out another name.
4. Continue the process, until you have selected the required number for your sample. If a name is drawn twice, it is returned to the container. The first 100 students chosen will make up the sample.

If you did it all over again, the names would not correspond to those of your initial sample, but the second sample would be as reliable as the first.

A more widely used approach of selecting a simple random sample is by means of a table of **random numbers** (or you can use computer-generated random numbers). The table of random numbers is made up of numbers that are in no specific order; think of them as if someone else mixed the numbers for you. It is relatively easy to use a random number table. Briefly, you start anywhere on the table of random numbers, then move in a particular direction and select your sample. For example, suppose the following numbers are from a table of random numbers (see Table 4.1):

```
81300
12228
92726
99026
90308
27638
24570
```

To select our sample of 100 students from the population of 500 we would do the following:

1. List the names of the first-year students and number each name from 1 to 500. For example:

```
  1.    Mary Antoine
  2.    Sam Austin
            . . .
500.    Rick Zagreb
```

2. Since the population is made up of 500 students, and you used up to three digits to number each one, you need to select three-digit numbers from the random numbers table to ensure that all have a chance of being selected.

TABLE 4.1

RANDOM NUMBERS

Nowadays computer spreadsheet programs and statistical packages all have a function that generates random numbers for any range.

If you do not have such a program, below is a list of computer-generated random numbers of five digits. The first column (01 to 40) is included to make it easier to read the numbers in the various rows.

01	09430	73223	70535	18533	79431	66128	23456
02	01563	48261	40090	42529	39321	88719	79737
03	91619	06271	86315	74543	54276	80612	11677
04	99980	97778	72852	85762	64551	10988	06827
05	93140	33141	48741	15264	13407	10486	41691
06	25598	14607	35369	88154	08681	24369	10585
07	68317	20603	02956	37784	61458	55566	78160
08	98846	67347	53576	33548	55446	45871	16090
09	84210	87145	74381	93241	07356	77914	44914
10	14451	23345	48777	76197	18693	73240	76948
11	95528	65911	46410	31626	78562	37872	85112
12	35754	89950	81300	92289	57256	68646	83260
13	80792	75646	12228	30562	72917	65055	97489
14	43644	97983	92726	55145	07336	22470	81040
15	60863	72144	99026	82130	47914	39931	50068
16	13443	60905	90308	37870	46354	71315	87354
17	98789	36197	27638	57789	74508	70089	62507
18	87884	94249	24570	10831	22028	20417	17769
19	65777	71115	18967	51052	93366	87433	21554
20	20891	92655	30080	26634	12020	58419	86744
21	21278	27361	84248	04471	99684	61911	44798
22	03846	55135	48911	91011	41471	70775	16108
23	39437	87310	82972	05570	91964	67980	79659
24	22306	91645	05060	73037	46983	25471	60492
25	13308	23580	93920	79172	44234	45317	11187
26	45281	54523	64743	31021	54823	40253	50301
27	25920	33294	64967	55091	43970	09307	97462
28	90149	85488	70964	90097	07011	12687	31212
29	87364	41973	79875	43923	72970	83110	48937
30	52631	71564	99594	22685	40374	22024	63070
31	43192	08144	48950	53592	39644	85520	61724
32	11889	30112	17316	22318	69227	63698	99177

33	55463	37010	88934	19056	92129	11090	98311
34	34349	13016	47883	43687	60928	72117	18027
35	87300	72345	49585	40915	96257	24810	26302
36	75181	01577	40904	75792	93851	93925	92334
37	78810	73992	63836	29333	44341	56843	70191
38	32099	75710	05649	39568	68069	10955	73474
39	30219	47586	88962	71482	13743	67061	46713
40	11142	52243	89842	25147	69038	48310	11928

3. Decide which approach you will use to create the three-digit numbers from the five-digit numbers. Will you use the first three or the last three or another approach? Assume that from the five-digit number you will only take the first three numbers. For the five-digit number 18659, you would only read the first three numbers, 186.

4. Decide on a pattern for selecting the numbers. Will you be moving up or down the column, across from left to right or right to left, or diagonally? Once you decide on the pattern you need to stay with it. Assume you decided to move down the columns.

5. Pick a starting point anywhere on the table of random numbers. Let us say you closed your eyes and with your pen pointed to the five-digit number 12228 on the table of random numbers. The first three digits read 122, and the student whose number is 122 is selected for your sample.

6. The next five-digit number reads 92726, and since the first three digits are 927, and is greater than 500, you would skip this number. You would continue to skip five-digit numbers until you reach one whose first three digits are in the range 001 to 500. In the table, that would be 27638, since the first three digits are 276. Thus, the student numbered 276 would be selected for your sample. You would continue this procedure until you had a random sample of 100 students.

If you picked another starting number or selected the same number but moved in a different direction, the 100 students selected would include different students from your earlier selected sample, but the results would be as reliable.

Systematic Random Sample

A **systematic random sample** involves selecting individuals at every fixed interval on your list of the population. Thus, you need to know the total number of the population and the number you want to sample. You simply divide the total number of the population by the number you want in your sample and determine the interval. However, you do not necessarily begin the systematic sampling procedure at the start of the list of names. Instead, you would begin the procedure by randomly selecting a name from those in the first interval of names. The randomly selected name is the starting name and from then on every name that falls at the determined interval is selected.

Suppose you have a complete list of all 250 faculty members of a community college and want to sample seventy-five. The following steps indicate how to select the sample:

1. Have the complete list of 250 faculty members.

    > Sanders
    > Trevisano
    > Goldberg
    > Trudeau
    > Brandon
    > Handy
    > Kim
    > Anderson
    > Lee ... and so on

2. Calculate the interval.

    > population/sample size = 250/75 = 3 (the interval)

3. Randomly select any name from the first three names on the list. You can close your eyes and point to one of the names, which then becomes your starting point. Or you can place the three names in a box, and the first one selected becomes your starting point.

    Assume the second name of the first three names was randomly selected. Your starting point and the first name selected for the sample would be Trevisano.

4. Begin the selection process with Trevisano. Count three more and select Brandon, and continue the technique until you have the seventy-five names for your sample. (Which would be the third name selected for the sample?)

If one of the faculty members that appears on the list is no longer at the community college, select the name just before or after it. One suggestion is to flip a coin and if it comes up tails select the name after; if heads, choose the name before.

Stratified Random Sample

Suppose you want to compare the future aspirations of male and female students in a health science program. Assume you have access to a student directory that also states the gender of the students in the program. How could you assure that the sample reflects the population in terms of gender? In other words, if females make up 60 percent of the student population, how could you assure that 60 percent of the sample consists of females?

You can do this by means of the **stratified random sampling** procedure, which is a modification of the simple and systematic random sample procedures. However, you will need a list of the population that can be rearranged according to the necessary groups or strata. Social scientists choose to stratify, or sort out, the population using a variety of variables such as gender, age, ethnicity, occupation, or income. Which groups or strata are chosen will depend on the research question or hypothesis.

For example, since you want to compare the future aspirations of male and female students, your population will be stratified according to gender. Assume the desired sample size is 100. There are different approaches in selecting a stratified random sample. A common approach involves the following steps:

1. Divide your list of 500 first-year students into two groups: males and females. Say there are 300 females and 200 males.
2. Make a continuous list of the names beginning with the 300 females followed by the 200 males, or vice versa.
3. Select a systematic random sample of 100, with a random start, from the list. (Careful, the simple random sample would not be appropriate here. Why?)

The result is a proper representation of each group in the sample. If necessary, you can complicate the stratification method by adding other characteristics. Suppose you knew the academic discipline of each student, you could organize each group of females and males by academic disciplines.

To carry out a stratified random sample, it is necessary to determine the proportions of each group in the population. From each list of the group, you then select the number of names for the sample that constitutes the proportion of that group in the population. For example, the proportions of females and males in the student population are 60 percent (300 divided by 500) and 40 percent (200 divided by 500), respectively. Since your desired sample is 100, you would want sixty females and forty males—the same proportion as in the population.

You would then select a random sample of sixty females from the list of females, and a random sample of forty males from the list of males (see Exhibit 4.1).

EXHIBIT 4.1

Stratified Random Sample

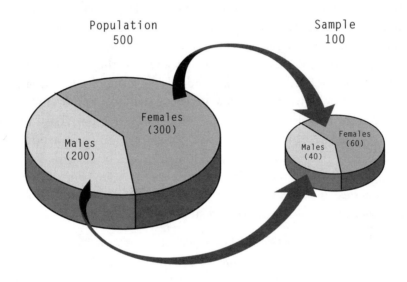

Multi-Stage Cluster Sampling

The previous sampling techniques have dealt with selections of samples from lists of populations. But what if you want to carry out a study of a population that cannot be easily listed? Or, what if it is difficult and costly to compile a list of the population?

For example, what could you do to get a sample of all the graduating high-school students in the province? Of course, you could get the lists of the graduating students in every high school, and then select a random sample. But that would be time consuming, costly, and difficult. To save time and money you could use **cluster sampling,** whereby you randomly select a sample of high schools (clusters) and then survey all of the graduating students at those schools. Another possibility is to use **multi-stage cluster sampling,** whereby you randomly select a sample of high schools, and then randomly sample students from the lists of graduating students at each of the selected schools.

Cluster sampling involves a single stage, where everyone in the selected clusters is in the sample, such as all the graduating high-school students in the selected sample of high schools. Multi-stage, as the name implies, involves various stages and selects subsamples from the clusters, such as selecting a sample of graduating students from within the selected high schools. An advantage of these procedures is that they save time and money. But a disadvantage is that they can result in a biased sample. The selected sample of high schools may have certain characteristics that are unknown to the researcher and which can have an impact on the results. For example, they might all be located in low-income districts.

Thus, in cluster sampling you select samples in stages. Cluster sampling is especially useful in selecting a sample that covers a population that is geographically dispersed. National samples are usually selected by means of a multi-stage cluster sampling procedure.

The essentials of cluster sampling can be demonstrated even in selecting a sample at a college or university. Suppose you want to carry out a study of first-year students in social science disciplines. Assume the student directory does not exist or is not useful. Now suppose that all first-year social science students are required to take the course Social Research, of which there are forty sections. You could compile a list of all the students in the forty sections and then select a simple random sample. But you do not have the time and money. Another approach is to do cluster sampling.

1. Compile the list of the forty sections of the course. Assume you want a sample of ten sections. Randomly select ten sections.
2. Survey the students in each of the ten sections.

Or you could add another stage in the sampling process.

2. (Replaces 2 above.) Compile a list of students for each of the ten selected sections.
3. Do a random sample of the students in each of the ten selected sections, whereby one fourth of the students in each section are selected.

The sample evolved in stages from forty sections to ten sections to randomly selected students in each of the ten sections. Cluster sampling will provide a reasonably representative sample of first-year social science students without requiring you to identify the entire population at the outset.

Census Feeds Passion for Data

Thousands Clamour to Sift Through Facts

Early last summer, even as they wrestled with huge budget cuts, six federal departments took a deep breath and scraped together $55.5-million for something they knew they couldn't live without: the long form of 1996 census that the government's fiscal hawks were telling Statistics Canada to chop.

It's testimony to the modern desperation for data. And on Tuesday, when census day arrives and the count of nearly 30 million Canadians begins, about six million will fill in that salvaged long form.

In the process, they will feed a voracious information age that has already made them the most studied population in this country's history.

So great is this passion for data in the waning years of this millennium that people such as Bruce Petrie, the assistant chief statistician of Statistics Canada, say information has become as indispensable as roads and bridges.

"It's a cornerstone of the infrastructure of modern society," he said.

The census, the most influential of Statistics Canada's surveys—and at a cost of $347.4-million this time around by far the most expensive—is the fundamental building block of this information infrastructure.

And, as might be expected in an era that is mad for numbers, the census that people are filling in this weekend and over the next few days, will gather yet more information about who Canadians are, where they live and what they do. Modern computers, with their vast electronic storage and calculation abilities, make analyzing greater amounts of data ever more possible.

That this information provides the basis for such democratic principles as parliamentary representation is well understood. So is the fact that billions in federal government transfer payments also rides on the

official census count.

Perhaps less catalogued are the thousands of other users clamouring to sift through census facts, including every federal government department and most provincial ones. Local governments won't build a school or plan a road without examining the census.

Academics, social agencies and advocacy groups line up for census data the second Statscan makes it available. Private businesses are also heavily dependent on census figures: moving companies want to know whether migration patterns suggest they invest in a new fleet of trucks; technology firms use it to find out whether Canadians are educated enough to accept a new generation of computer software.

But it's not just the census that feeds the giant maw. Statscan has launched three massive studies in recent years that move beyond the census's one-time-only snapshot of its subjects. In all, these three longitudinal surveys will capture information on 140,000 Canadians over periods of up to 20 years. And that's in addition to all the other regular surveys Statscan conducts— counting the unemployed every month, for example— and the vast polling and market research conducted by private enterprise.

A measure of the Canadian taste for numbers lies in the data about Statistics Canada itself. The agency has a budget of $423-million this fiscal year, of which $180-million will be spent on the census. It boasts 5,062 regular employees, as well as roughly 1,500 sporadic interviewers. Another 45,000 employees have been hired temporarily to conduct Tuesday's census. Later this year, about 5,000 more will be taken on to process some of the information the census gathers.

"We love to quantify," said Robert Glossop, a sociologist are the Vanier Institute of the Family in Ottawa, which is a heavy user of census data. "This society values numbers. There is, in a sense, only one calculus."

One of the best examples of numbers as validation is the question about unpaid work that appears on the 1996 census for the first time. Statscan admits that it was muscled into putting the question on the census form by a lobby group of women led by Carol Lees of Saskatoon. They felt their work was not being formally recognized as it was left off the official count. (It is counted in other, smaller surveys, but nothing with the heft of the census.)

Ms. Lees refused to fill out her 1991 census questionnaire because it lacked a place to fill in information about household work, and Statscan threatened her with fine or jail. In turn, she set about organizing a boycott if the agency refused her request. Last summer, she won the showdown.

"If we are not present in the statistical record, we are not present in the public policy," said Ms. Lees. "We have been left out of information gathering."

She points to the national child-care debate as proof of the power of numbers. Because there aren't any regular, accurate ones on the extent of unlicenced home care, including that done by parents, the debate has centred instead around such quantifiable things as the number of day care spaces and the characteristics of the counted labour force.

"We are not even a part of that debate," she said. "I insist we must be part of the debate and the only way we can be included is to be named and numbered."

Government departments, too, are terrified at the thought of not having good census data, as last summer's scramble for funds for the long form demonstrates.

But Mr. Petrie of Statscan says that this financial stress underlies the modern thirst for data. When every dollar any level of government spends is under scrutiny, that dollar has to go—and be proved to go— to the citizen who can make the best use of it.

Mr. Petrie said: "The objective is to better target."

But the need for more census data is coming from forces within the Canadian population itself, too. Shifts in the rate of common-law unions, elderly Canadians living alone and two-job families have left policymakers scrambling and social critics demanding data from the census and from other surveys that use the census data as a jumping-off point.

"The whole notion of the family is very charged," said

Pamela White, who is in charge of what questions will appear on Tuesday's census. "The interest here is what is happening on the home front."

Immigration, too, is resulting in huge, new changes for Canadian society, said Mr. Petrie. Not only are immigrants arriving in Canada from a whole host of new countries, they are forming a larger and larger proportion of the growth in the Canadian population.

That is one of the reasons for the controversial new question on race to be given to every fifth household in Canada. It asks which of 10 population groups one belongs to, including White, Chinese, Black and South Asian.

If the data prove reliable—and so far the backlash against the question has been mild—then Canadians will be able to find out, for example whether Black men and White men tend to earn the same income or own the same kind of homes.

Statscan is asking the question to fulfill its legislative requirements to provide data to support the Employment Equity Act, but a partial list of users who have already signalled interest in the race question and the one on ethnic origin runs to 17 federal agencies and departments alone (including Citizenship and Immigration Canada, Health Canada and Revenue Canada), all provinces and territories and about 68 other groups such as Black United Front, German Canadian Congress and *Jeunesse acadienne.*

Even something as seemingly innocuous as the postal code question arouses passionate interest among potential users of census data. Before, it was collected only on every fifth form, representing about six million Canadians. On Tuesday, it will be a requirement for each of nearly 30 million Canadians.

Why the change? The genius of the census, and the source of its power, is cross-tabulation. That means that when all the millions of pieces of information extracted from the forms (apart from names, which are kept strictly confidential) are crunched together in database, then any one of those can be matched with any other.

This massive, plastic census database can then be sliced any way a user wants, as long as the information produced does not identify an individual Canadian.

In the case of the postal code, this means that the private sector, for example, can find out even more detailed information about the people who live in any small geographic area, sometimes as small as a neighbourhood.

Want to find out how many middle-income, two-job families with children live around the site of a potential pizza parlor? Consult census data by postal code.

Want to figure out where to put a community centre for seniors on welfare? Easy, using census data by postal code.

In fact, so pervasive is the dependence on census data that few government reports or programs or policies are made in the absence of these numbers. And the effect of what the census finds out, while sometimes difficult to point to, is seamlessly woven into the lives of nearly every Canadian.

"Directly or indirectly, the census will affect all of us in a number of ways," said Mr. Petrie. "Collectively, a lot better decisions should be made as a result of it."

Of course, the down side of Canada's love affair with

numbers is the assumption that having good information means it will be used well. In fact, said Ellen Gee, chairwoman of sociology and anthropology at Simon Fraser University in Burnaby, B.C., policy debates often rage in a vacuum, even when statistics are at hand.

"When policies get made, sometimes it seems like they are made on politics alone and that research doesn't figure," Dr. Gee said.

She points to the thesis among some immigration policy-makers that encouraging young immigrants will somehow help stem the aging of the Canadian population. In fact, at the kind of immigration numbers Canada now allows, immigration plays a minuscule role in changing the country's age structure, the research indicates.

Not only does the census provide massive amounts of information necessary for governing and policy making, but shifts in the census questions reflect social changes. What are some of the shifts mentioned in this report?

Source: Alanna Mitchell, "Census Feeds Passion for Data," *The Globe and Mail* (11 May 1996), pp. A1, A6. Reprinted with permission.

Nonrandom (Nonprobability) Sampling Procedures

Nonrandom sampling procedures provide a weak basis for generalizing from the sample to the population. However, their importance in research should not be disregarded. Various reasons exist for using nonrandom sampling procedures; in most instances their use is due to the objectives of the research and the lack of resources. Students are especially likely to lack the time and resources to carry out a study based on a random sample, and may therefore have to resort to a nonrandom sampling procedure. In carrying out your own research, first consider what resources (time, money, sampling frame, and so on) you would need to draw a random sample. If you are unable to draw a random sample, for whatever reasons, consider a nonrandom sample that best serves the purpose of your study and explain why you are using it.

Five common procedures of nonrandom sampling are described below with examples of situations in which you may need to use them.

Accidental Sampling

In one social science discipline, history, sampling tends to be the exception rather than the rule. This is because history (and other historical sciences like archaeology and paleontology) works with ready-made samples: the historical remains that have been accidentally left behind. The further back in time one studies, the fewer the number of items that have escaped wear and tear, destruction, and burial. All you can study is what remains, what has been saved, and what has been discovered from an original population of documents, buildings, monuments, and other artifacts. This is called **accidental sampling.**

An enormous amount of effort goes into describing these remains, and establishing as clearly as possible how they were located and discovered. Each piece of information is used to cross-check every other piece and build up a picture of life in the past. The logic of sampling still holds. That is, historians are trying to draw conclusions about a population from a subgroup of that population. However, for historical work there is no choice but to use whatever evidence has survived over time.

Convenience Sampling

Convenience sampling involves selecting for the sample whomever or whatever is convenient for the researcher. This method is roughly equivalent to "person-on-the-street" interviews by reporters and journalists who want to give a sense of what some people think about an issue. Journalists operate under severe time pressure to get a story out while it is still "hot" and consequently they are forced to use shortcuts in gathering information. We cannot and should not assume, however, that the opinions of the persons interviewed reflect those of everyone else. The same can be said about any sample that was conveniently selected.

Suppose you want to do a study on nutrition among college or university students and only survey students in one of your classes. Are the students surveyed representative of all college or university students? You have no way of knowing. The students were selected because they were available and because it was convenient for you to carry out the survey on them. The sample results could be highly misleading.

Likewise, assume you want to carry out a study on the opinions of students at your college or university and interview every tenth student that you meet in the cafeteria on a Wednesday afternoon. But are the opinions of the students you interviewed representative of all the students in the college or university? You have no way of knowing; you selected the sample from whomever happened to be in the cafeteria on a particular day and time. The information only tells you about the opinions of students in your sample and you cannot generalize to all the students in the college or university.

Thus, the results obtained from a convenience sample only pertain to the sample itself. There are many reasons why researchers may resort to a convenience sampling approach. One common usage is to pretest questionnaires. In this case the researchers are concerned with checking out how well the questionnaire works in terms of the clarity of questions and any problems arising from the format. (We cover questionnaires in Chapter 5.) There is no attempt to make generalizations from the results. As long as the questionnaire is tried out with a test group similar to the population being studied no special sampling techniques beyond convenience need be used.

Convenience sampling is also used in advancing our understanding of particular issues. For example, suppose you wanted to carry out a study on people who at one time in their lives were homeless. It would be virtually impossible to draw up a list of all such persons from whom you could draw a random sample. You may instead resort to a convenience sampling procedure whereby your sample consists of persons whom you know have at one time been homeless. Although you cannot generalize to all formerly homeless persons, the information gathered is nevertheless useful.

Another area where convenience samples are often used is in psychology. Psychologists often use student volunteers as subjects in their experiments and tests. They argue that the kinds of phenomena they study—cognition, memory, language learning and use, etc.—are found in all healthy, normal human beings. Differences between students and nonstudents, or between students who volunteer for the experiments and those who do not, are viewed as irrelevant to the issues studied in their experiments, so the use of convenient groups of highly accessible students is acceptable. As well, when psychologists perform experiments other procedures aid the validity of their research, so that generalizations from the results are possible (see Chapter 6).

Purposive (Judgmental) Sampling

Purposive sampling involves selecting for the sample whoever or whatever in the researcher's judgment has characteristics that meet the purpose of the study. Suppose you want to study female students who are single parents. It may be difficult and time consuming to compile a list of all such female students and draw a random sample. Therefore, if you have limited time and resources, you may decide to select all female single parents who are members of, say, the Mature Students Association at your college or university, or who have children in the college or university day care, or both. You purposely select these female students because you assume that they are typical of

BOX 4.3

How Was the Sample Selected?

Two studies have been carried out on the spending habits of university students in Canada. One is based on 3000 interviews and the other on 500 interviews. Could you tell on the basis of the size of the sample which is the more reliable study? Do not be deceived into believing that just because a sample is large it is more valid than a smaller one. It is worth asking, how was the sample selected?

To illustrate, consider the widely cited case of the now-defunct upscale American magazine the *Literary Digest*, which conducted a postcard poll during the 1936 U.S. presidential campaign. The *Digest* mailed out ten million ballots to telephone subscribers and automobile owners, of which two million sent in their ballots. From these, the *Digest* predicted that the Republican candidate, Landon, would get 57 percent of the votes to 43 percent for the Democratic candidate, Roosevelt. The reverse occurred: Roosevelt won by a landslide with 61 percent of the vote. Clearly, one of the many errors of the *Digest* poll was that its sample mainly consisted of one socioeconomic group: telephone subscribers and automobile owners in 1936, a time when the impact of the Depression was still being felt.

Meanwhile others, such as George Gallup, were developing new sampling methods aimed at making samples more representative of the electorate. The samples were also far smaller than that of the *Digest*. Mainly because of their sampling technique, Gallup and others correctly predicted that Roosevelt would win.

Thus, do not assess the reliability of a sample based on size, but rather on how the sample was selected. (For example, see the sample size of the Quebec referendum polls in Box 4.1).

The random sample gives everybody the same statistical chance of being selected; its aim is to be representative of the target population. The nonrandom sample is less statistically accurate and we do not know how representative it is of the target population. But a random sample is nevertheless also prone to providing poor results. Do not judge the quality of a study solely on the sampling technique.

Further, if the results of the study are intended to reflect the opinion of a larger group than the sample, then we need to restrict our findings to the target population. For example, a random sample selected from adults in Toronto can reflect the views of adult Torontonians, but not all adults in Ontario or Canada.

female students who are single parents. You will never know for sure, but the study may still be of practical interest.

Likewise, suppose your study on homeless persons concerns single women over 60. For your sample you purposely select women over 60 who are aided by a service agency in your community because in your judgment they are typical of homeless women over 60. You may have various reasons for assuming this, but you can never be certain that they are typical. But representativeness may not be your concern. The aim of your research may be to test a theory or to further our understanding of homeless women and gain insights that challenge widely-held assumptions.

Quota Sampling

Quota sampling involves selecting quotas (or proportions) of each defined subgroup from the population. Therefore, we need to know the proportion of each subgroup in the population, such as the proportion of males and females, or of other features such as age, academic discipline, or place of residence. Note that despite the effort, quota sampling is a nonrandom sampling procedure; do not confuse it with stratified random sampling. A list of the population from which to draw the sample is missing in the quota sampling procedure.

Suppose you want to find out which political party is favoured by college or university students and you have reasons to believe that support may vary according to gender. Let's say a directory of students does not exist or that you do not have the time and resources to draw a random sample. But you find out from the registrar that the student population consists of 55 percent females and 45 percent males. Assuming you want a sample of 100, your sample should have fifty-five females and forty-five males. You then seek out in your college or university, such as in the cafeteria on a Wednesday afternoon, fifty-five females and forty-five males for your sample.

The study would be further complicated if some other feature, say an academic year, was also relevant for your study. You would have to determine the relevant proportions of the various subgroups with the desired features; for example, the proportions of first-year males, first year-females, and so forth. Then you would determine the appropriate number of each subgroup needed for your sample that would correspond to the proportion of each subgroup in the population. For instance, if first-year males make up 8 percent of the student population at your college or university and your sample is to consist of 100 students, only eight students in the sample should be first-year male students.

Quota samples are common in market research and opinion polls, mainly because they are quicker, easier, and less expensive to obtain than random samples. But they have various inherent problems. The information from which the proportions are determined may be inaccurate or outdated. And even if the appropriate proportions are selected, biases may exist among the persons chosen for the sample. For instance, after having examined the results, you might learn that all eight first-year male students in your sample were members of a specific political party. By contrast, in a stratified random sample this would be less likely to occur, since the samples for each strata are selected randomly.

Snowball Sampling

Snowball sampling involves first selecting persons who have characteristics that meet the requirements of the study and then asking them for further contacts. Like a snowball that grows larger when you roll it in wet snow, a snowball sample grows ever larger from the initial contacts on.

Suppose you want to do a study on racism and wanted to interview college or university students who attended a march in support of white supremacism. You were able to find two students at your college or university who attended the march and were willing to be interviewed. You might ask each for other names of march participants and you would do the same with these other subjects. You would continue the process until no more new names were suggested or until you felt the sample was of a sufficient size. You cannot be sure, however, that the sample is reflective of all the students who participated in the march. Moreover, unbeknownst to you, a bias may have entered into the sample from the outset. For instance, the first two students could have been members of a clandestine white supremacist organization and suggested names of other students who belonged to the same organization. But despite this drawback, you would have gained information about the racist beliefs of such students that might not have been available to you without snowball sampling.

Snowball sampling is, in fact, essential for studying minority, unpopular, or unofficial beliefs such as racism. Where beliefs or actions are controversial, unpopular, marginal, or hidden for other reasons, snowball sampling is often the only way to get to talk with a group of individuals associated with such beliefs and actions. Sociologists interested in studying criminals, cult groups, or political extremists often use snowball sampling techniques.

Likewise, suppose you are doing a study on leadership among ethnic communities and need to interview leaders of an ethnic community with which you have little contact. Assume you are able to obtain the names of executives of some associations in that community. You could first interview them and then ask them for names of other leaders in the community, and so forth. The underlying assumption is that leaders of an ethnic community would know each other. As you can imagine, the snowball sampling procedure could lead you astray and to a biased group of leaders, but you would still have learned about some aspect of leadership in that community. Political scientists studying power elites and other leaders use the snowball sampling technique. Being referred to the next leader not only helps the researcher to gain access, but also gives the researcher credibility and helps promote trust between the researcher and the people being interviewed. Where trust is an important consideration in research, the snowball technique may be the only practical method of sampling.

HOW LARGE A SAMPLE?

How large should the sample be? This depends on many factors, including the sampling method, how accurate you want to be, and the variation in the population. Thus, the answer will partly depend on the researcher's purpose and the characteristics of the population. For both nonrandom and random samples, another major factor affecting sample size will be the time and resources available for your research.

For nonrandom samples, the size of the sample is not a major issue, since the results cannot be generalized to a population. Nonetheless, as a student you may find yourself using such a sample for a class project, such as a social survey. Experience tells us that in such a situation it is best to have at least thirty respondents in order to be able to make some simple analyses.

Sample size is of particular concern in random sampling procedures, since you want to generalize to the population. Depending on the research objective, the more characteristics being taken into account about the population, the larger the sample. For example, if your study requires a sample of students from all the different programs at your college or university, then you are likely to require a larger sample than if you were selecting students irrespective of their program or other characteristics. The greater the variation in the population that has to be present in the sample, the larger the sample—or else the lower the accuracy of the results. Various statistical formulas can be used to compute the appropriate size of the sample in random sampling procedures, but these are beyond the scope of this chapter. Instead, let us explore certain factors to consider in examining sample size.

BOX 4.4

Types of Samples

RANDOM SAMPLING

Designed to give everyone in the target population an equal chance of being selected. Aims to be representative of the target population. Permits the use of various statistical techniques for estimating error and making inferences.

Simple Random
- everyone in the target population has an equal chance of being selected, such as selecting names out of a hat
- rarely used because it is less efficient than systematic sampling.

Systematic Random
- selecting a sample from a list at certain intervals, say every tenth person on a list, using a random start
- an efficient technique provided that you have an appropriate sampling frame (i.e., a list of the individual units in the population)

Stratified Random
- dividing the target population into groups (strata) and selecting samples from each one, for example when you want the sample to represent both men and women
- necessary to ensure the representation of subgroups in the sample

Multi-stage Cluster
- will sample at different stages, for example in the first stage select a sample of city blocks, second stage select specific dwellings in those blocks, third stage select a sample among the people residing in those dwellings
- necessary when your sample frame does not list individuals but some other kind of unit such as households or schools

NONRANDOM SAMPLING

Any sample for which it is impossible to give each person in the target population an equal chance of being selected. The sample is usually biased.

Accidental
- where the sample emerges from uncontrolled events such as historical wear and tear and accidents

Convenient
- choose whoever is most convenient to be interviewed, similar to the "person-on-the-street" interviews often used by television reporters
- used for pretesting survey questionnaires

Purposive
- choose people difficult to find in a target population, for example selecting members of the college's gay and lesbian club to find out about discrimination against homosexuals and lesbians in your college or university

Quota
- choosing a certain number of respondents within various groups, for example a certain number of females in different age groups and a certain number of males in different age groups

Snowball
- selecting persons with characteristics that meet the purpose of the survey, and then having them provide names of others like them to contact, and so on
- only possible way of studying certain social groupings such as deviants or elites

In a study at a college of 1000 students, which findings would you be more confident in accepting: those based on a random sample of 100 students or those based on a random sample of 500 students? The random sample of 500 is more accurate. But why? The results from a random sample of 500 are likely to be closer to the "true value" of the characteristics of the population. Thus, we recognize that random samples, despite their attempt at being representative of the population, are subject to **a margin of error** (or sampling error); a difference between the "true" value of a characteristic of the population and the value estimated from a random sample of the population. (Careful sampling error does not refer to a mistake that you intentionally or unintentionally made.) For example, suppose the average age of your sample of 500 students is 19.2 years, but the average age of all 1000 students in the college is 19.8. The sample average age is close to that of the population value, but is off by 0.6 years from the population value.

But, you might rightly ask, how can you know the margin of error if you do not know the true value of the population? With regard to the above example, how could you assess the margin of error if you did not know that the average age of the population is 19.8 years? Researchers do this by establishing a **confidence interval,** a range in which they expect the true value to fall. Again, take the example above. The sample average age of the students was 19.2, and if the confidence interval is +1.2 to –1.2 from the average age, we expect the average age of the population to fall between 18 years and 20.4 years.

It is also possible to measure how confident we are that our results will fall in this range; this is known as the **confidence level.** For example, rather than simply saying that we expect the average age of the population to fall between 18 years and 20.4 years, we can be even more precise by noting that we are 95 percent confident. In other words, if various random samples were drawn from the same population of students, we are confident that 95 percent of the samples, or nineteen out of twenty samples, would have an average age that would range from 18 years to 20.4 years, while another 5 percent of the sample would have average ages outside the range. Note that we do not know the actual average age of the population, since we only collected information on a sample of the population. Yet, by means of certain computations beyond the scope of this book, we are able to state that we are 95 percent confident that the average age of the population falls in the confidence interval of the sample. (Or we could use another confidence level, such as 99 percent and so on.)

The rules of probability also tell us that for large populations, say 10 000 or more, we can achieve about the same degree of accuracy with roughly a sample size of about 1000 to 1100, irrespective of whether the population consists of 10 000 or 10 million or 100 million. For example, to achieve a sampling error of plus or minus 3 percent at a confidence level of 95 percent, we would need a sample of about 250 for a population size of 500, a sample of about 1000 for a population size of 10 000, but only a sample of about 1100 for a population size of one million. National polls in Canada usually accept a margin of error (sampling error) of plus or minus 3, at 95 percent

BOX 4.5

What Is the Margin of Error?

The television announcer just informed us of the latest poll results. Candidate Humble is preferred by 52 percent of voters while Candidate Vanity is preferred by 48 percent. Who was likely to have won if an election was held when the poll was conducted?

The results in themselves provide insufficient information. After telling us the overall results the television announcer is likely to state the margin of error, and then point out that according to the polling agency the results are too close to call a winner. Why? There are four percentage points separating the two candidates! Could it be because of the margin of error?

The best way to understand margin of error is by way of examples. Assume we are told that the poll had a margin of error of plus or minus 3 percent, 19 times out of 20. The information provided tells us that the researchers are confident 19 times out of 20 (or have a 95 percent confidence) that the sample is from plus to minus 3 percentage points of the results they would have had if they interviewed the entire target population. Careful, it does not mean that a mistake of 3 percentage points occurred 19 times out of 20.

Again let us use the example of Candidates Humble and Vanity. With plus or minus 3 percentage points, the expected support for Candidate Humble is between 49 percent (52 – 3) and 55 percent (52 + 3), and for Candidate Vanity between 45 percent (48 – 3) and 51 percent (48 + 3). Hence, we cannot infer from these figures which candidate is more popular. Why? (Take note of the overlap.)

Another example is the last poll taken before the 1995 Quebec independence referendum with a sample of 1003 (see Box 4.1). A sample of this size has a margin of error of plus or minus 3.1 percentage points, 19 times out of 20. Among those who stated a preference, 41.4 percent said they would vote Yes and 46.8 percent said they would vote No. But the margin of error tells us what the range of the final results might be. With a margin of error of 3.1 percentage points, the results among those who stated a preference were expected to fall between 38.3 percent and 44.5 percent for the Yes and between 43.7 percent and 49.9 percent for the No. Why was it too close to call? (Researchers may also take into account other factors in determining how close the expected results are. See Box 4.1 for an example.)

When a sample is broken down into subgroups, such as by gender, age, or location, the margin of error rises. Suppose the above results for our two candidates covered the whole country. Now assume that we also had the results by region. In the Atlantic region support for Candidate Humble is 46 percent and Candidate Vanity 54 percent, with a margin of error of plus or minus 6 percentage points. Then in the Atlantic region support is expected to be between 40 and 52 percent for Candidate Humble and from 48 percent to 60 percent for Candidate Vanity. Can you tell who is likely to win in the Atlantic region?

Thus, the margin of error is determined on the basis of what to expect in a perfect survey. However, perfect surveys do not exist. And if subsamples are considered then their margins of errors are greater than that of the overall survey. The margin of error alone is insufficient in judging the results. We need to always interpret the results with caution; there can be many serious flaws in how the study was conducted.

[The aim here is to help you grasp what is meant by the concept of margin of error. To produce a confidence statement, it is necessary to have an elementary understanding of statistics. Chapter 9 provides a brief introduction to statistics.]

confidence level, and therefore consist of a sample of about 1100 people. Other factors may have to be taken into account, such as provincial or regional social variations, which can affect sample size and confidence level.

Thus, especially in the case of student projects, in general the larger the random sample, the more accurate and more confident you can be in the results. But your confidence in your survey does not depend only on the size of your sample and the procedure used in selecting the sample. Among other factors, it will also depend on the technique selected and the quality of the research method. If, for example, you are studying a sample over a long period of time (such as studying changes in the career plans of students as they go through school), you need to allow for a certain amount of shrinkage in your sample. Students will move away and transfer to other schools, drop out and get jobs, and so on. The longer the time period of your study the greater the problem of shrinkage, known as **mortality,** will be. Therefore, the sample you begin with will have to be larger than necessary.

A similar problem occurs when you are investigating sensitive, intimate, or controversial subjects such as sexual behaviour. You are likely to have a large number of outright refusals to answer as well as incomplete and even spoiled questionnaires, which will require compensation through a larger initial sample. As you can see, the problem of sample size is a complex one for which there are no simple answers.

WHAT YOU HAVE LEARNED

- Sampling is an almost universal part of any act of gathering information.

- The essential problem of sampling is to attempt to select a representative sample from a population.

- In order to be able to generalize from a sample, one of a number of types of random sampling has to be used.

- Nonrandom sampling techniques are valuable research tools even though they do not permit generalizations to be drawn.

- Many factors affect the size of a sample required for a particular study.

KEY WORDS

sampling	cluster sampling
population	multi-stage cluster sampling
sample	accidental sampling
random sample	convenience sampling
purposive sampling	purposive sampling
nonrandom sample	quota sampling
sampling frame	snowball sampling
simple random sample	margin of error
random numbers	confidence interval
systematic random sample	confidence level
stratified random sample	mortality

REVIEW QUESTIONS

1. What is the essential problem of sampling?
2. What are the two types of sampling procedures? What distinguishes them?
3. What is a sampling frame and why is it important?
4. What is a stratified random sample and why would you use it?
5. When are cluster sampling and multi-stage cluster sampling procedures needed?
6. Which kinds of studies use snowball sampling and why?
7. What factors affect the size of a sample?

RECOMMENDED READINGS

Satin, A., & Shastry, W. (1993). *Survey sampling: A non-mathematical guide.* (2nd ed.). Ottawa: Statistics Canada, Catalogue Number 12-602.

A basic guide on survey sampling published by Statistics Canada and intended for individuals with no formal training in statistics. It illustrates the main concepts and methods of survey sampling, mainly by means of examples.

Slonim, Morris J. (1966). *Sampling.* New York: Simon and Schuster.

A concise, humorous introduction to sampling designed for readers without any statistical knowledge.

Social Survey

WHAT YOU WILL LEARN

- the aim and purpose of surveys
- how to judge surveys conducted by others
- how to construct a questionnaire
- how to administer a survey

INTRODUCTION

Quebec teens, be they francophones or anglophones, are far more open than teens elsewhere in the country to premarital sex and homosexuality (Bibby and Posterski, 1992, p. 116).

The past decade witnessed an especially sharp increase in the labour force participation of women with children (Parliament, 1994, p. 257).

Canadians are taking better care of themselves today than they did just a few years ago. They are smoking less, drinking less, and exercising more (Millar, 1994, p. 91).

Only about half of household property crimes ever come to the attention of the police (Sacco and Johnson, 1994, p. 395).

Perception of the seriousness of AIDS generally increases with age (Strike, 1990, p. 85).

The above statements are all examples of results obtained from surveys. It is very likely that in your lifetime you have participated either directly or indirectly in a social survey. The survey method has become one of the most popular techniques of collecting data in the social sciences. The survey is also widely used by government agencies, market researchers, political parties, community groups, and media organizations.

Of the various social science methods, the survey is the most familiar to the general public; survey data have become part of our everyday sources of information. The media regularly report the results of surveys on a wide range of topics, and TV documentaries, magazine articles, and newspaper editorials often include survey data.

The media regularly fund surveys on a variety of topics. During election campaigns, for example, numerous polls are funded by newspapers and television stations. But while most surveys are properly carried out, at times the media report findings that are based on poorly designed surveys whose results are not trustworthy.

Unfortunately, despite the popularity of survey research, the public is generally unaware of the criteria that determine if a survey is meaningful or meaningless. And because of the popularity of survey research, many may wrongly assume that to conduct a survey requires little thought and effort. There is the added problem that at times they may have been asked to take part in a bogus survey that is disguised as research but is instead part of a sales campaign.

Dial-in-polls, which some may wrongly assume are acceptable scientific research, have also been growing in popularity. Television and radio programs invite listeners to call a phone number to register their vote on a particular issue, usually with a yes or no response to a question. Do you agree with the government's latest budget? Should pornography be illegal? Should the Toronto Maple Leafs get a new coach? And so on. A short time later, the responses are compiled and reported. But while the announcer may state that the poll reflects only the views of those who chose to call, the impression often left is that the results are representative of the public's opinion. Why are these polls not valid as scientific research? Similarly, why should little importance, if any, be given to results of surveys based on questionnaires included in popular magazines? (See Box 5.1.)

CASUAL AND SCIENTIFIC INQUIRY

The Casual Inquiry

Suppose you want to find out whether students at your college or university who do not work part time do better in school than students

BOX 5.1

Sex Survey: Is This Social Science?

Among the feature topics highlighted on the cover of an issue of the popular fashion magazine *Flare* was one called: "Sex Survey: Canadian Women Tell All!" (Young, 1994).When we turn to the article titled "Sex File" our tendency is first to read the results noted in large print, including: "Is penis size important? Only 2% said yes!" There is much more. We are told about females' favourite sexual fantasies, how they describe sex, what percentage have had a one-night stand, who they would consider to be a "million-dollar lover," and where is the most interesting place they had sex.

Interesting! Yes, but. Our curiosity may prevent us from asking questions about the quality of the data.

We are informed that the survey was based on the responses of 2000 readers who took the time to fill out and mail a questionnaire that appeared in an earlier issue of the magazine. Moreover, we are told, without any explanation, that the responses of only about 1000 were used in tabulating the sex survey results. Can we generalize from the information collected from these readers of the magazine to all Canadian women? To all the readers of the magazine? Although 2000 readers responded, we do not know which women, assuming only women responded. Despite the large number of respondents, they did not necessarily represent the magazine's readers and certainly did not represent all Canadian women.

The magazine's sex survey relied on readers who chose to complete and return the questionnaire. They are likely to give a distorted picture of the general reader of the magazine, and of Canadian women, especially since the survey concerns a sensitive topic, which in many ways was also trivialized. The findings would have been more believable if the respondents had been selected by researchers to be representative of either all the readers of the magazine or all Canadian women.

Thus, it is essential to consider the quality of the survey to determine whether the results are credible. Articles on sex surveys may sell magazines, but if the data collection method is flawed, we have to seriously question the results.

who do work part time. What could you do to find out? A quick and easy way, and one with many flaws, is to collect information from students you know who work part time and those who do not have jobs. Assume you wanted to draw conclusions about all the students at your college or university, but collected information from only ten students, five of whom worked part time and five of whom did not. Also assume the students were your friends, and while having lunch in the cafeteria you asked them what their overall grade averages were.

For the social science researcher this approach has numerous weaknesses. Consider a few of many questions a social scientist would ask about the research:

- Which group were you interested in studying?
- Whom did you interview?
- How were the students chosen to be interviewed?
- How were the interviews conducted?
- What question(s) did you ask them?
- How did you determine their academic performance?
- How many courses were the students registered in and how many did they regularly attend?
- Were they day students or evening students?
- How many hours did the students work?
- If they worked, what were the main activities of their jobs? Were they related to their studies?
- Is the information collected sufficient to make generalizations about all the students in the college or university?

The obvious answer to the last question is "no" (see Chapter 4). The example illustrates a serious but common error in everyday personal inquiry. After having spoken to a few students, the tendency might be to look for a general pattern in the relationship between grades and part-time work. Suppose the five students who worked part time had lower grade averages than the five students who did not work part time. The tendency is to conclude that all students in the college or university who work part time have lower grades than students who do not work part time, and therefore that working part time results in poor academic performance. Both conclusions are highly suspect; in particular, they are based on the limited information gathered from casual conversations with ten students. Moreover, are there measures of academic performance other than the grade?

The example above, although flawed, contains some of the main ingredients of a **social survey:** asking questions to a selected number of people, usually to draw conclusions about a larger group of people.

However, the survey is far more complex and demanding than an everyday casual inquiry.

The Scientific Inquiry

Let us consider briefly the main components of the social survey. Later we will explore them in greater detail. Again, suppose you want to find out whether at your college or university students who work part time do better in school than students who do not work part time.

Because of time and cost it may be impossible, and unnecessary, to interview all the students. Instead you can select a subgroup of students (say about 300 students) to represent all 6000 students at your college or university. You might, for example, select for interview every twentieth student from a list (the sampling frame) of all the students. As you will recall from Chapter 4, this is the systematic random sampling procedure which, if properly carried out, lets you generalize the results from a few hundred students to all the students in the college or university. In other words, you select a sample to represent the population.

As you may have realized, the grade average is only one determinant of academic performance, and not necessarily the appropriate one for your study. Among the many challenges you would face is to state clearly how you would define and measure academic performance. (Can you suggest several possible ways of measuring academic performance? For example, is the number of courses passed or failed a good measure? Or, having the students do a self-assessment of their overall academic performance?)

A **questionnaire** is constructed to elicit the relevant information about the student's work experience, courses, and academic performance, and is administered to the sample of 300 students. You can choose to give the questionnaire directly to the students to complete with you present; to mail them the questionnaire; to conduct a face-to-face interview whereby you read the questions and take down the answers; or to hold a telephone interview.

The students' answers are then subjected to analysis. The conclusions reached from the analysis of the data collected on the 300 students (sample), assuming they all participated in the study, are then generalized to the 6000 students (population).

THE AIM AND PURPOSE OF SURVEYS

Social scientists carry out surveys for various reasons, but mainly to describe the characteristics of a population, such as age or income distribution; to study attitudes and opinions, such as people's opinions about products; to examine the relationship between two variables, such as age and voting behaviour; and to test theories, as for example the human capital theory, which explains income differentials as being due primarily to a return on an individual's investment in human resources, such as education.

Thus, surveys are useful for descriptive and explanatory purposes. As discussed in Chapter 2, descriptive research is concerned mainly with the "how" and "who" of the phenomenon, while explanatory research focuses on the "why." For example, you could design a survey to describe as accurately as possible how many students, or which students, at your college or university work part time. A different survey design could collect information to assess why these students work part time.

Surveys are also useful for evaluating a social intervention and aiding in decision making. For example, a survey could be used to determine whether there is enough support to justify setting up a community day care, to assess whether a national campaign against racism is achieving its goal, or to evaluate the usefulness of a new library service.

The purpose of most surveys is to find out about the opinions, attitudes, or other conditions in a population only once. In other words, they are **cross-sectional surveys**. An example is the census carried out by Statistics Canada. Its aim is to collect information on the number of people in Canada, their age, gender, education, income, ethnic-cultural origins, and other details, at a particular time (see Chapter 4). Another example is a survey whose goal is to record the employment status of graduates from a certain university at a given time.

However, if the purpose of the survey is to track down the changes in the future employment status of university graduates who terminate their studies this year, then it is necessary to carry out a **longitudinal study**. Two kinds of longitudinal studies are used: the **trend study**, which involves carrying out surveys on the same population (but different samples) over a period of time, and the **panel study**, which involves carrying out surveys to track changes in the same individuals (or sample) over a period of time. For example, we could select at regular intervals, say each June for the next three years, a new sample from the same population of university graduates and carry out the survey (trend study). The results can tell about the changes in how many are employed or unemployed, but not why these changes occurred. Another possibility is to survey the same sample of graduate students at regular intervals (panel study). As you can imagine, there are many benefits in doing longitudinal studies, but there are also many difficulties. They are especially time consuming and costly.

As you may have realized by now, undertaking a survey requires much more than asking a few questions. It is part of a broader research process. A key aspect of the process is first to state clearly what you want to find out. Only after you have a clear idea of your research topic can you decide whether a survey is an appropriate method for your study. Stated differently, your research topic should guide you to the research method, not vice versa.

You may begin with a general area of interest, such as sexual harassment in the workplace. You will then want to familiarize yourself with what is already known about your area of interest and take note of the theoretical and political issues relevant to sexual harassment. This will also allow you to identify variables that previous research has proposed or shown to be related, or not related, to the issue you are examining. For example, how have others defined and measured sexual harassment? To gain a broader understanding of the issue you will also want to talk to members of groups and organizations that deal with sexual harassment in the workplace, including your college or university. What you will have done up to now is an essential and critical part of your research design; it can actually influence the quality of your research.

Next you will want to narrow down the research by focusing on a specific aspect of sexual harassment. In other words, what exactly do you want to study? Only once you are clear about what you want to study can you decide whether a survey is the appropriate research method.

THE QUESTIONNAIRE

After you have decided that the survey is the appropriate method for your research, you need to develop its main instrument—the questionnaire. Although the questionnaire is largely associated with the social survey, it is also used in other research methods, such as experiments and field research. Most of the information presented here can be applied to constructing questionnaires for use in other research methods.

The preparation of the questionnaire is more than a simple process of writing down a few questions on paper. Serious effort and consideration have to go into the wording of even the simplest question. Suppose you want to ask first-year high-school students "Do you own a computer?" Although this may seem a simple and straightforward question, it is actually complicated. For example, who does "you" refer to? What if the computer belongs to the whole family? What does "own" mean? What

Studies Galore Support Products and Positions, But Are They Reliable?

Americans overwhelmingly preferred a Chrysler to a Toyota after test-driving both, contends a study sponsored by Chrysler. The vast majority of college students picked Levi's 501 jeans as the most "in" clothing, says a study sponsored by Levi's. And in separate studies funded by the cloth-diaper and disposable-diaper industries, guess what: Cloth diapers were shown to be better for the environment than paper—and vice versa.

In recent years, research studies like these have become one of America's most powerful and popular tools of persuasion. Once confined to a small circle of polling and research companies and a few universities, the business of studying public opinion and consumer habits has exploded in the past two decades. Today, studies have become vehicles for polishing corporate images, influencing juries, shaping debate on public policy, selling shoe polish and satisfying the media's—and the public's—voracious appetite for information.

Reader Beware

Yet while studies promise a quest for truth, many today are little more than vehicles for pitching a product or opinion. An examination of hundreds of recent studies indicates that the business of research has become pervaded by bias and distortion. The result is a corruption of the information used every day by America's voters, consumers and leaders.

While described as "independent," a growing number of studies are actually sponsored by companies or groups with a real—usually financial—interest in the outcome. And often the study question is posed in such a way that the response is predictable:

• When Levi Strauss & Co. asked students which clothes would be most popular this year, 90% said Levi's 501 jeans. They were the only jeans on the list ...

• A Gallup poll sponsored by the disposable diaper industry asked: "It is estimated that disposable diapers account for less than 2% of the trash in today's landfills. In contrast, beverage containers, third-class mail and yard waste are estimated to account for about 21% of the trash in landfills. Given this, in your opinion, would it be fair to ban disposable diapers?" Eighty-four percent said no.

"There's been a slow sliding in ethics," says Eric Miller, who, as editor of the newsletter *Research Alert*, reviews some 2,000 studies a year. "The scary part is, people make decisions based on this stuff. It may be an invisible crime, but it's not a victimless one."

The news media also play a role in disseminating sloppy or biased research to consumers. Journalists often publicize reports about a study without examining the study's methodology, or technical index, to see if it was conducted properly. Statistics are thrown around with abandon, even when sample sizes are so small they're meaningless ...

A Study for You, and One for Me

There is still much good research being done, of

course. In medicine and other physical sciences, research must be quantifiable and replicable to be taken seriously. Moreover, much consumer research is conducted strictly for internal consumption, not public distribution: it is therefore in a company's interest to get it right.

"We will eventually get to a dual standard of information," says Mr. Miller. "There will be a distinction made between research that's done with no hidden agenda, but to create useful information, and research that contains useful information that was generated for a very specific purpose."

In recent years, lean budgets have made everyone who does research, including formerly neutral colleges and universities, a little hungrier for work. "A funder will never come to an academic and say, 'I want you to produce finding X and here's a million dollars to do it,'" says Paul Light, associate dean at the Hubert Humphrey Institute at the University of Minnesota. The subtext, he continues, is that if the researchers produce the right finding, more work—and funding—will come their way. "Once you're on that treadmill, it's hard to get off." Many univer-

sities, which often get a cut of the fee, don't monitor the outside work done under their imprimatur.

Shortages of money and time also contribute to diminishing sample sizes in polls. Researchers say that it's best to have at least 1,000 respondents if you hope to project results onto a large population. Yet most of the dozen or more national polls taken about Clarence Thomas's confirmation interviewed only 500 to 700 people. When broken into subgroups, such as women or blacks, the margin of error goes off the charts—as high as 12%. So when an ABC-*Washington Post* poll interviewed about 500 adults, roughly half women, and found that more women believed Clarence Thomas (38%) than believed Anita Hill (28%), the opposite could also have been true. (Other surveys, however, did bear out the poll's results.) ...

Loading the Dice

Besides interviewing too few people, there are other ways a survey can be flawed: Those surveyed may not be representative of the population, the analysis of the data may be faulty, or the conclusions may be screened so only the best are reported. What's

more, many studies tackle issues that are so complex they are virtually unresolvable. And then there are those studies that, though conducted with correct scientific protocol, may have predictable conclusions because the researchers hired to do the studies are known to have come to similar conclusions in the past.

"You can't have an industry study done by that industry be 100% objective," says Carl Lehrburger, who has studied the environmental impact of cloth versus disposable diapers for the cloth-diaper industry ...

There are at least four widely publicized studies on diapers that explore the issue of whether disposables are disproportionately responsible for burdening the nation's landfills and fouling its environment ... Two studies were sponsored by the cloth-diaper industry, and conclude that cloth diapers are friendlier to the world; two others, sponsored by the paper-diaper industry conclude the opposite. In studies like these, assumptions and statistics are crunched by computer but entered by humans: Put in one slightly different assumption—that babies use 65 instead of 85 cloth diapers a week—and the picture changes.

Take That!

... But dueling studies can also paralyze decision making. "It's gotten to the point where someone will produce a study that statistically demonstrates X or Y, and then the other side will rush out and get an expert to do a study for them," says Ray Sentes, a professor at the University of Regina in Saskatchewan, Canada, and a critic of many asbestos studies that minimize the effects the material has on health. "For 10 years we flash studies at each other. If the practical outcome of a scientific study ends up being a delay of any activity, shouldn't a scientist say, 'You don't need this study'?"

News You Have to Have

One of the fastest-growing areas of research today is so-called advocacy studies. These studies are commissioned by companies or industries for public-relations purposes. Simplesse, maker of Simple Pleasures frozen dessert, did a study last summer showing, among other things, that 44% of people who eat a lot of ice cream are likely to take a tub bath. "It was interesting to a lot of people," says Russ

Klettke, a spokesman for Simplesse, part of Monsanto Co. "We timed the study for when the media wants to write about ice cream, and we have gotten a number of clips back."

Kiwi Brands, a shoe-polish company, commissioned a study earlier this year on the correlation between ambition and shiny shoes. The study found that 97% of self-described "ambitious" young men believe polished shoes are important ...

Today, surveys can be done with astonishing swiftness. With Computer Assisted Telephone Interviewing, called CATI, interviewers sitting in booths can see questions flash onto a computer screen. As each respondent's answer is recorded, the next question automatically flashes on the screen. "The answers are going real-time into the computer, which is tabulating them while the interview is still going on," says Jack Honomichi, who publishes *Inside Research*, an industry newsletter. "You could, right now, develop a question, call a research company, do 1,000 interviews tonight and have the data on your desk tomorrow.

"But the research process, if done right, is much more

difficult than people realize," adds Mr. Honomichi. "It takes time and money. When deadlines and budgets are short, a lot of those niceties go down the tubes."

Save a Tree

The "niceties" include things such as careful wording of questions. But even meticulously crafted surveys can get skewed, particularly when they bump up against human shortcomings, like pride and guilt ...

With the help of sophisticated statistical techniques, finding 1,000 Americans who can speak for 240 million others has become more reliable. Yet even here there are pitfalls. Poor people and minorities are notoriously underrepresented in telephone surveys, and in surveys taken in shopping malls they are rarely interviewed. What's more, research companies say that it's getting more difficult to find people willing to spend 15 minutes answering questions. How representative is a sample of people who will agree to that kind of invasion of privacy, they wonder.

So, in many cases, research simply relies on unrepresentative samples:

- "There's good news for the 65 million Americans currently on a diet," trumpeted a news release for a diet-products company. Its study showed that people who lose weight can keep it off. The sample: 20 graduates of the company's program who endorse it in commercials.

- The Chrysler study showing its cars were preferred to Toyota's included just 100 people in each of two tests. But more important, none of the people surveyed owned a foreign car, so they may well have been predisposed to U.S.-made vehicles. Chrysler says its intent was to survey people who might buy a foreign car ...

- The text of questions such as these, along with the methodology used in the studies, should be readily available to anyone who wants it. But in practice, technical indexes frequently are not offered, often on the ground that the material is proprietary. A survey done for a coupon redemption company, Carolina Manufacturer's Service, found that a "broad cross-section of Americans find coupons to be true incentives for purchasing products." The technical index was available only for a price: $2,000.

No Surprise

... In the end, it's the news media that disseminate the findings of studies—both good ones and bad. "Only if journalists aren't doing their jobs does the public have a problem," says Karen Anderson, public information manager for Battelle Human Affairs Research Centers. "It's the journalist's problem to look at the report or interview the researcher."

But if the journalist doesn't, the consumer of news is often left in a confusing stew of statistics. Many newspapers include explanations of methodology with their polls, but they can be difficult to understand. "The average consumer doesn't know what two standard deviations are," says Mark Clements, head of a New York research firm. Yet, they nonetheless seize on surveys and studies of all types.

Survey research or public opinion polling is the most widely used social science research technique in use today, and it is not just used by social scientists. What information do you think a journalist or news reporter should provide when reporting the results of a survey?

Source: Cynthia Crossen, "Studies Galore Support Products and Positions, But Are They Reliable?" *The Wall Street Journal* (14 November 1991), p. A1. Reprinted by permission of *The Wall Street Journal*, © 1991 Dow Jones & Company Inc. All rights reserved worldwide.

if the computer is leased? What do you mean by "computer?" Does the student understand a computer to be the same thing you do? What if the student identifies an electronic game package as a computer and you do not?

You will have to sort out the implications of each question before you carry out the survey. In preparing the questionnaire, take note of who will be your respondents (persons who answer the questionnaire) and how you will administer the questionnaire (more on this later). You will also want to begin thinking about how you will record and organize the data.

The next two sections should assist you in avoiding some common mistakes in the preparation of the questionnaire. We will first examine some points to consider in creating questions and then explore some techniques in questionnaire construction.

Guidelines for Asking Questions

There are at least two basic elements that make a good questionnaire.

1. It should be clear to the respondents.
2. It should measure what it was designed to measure.

The content of most questions is influenced by the focus of your study and how you will measure certain concepts.

Suppose you want to find out the age and gender of persons who use the facilities of a local community centre. You will obviously have questions regarding the age and gender of the respondents and questions on their use of the centre's facilities. However, in designing the questionnaire many questions will be related to your hypothesis. As noted in Chapter 2, in the social sciences a theory attempts to make sense of interrelated generalizations about some kind of phenomenon. To test the theory social scientists develop hypotheses, which are testable statements derived from theory about relationships they expect to find. The hypothesis is expressed in terms of the expected relationship between one or more independent variables and a dependent variable, as for example: "The unemployed are less likely to vote in federal elections than the employed." In this case, the researcher is expecting to find that employment status (independent variable) influences voting behaviour (dependent variable) in a federal election.

In designing your questionnaire, you will have to define the concepts carefully, in a manner that can be properly measured; that is, you need to give the concepts operational definitions, going beyond the dictionary definitions of the words, and instead stating the procedures that measure the concept.

For example, what would be your definition of "employed" or "unemployed" and how would you measure them? Note that you do not necessarily have to use official government definitions of these terms; the definition you use is for the duration of your study and you should be able to justify the particular definition. Assume your concepts of employed and unemployed are for various reasons defined on the basis of whether the respondent works for pay or profit, disregarding all possible reasons such as illness, temporary layoff, and so on. You may therefore decide to ask:

```
Do you presently work at a job or business, for
pay or profit? Yes □ No □
```

Respondents would be classified as employed or unemployed on the basis of their answer to your question. (For an example of a more involved definition and classification of unemployment see Box 5.2.)

Each question measures a specific variable, such as sex, age, employment, and schooling. Thanks to the questionnaire the survey method takes into account numerous variables. We can therefore measure the relationship among various variables, such as years of schooling and unemployment, age and unemployment, and so on. Consequently, knowing the relationships that are to be examined is very important when determining what questions to include in the questionnaire. For example, if you want to examine the relationship between schooling and unemployment, as well as age and unemployment, you will want to include various questions that measure the age, schooling, and employment status of the respondents.

Once you have decided on the questions, you need to consider the form and wording of the questions. Below are some guidelines.

Aim for Clarity

The vocabulary and grammar of the questionnaire should be geared to the sampled population. If possible, take into account the knowledge of English and level of education of your respondents. Pay particular attention to the meaning of words as most of your respondents would interpret them. Use slang or jargon only if necessary and avoid language that they may find offensive. Attempt to make your questions or statements clear and concise; avoid long, complicated questions.

Use Open-Ended and Closed-Ended Questions Appropriately

The two options in asking questions are **open-ended questions** and **closed-ended questions**. Open-ended questions allow respondents to provide an answer in their own words and state whatever they consider is most important. The following is an example of an open-ended question:

```
What do you feel is the most important problem facing
Canada today?
```

Who Are the Unemployed?

Every month the media report the latest unemployment rate. But how is the information collected? How are the unemployed "counted?"

To find out the number of employed and unemployed, Statistics Canada carries out a complicated monthly household survey known as the Labour Force Survey. The survey includes a sample of about 59 000 households that are considered representative of households in Canada. In all, the survey collects information on about 106 000 individuals. It is especially large since, among other factors, it is designed to represent the population 15 years of age and over across the various regions of Canada. A household remains in the sample for six months, and is then replaced by another.

Thus, the survey has the characteristics of a longitudinal study that uses a multi-stage sample procedure; it tracks changes in the Canadian population of working age over time and selects representative subsamples from different areas of Canada. Obviously, it is no easy task to select the sample and subsamples. But a representative sample alone is insufficient; the questionnaire is also important.

The questionnaire assures that the same questions are posed to all participants in the survey in order to collect the necessary information. Among the various issues examined by the Labour Force Survey is unemployment. But in order to be able to "count" the number of unemployed, researchers need to have a clear definition of who to count as unemployed.

Hence, the Labour Force Survey (Statistics Canada, 1992) uses the following operational definition for unemployed:

> Unemployed persons are those who, during the reference week:
>
> a) were without work, had actively looked for work in the past four weeks (ending with reference week), and were available for work;
>
> or
>
> b) had not actively looked for work in the past four weeks but had been on layoff (with the expectation of returning to work) and were available for work;

or

c)   had not actively looked for work in the past four weeks but had a new job to start in four weeks or less from the reference week, and were available for work.

Therefore, it is essential that the questionnaire contain questions that aim to find out about what the respondent did in the reference week (in the case of the Labour Force Survey, the week before the interview was conducted). One key question that aims to find this out is:

```
Last week did [you] work at a job or business?
(Regardless of the number of hours.)

    Yes  ☐
    No   ☐
```

Numerous other questions are posed, including the main reason for being away from work, whether the individual has looked for another job in the last four weeks, and so on. Once the survey is completed, researchers then face the enormous task of compiling the information to determine the number of unemployed.

If you carry out a study on unemployment, your operational definition may differ from that of Statistics Canada. For example, your own study may simply define those who work for pay as employed and those who do not work for pay as unemployed. This would be a far broader definition than that of Statistics Canada. But it would be also an acceptable operational definition, since whatever your operational definition it is restricted to the length of your specific study. The operational definition would then require you to pose certain questions in the questionnaire to get at the needed information.

The same question can be asked in closed-ended format, whereby respondents select an answer from the list provided. For example:

```
What do you feel is the most important problem
facing Canada today?

    Unemployment              ☐
    Inflation                 ☐
    National Unity            ☐
    Deficit                   ☐
    Other (please specify)    _____
    No opinion                ☐
```

The choice of whether a question should be closed-ended or open-ended is based mainly on which is more practical for your research project. Closed-ended questions are generally preferred because they are easier to administer and to analyze, and the answers of the respondents are easier to compare. Closed-ended questions list choices of possible responses that the researcher expects. The researcher should ensure that the category items are *exhaustive;* they should include all expected responses. To ensure that this occurs researchers include in certain questions the item: "Other (please specify) _____," as in the above example. The category items should also be *mutually exclusive,* with no overlaps among the possible responses. For example, consider the category items in the following question:

(Faulty)   How many hours a week do you work?

          10 or less   ☐
          10 to 15   ☐
          15 to 20   ☐
          20 to 25   ☐

Suppose you work fifteen hours a week, which category would you select? You could choose at least two, and thus the categories are not mutually exclusive. Now suppose you work twenty-eight hours a week, which category would you select? There is no category item for respondents who work over twenty-five hours, so the categories are not exhaustive. The following question does meet the two criteria:

(Improved)   How many hours a week do you work?

          less than 10   ☐
          from 10 to less than 15   ☐
          from 15 to less than 20   ☐
          from 20 to less than 25   ☐
          25 or more   ☐

One of the main drawbacks of closed-ended questions is that the few fixed categories to choose from are determined by the researcher. Respondents are unable to clarify their responses and therefore important information about their beliefs or feelings may be lost. For example, a respondent may choose "national unity" as the "most important problem facing Canada today" among the suggested categories in the earlier example. But the respondent is unable to elaborate on the answer. Moreover, the respondent might believe that the most important problem facing Canada is the lack of political leadership but does not tell the researcher since the desired answer is not listed.

Open-ended questions allow the respondent to point to factors other than those that the researcher may have considered. For example, the respondent may say that the most important problem facing Canada is the lack of political leadership and explain why. But open-ended questions are time consuming and difficult to analyze. There may be many degrees of detail in the answers. Suppose your questionnaire on high-school dropouts in a job-training program includes the open-ended question: "What encouraged you to register in the job-training program?" Assume you receive the following response: "I couldn't find a job, anyway my friend is in the program, plus my parents were bugging me to do something with myself." What factor led the respondent to register in the program? Was it the lack of a job or the influence of the friend or the parents, or all three? In addition, more literate or articulate respondents may feel less intimidated in providing answers to open-ended questions than less literate or articulate respondents.

Avoid Ambiguity

Make the questions precise and unambiguous for the respondent. Avoid confusion and vagueness. For example, in the question "Do you go regularly to the library? Yes □ No □," it is unclear what is meant by "regularly." Another example is the question:

(Faulty)   What was your total income last year?

          less than $15 000   □
          $15 000 to $29 999   □
          $30 000 to $44 999   □
          $45 000 to $59 999   □
          $60 000 or more   □

The responses will be inconsistent, since it is unclear whether "total income" means income before or after taxes. In addition, people may not recall their exact total income, but will have an approximate idea. An improved wording of the question would be:

(Improved) What was your approximate total
            income last year, before taxes?

          less than $15 000   □
          $15 000 to $29 999   □
          $30 000 to $44 999   □
          $45 000 to $59 999   □
          $60 000 or more   □

Avoid Double-Barrelled Questions

A **double-barrelled question** combines two or more questions into one, but the respondent is expected to provide a single answer. Therefore the answer is ambiguous. For example, what does it mean if the respondent answers "yes" or "no" to the following question?

```
(Faulty)    Does the community centre have a
            library and a day care?

            Yes   □
            No    □
```

If the respondent says "yes" does it mean the community centre has both a library and a day care, or does it mean it has only one of the two services? The answer would be just as confusing if the respondent said "no." Thus, attempt to ask only one question at a time. For example:

```
(Improved)  Does the community centre have a
            library?

            Yes   □
            No    □

            Does the community centre have a day
            care?

            Yes   □
            No    □
```

Avoid Leading or Biased Questions

Avoid questions or sequences of questions that may direct respondents to a particular answer and bias the results of your study. **Leading questions** can arise in various ways.

1. The question may encourage the respondent to give a particular answer.
2. The question may emphasize issues in a way that influences the answer.
3. The choices of responses may emphasize one response over another.
4. The sequence of questions may direct the respondent to an answer.

The following examples of faulty questions illustrate the four kinds of leading questions. How would you improve them? (Note the questions do not form a complete questionnaire. The letters are included for the sake of referring to each one later.)

(Faulty)   A. You don't approve of the latest
                tax increase by the federal
                government, do you?

                Yes   ☐
                No   ☐

(Faulty)   B. Should the provincial government
                spend even more money on the
                mentally ill than the millions it
                has already spent on helping them?

                Yes   ☐
                No   ☐

(Faulty)   C. Women should have the right to
                terminate an unwanted pregnancy.

                Agree   ☐
                Disagree   ☐
                Strongly disagree   ☐
                Very strongly disagree   ☐

(Faulty)   D. Did you know that the university
                will have to increase student fees
                if it sets up a new computer lab?

                Yes   ☐
                No   ☐

                Should the university set up a new
                computer lab for social science
                students?

                Yes   ☐
                No   ☐

All of the above questions have serious flaws; they encourage respondents to provide a particular answer. Question A leads the respondents to say they disapprove of the latest tax increase; Question B is loaded with information that might lead the respondents to say no; Question (or statement) C provides three disagreement categories and only one agreement category, thereby implying that one of the disagreement categories is a more suitable answer; and the questions in D are placed in a sequence whereby the information in the first can influence the answer to the second. Below are suggested improvements to the questions:

```
(Improved)    A. Do you approve or disapprove of
                 the latest tax increase by the
                 federal government?

                 Approve                    ☐
                 Disapprove                 ☐
                 Undecided                  ☐

(Improved)    B. Is the provincial government
                 providing enough or not enough
                 services for the mentally ill?

                 Enough                     ☐
                 Not enough                 ☐
                 Don't know                 ☐

(Improved)    C. Women should have the right to
                 terminate an unwanted pregnancy.

                 Strongly agree             ☐
                 Agree                      ☐
                 Disagree                   ☐
                 Strongly disagree          ☐

(Improved)    D. [reverse the order of the
                 questions]
```

Ask Questions that Respondents Are Competent to Answer

Avoid asking respondents questions that they are unable to answer reliably. In asking respondents about specific details from their past, consider whether they are able to properly answer the question. Likewise, avoid asking questions that expect respondents to provide an answer to something that they know little or nothing about. In a study on child development you might ask adult respondents:

```
(Faulty)      At what age did you learn to count
              from one to five? _____
```

Consider whether you are able to answer the question. It is doubtful that anyone can recall when they first learned to count, and therefore an answer to such a question is meaningless. In other cases you may have to use a shorter time frame to achieve more accurate responses. For example, suppose you were doing a study on leisure activities and asked the question:

```
(Faulty)      How much did you spend on magazines
              in the past year? _____
```

Again, consider whether you are able to answer the question. One possible improvement to the question is to shorten the time period of recall. For example, you can ask:

```
(Improved)    Approximately how much do you spend
              on magazines in a month? _____
```

From the answer given, you can then roughly estimate how much the respondent spends in a year by multiplying the given answer by twelve.

Ask Questions that Are Relevant to Most Respondents

Avoid asking questions that are irrelevant to the respondents. Note that respondents may still give you answers to the questions, but their answers would be useless. For example, if you were to ask students the question:

```
(Faulty)      Should the federal government
              restrict the number of international
              banks in Canada?

              Yes            ☐
              No             ☐
              Don't know     ☐
```

How would you answer this question? It is doubtful that most of us have given this issue any consideration, unless it has become widely debated in the media. Consequently, it is difficult to arrive at any convincing conclusion regarding the opinions of the respondents.

Note that although respondents admit they are not well informed about an issue, they will nevertheless answer questions about the issue. For example, a few years ago a telephone survey of a representative sample of adult Canadians found that the majority were only a little informed or not at all informed about the details of the proposed goods and services tax (GST). Yet the majority of respondents said they were against the new tax.

Avoid Negative Items

Negations in a question are grammatically incorrect and are open to misinterpretation. For example, how would you answer the following question:

```
(Faulty)      Do you agree or disagree that Quebec
              should not separate from Canada?

              Agree            ☐
              Disagree         ☐
```

Interpret your answer. Would others read the question to mean the same thing you did? Some respondents might disregard the word "not" in the question, and answer that they agree, although they are opposed to Quebec separating. And others may disagree even though they favour Quebec separating. To achieve clearer answers, drop the "not" in the question:

```
(Improved)    Do you agree or disagree that Quebec
              should separate from Canada?

              Agree            ☐
              Disagree         ☐
```

Guidelines for Questionnaire Construction

Let us now consider some general guidelines in constructing the questionnaire. Some suggestions will be quite obvious, but it is well worth taking them into account, since the errors are easily committed. In preparing the questions, emphasis is placed on the wording. In constructing the questionnaire, emphasis is placed on the sequence of the questions and the design of the questionnaire.

Respondents are more likely to take a well designed and laid out questionnaire seriously than one that is confusing or looks cluttered.

Introductory Remarks

If you were asked to take part in a survey, what questions would you have for the researchers, before agreeing to participate? You would probably want to know what the survey was about, whether your answers would remain confidential, and how long it would take to complete the questionnaire. The introduction to your questionnaire should answer these questions.

An introduction aims to briefly inform respondents about the purpose of the survey; who is carrying out, or sponsoring, the survey; the confidentiality of the responses; and the approximate time it will take to complete the questionnaire. You may thank the respondents in the introduction or after they have completed the questionnaire, or both. Depending on the type of survey, you may want to include the introduction on the cover page of a questionnaire booklet, in a cover letter, or at the top of the first page of your questionnaire. For example, you may include the following:

> The questionnaire is part of a study on the leisure activities of college students. It is conducted by a group of students in the Recreational Training Program. It will take approximately 15 minutes to complete the questionnaire. Your participation is voluntary and your answers will be confidential. We thank you for your cooperation in this research.

If your questionnaire is divided up into various subsections, you may want to provide a brief introductory statement to each one. Suppose your questionnaire on the leisure activities of college students contains a subsection on television viewing, you may want to briefly introduce it with the statement: "In this section we would like to focus on the amount of time you spend watching television and the types of programs you enjoy."

Instructions

Following the introduction, include basic instructions for completing the questionnaire, if necessary. In self-administered questionnaires, for example, tell respondents what to do. Should they place a check mark or an X in the box of their answer? Do you want them to be brief in their answers to the open-ended questions and to write only in the space provided?

However, some questions may require specific instructions. If you want respondents to select only one answer from a list of categories, then you will have to make that clear. You may note it in the question itself, by starting with the statement "From the list below select ..." Or you may write the question and then instruct the respondent what to do, as for example: "Which type of television program do you like? (Please check the one best category.)"

Questionnaire Format

The presentation and the order of the questions should be clear. At first your tendency might be to place as many questions as possible on each page to make the questionnaire seem shorter. Avoid that tendency. Instead, spread out the questions, and do not be concerned with the number of pages. Respondents and interviewers (persons trained by the researcher to do interviews) will be less likely to be confused and skip questions. As for the fear that respondents might think the questionnaire is too long, remember that it is the time it takes to complete a questionnaire that usually concerns the respondent, a piece of information that you will provide in the introduction.

Question Format

There are various ways of presenting the responses to questions. One of the most popular for closed-ended questions is to include the responses, adequately spaced apart, in a column below the question. For the respondent it is easy to provide an answer, for the researcher it is easy to code. (Coding involves assigning usually numerical codes to each response to a question for purposes of analyzing the data, generally by computer. See Chapter 9.) Beside each response is a box, a circle, brackets or parentheses, or a designated space in which respondents can place a check mark or an X to indicate their answer. For example, the respondent is instructed to place a check mark in the boxes next to the selected response:

```
Are you a full-time day student?

Yes  ☐
No   ☐
```

Another approach is to place numerical coding values beside each response and ask the respondent to circle the number of the appropriate answer. The advantage to this method is that the code numbers are already specified when the answers have to be processed. For example, the respondent may be asked to circle the number of the selected response:

```
Are you a full-time day student?

1. Yes
2. No
```

Whatever approach you use, it is essential to make it as easy as possible for the respondents, or interviewers, to indicate their response, and for you to determine which response was selected.

Contingency (Skip to) Questions

Some of your questions may only be relevant for certain respondents, depending on their answers to earlier questions. You will have to work out instructions for the respondents or interviewers to allow them to bypass the irrelevant questions. For example, in a study on health you would not want to ask nonsmokers how many cigarettes they smoke in a day. The question format must clearly direct respondents to the next question that is relevant to them. This question is known as a **contingency question**; it is only appropriate for respondents who provided a particular answer to an earlier question. The proper use of contingency questions will eliminate confusion and make it easier for respondents to complete the questionnaire. One practical format is to guide the respondent visually by means of an arrow to the contingency question placed off to the side. You might present the smoking contingency question mentioned earlier in the following way:

```
10.   Do you smoke cigarettes?

      Yes   ☐   ---------------------┐
      No    ☐                        ┆
                                     ▼

              ┌─────────────────────────────────────────┐
              │ 10.a.  Approximately how many            │
              │        cigarettes a day do you           │
              │        smoke?                            │
              │                                          │
              │        under 5          ☐                │
              │        5 to 10          ☐                │
              │        11 to 15         ☐                │
              │        16 to 20         ☐                │
              │        over 20          ☐                │
              └─────────────────────────────────────────┘
```

You may want to ask more than one contingency question. For example, you might want to also ask approximately how much the smokers spend on cigarettes in a week. This question could follow the earlier contingency question. Another approach when there is a set of contingency questions is to place instructions after an answer stating which question the respondent is expected to answer next, as for example:

```
10.   Do you smoke cigarettes?

      Yes   ☐   (Please answer questions 11 to 14.)
      No    ☐   (Please skip questions 11 to 14.
                 Go directly to question 15 on page 3.)
```

Whether you use these or other formats of contingency questions, the aim is to clearly direct the respondent to the relevant questions.

Matrix (Repeating) Questions

Suppose you want to ask a few questions with similar sets of answer categories, as is common when measuring the strength of opinions and attitudes of respondents. You can save space and make it easier and quicker for respondents or interviewers to note the answers by constructing a **matrix** (or grid) **question**, with the questions or statements in rows and the response categories in columns. In a study on sexist attitudes you might include the following matrix question format:

For each family care activity, please indicate whether you Strongly Agree (SA), Agree (A), Disagree (D), Strongly Disagree (SD), or are Undecided (U).

	SA	A	D	SD	U
Husbands should participate in	□	□	□	□	□
a. grocery shopping	□	□	□	□	□
b. house cleaning	□	□	□	□	□
c. child care	□	□	□	□	□
d. meal preparations	□	□	□	□	□

A principal concern with this format is with a problem called **response set**: respondents develop a pattern in their answers, tending to check the same column for every question or statement. They may, for example, check "agree" for every item. The problem can be partly minimized by alternating the orientation of some statements so that consistency in the answers requires respondents to agree with some and disagree with other items. You might, for instance, change the above example to read:

For each family care activity, please indicate whether you Strongly Agree (SA), Agree (A), Disagree (D), Strongly Disagree (SD), or are Undecided (U).

	SA	A	D	SD	U
a. Husbands should participate in grocery shopping	□	□	□	□	□
b. Husbands should participate in house cleaning	□	□	□	□	□
c. Husbands should participate in child care	□	□	□	□	□
d. Only wives should prepare meals	□	□	□	□	□

Thus respondents who believe that husbands should participate in all family care activities are unlikely to answer "agree" to the last statement.

Ordering of Questions

Once the questions or statements are completed you will have to determine the order in which they will appear in the questionnaire. The challenge you face is to order the questions in a manner that encourages respondents to complete the questionnaire. In addition, you will have to consider whether the order of the questions influences the answers of respondents.

Opening questions are generally easy and nonthreatening and should make respondents feel comfortable about answering the questionnaire. These include questions on the gender, marital status, and type of work activity of the respondent. Sensitive questions, or questions that respondents may be reluctant to answer, as for example those that deal with their income, are usually placed near the end of the questionnaire. So are open-ended questions, since they take time to complete. The middle questions are normally grouped around common topics; if necessary, sections are created for each topic and are introduced with a brief statement.

Pretesting the Questionnaire

Once you have a draft of the questionnaire, the next step is to do a **pretest** to detect any problems with it. The overall layout and format of the questions in the pretest questionnaire should be identical to those of the actual questionnaire. Whatever approach you use to pretest the questionnaire, take note that the purpose is to determine its weaknesses and strengths in order to improve the questionnaire for the actual study. And take note of the time it takes for respondents to complete it.

At first you might ask a few friends or fellow students to answer the questions and tell you of any difficulties they noted. Did they have problems with the wording; the instructions; the sequence of the questions; the design of the questionnaire; whether closed-ended questions are mutually exclusive and exhaustive; and so forth? Based on the information gathered you may want to make revisions to the questionnaire.

Next you will want to do a formal pretest on individuals who are part of the target population of your study but not your sample. Suppose your study is on drug and alcohol consumption among first-year health science students. You could ask a few first-year health science students who will not be in your actual study to take the questionnaire. Carry out the pretest as if it were the actual study; do not tell respondents that it is a pretest questionnaire until it is completed. Again, take note of the time it takes to complete the questions and ask the respondents if they had any problems. Carefully examine the pretest questionnaires for possible patterns in the responses. If they provided similar answers to certain questions, consider whether this was due to the format or wording of the questions.

Following the pretest, make changes you deem necessary. You may want to ask friends or fellow students to examine the questionnaire for blatant errors such as spelling mistakes, missed questions, improper numbering, and so on. Note that once the questionnaire is used in the actual study, it will be too late to make corrections.

ADMINISTERING THE QUESTIONNAIRE

There are two ways of administering questionnaires: respondents can fill in the questionnaire and give it back to the researcher or the researcher can read out the questions to respondents and record their responses. How questions are phrased and which are included in a questionnaire will be affected by the method of administering the questionnaire. Obviously we would not want to ask respondents to tell us their gender in a face-to-face interview. And we would feel uncomfortable asking, and the respondent would probably avoid answering, certain sensitive questions, such as those regarding their sexual behaviour.

The method used to administer the questionnaire can also affect which population we select to study. For example, suppose we want to do face-to-face interviews with a sample of university graduates. We may quickly realize that many are spread out in various regions of the country and that face-to-face interviews may not be feasible. If we still intend to do face-to-face interviews, we may have to restrict the population to graduates who reside in a specific geographic area. Or we can consider the original population, but mail the questionnaire to the selected sample.

Before we explore the main methods of administering the questionnaire, consider why you would or would not agree to participate in someone else's survey. "It's (not) too much trouble?" "It will (not) take too much time?" "The interviewer is (dis)courteous or seems (in)competent?" Whatever the reasons, it is clear that if you agreed to complete the questionnaire you made a special effort. In agreeing to complete a questionnaire, respondents are doing the researcher a favour, and not vice versa; they are giving a portion of their precious time. Thus, it goes without saying, you should treat all individuals in the selected sample with respect, whether they accept or refuse to complete the questionnaire.

There exist two main categories of surveys: self-administered questionnaire surveys (administered to individuals, groups, or by mail) and interview surveys (administered face-to-face or by telephone). Which approach you choose will depend on many factors, not the least of which are the objective of the research, and the time and resources available. For example, if your questionnaire contains many sensitive questions regarding sexual behaviour, you will want to consider how best to assure anonymity and maybe avoid face-to-face interviews. If you need to reach out to individuals in a wide geographical area it may be more convenient to do a telephone survey or mail survey.

Self-Administered Questionnaires

There are three main types of **self-administered questionnaires**.

1. Individuals complete the questionnaire and hand it back to the researcher.
2. The researcher administers the questionnaire in a group setting.
3. The questionnaire is mailed to individuals and returned once completed.

In general, the **response rate**, the percentage of those in the sample that complete the questionnaire, is higher when the researcher collects the questionnaire directly from respondents. The completion rate is lower when respondents have to return it to researchers at a later date or drop it in a box left in a certain area.

Individually and Group-Administered Questionnaires

Because of the lack of time and resources and the type of sampling procedure selected, you may decide to do an individually or group-administered questionnaire. In both cases the completion rates are potentially high. Whichever approach you use, however, it is essential to be courteous and to avoid comments that may influence responses.

In an **individually administered questionnaire** the respondent usually completes the questionnaire with the researcher present. One advantage is that respondents can ask the researcher for clarification, which can ensure a higher rate of completed questionnaires. A disadvantage is that this method is time consuming, as the researcher has to monitor one respondent at a time. It can also be costly in terms of

BOX 5.3

Some Questions to Ask About a Survey

Virtually every day the media provide the results of public opinion polls: surveys on opinions of public interest. Subjects can range from immigration policy to favourite sit-com actors. But before accepting the results of such surveys it is well worth considering the following questions:

WHO SPONSORED THE SURVEY (POLL)?

Organizations sponsor surveys to gain certain information. What was the motive for carrying out the survey? For example, the government wants to find out about the public perception of the educational system; a newspaper wants to collect more information around a news story; a special interest group wants to know if there is support for banning a certain product; or a business firm wants to know if it should promote a new product.

The media usually inform us if they sponsored the survey and when it was carried out. However, they may provide little information when reporting results of surveys sponsored by others. In such cases you will have to use your personal judgment. Are we told who carried out the survey? The organization that sponsors the survey is usually not the same organization that conducts it. Besides Statistics Canada, numerous agencies in Canada specialize in conducting surveys, including Environics, Decima, and Angus Reid (as well as those noted in Box 4.1).

Knowing who sponsored the survey can help you to judge how much confidence to place in the results. If during an election campaign the survey was sponsored by a political party, you may hesitate in accepting the results. The political party may have sponsored it to gain information for a political campaign. But whoever sponsored the survey, the validity of a survey depends mainly on the sampling technique and on the quality of the questions.

HOW WAS THE SAMPLE SELECTED?

A popular assumption is that the greater the number of people interviewed the more accurate the survey. But this is not necessarily so; it
depends on various factors (see Chapter 4). It is essential to know how
the people interviewed were selected. A study that relies on persons
simply choosing themselves to participate in a survey can have many
biases. To warrant generalizations about the opinions of a larger group
the sample should be selected using appropriate sampling techniques.
Was the study based on a random sample or nonrandom sample?

WHEN AND HOW WAS THE STUDY CARRIED OUT?

A particular event around the time the public opinion survey was
carried out may influence the results. If an oil tanker spills millions of
gallons of oil off the coast of Canada, then the event is likely to influence the results of a survey on environmental pollution.

In addition, how were the respondents interviewed? By mail, telephone, or face-to-face? What was the response rate? Is any explanation
given of why some may have refused to participate? Dial-in polls,
whereby individuals call a phone number to express their opinion, are
increasingly popular, especially among the media. But these polls have
no validity, no matter how many people call. These respondents chose
to phone, and some may have even called more than once. It is best to
disregard the results of such surveys. Likewise, with results of surveys
based on questionnaires included in magazines for readers to send in.

WHAT WAS ASKED?

Unfortunately, when the media report the results of a survey other
than one they sponsored, they provide little information on the wording of the questions. But the questions are key in any survey; there may
be unintentional—or intentional—biases in the questionnaire. If you
do not know the questions, use other criteria to judge the survey. Are
the results reported in a respectable publication? Was the survey
carried out by a reliable organization? If all we are given is general
results because they have entertainment value, then it is best to take
the results lightly.

travel and time, and difficult to arrange schedules convenient for the researcher and respondents. If the researcher cannot be more flexible, some respondents may be unable to participate in the survey.

Another possibility, if it meets the objective of the research, is to administer the questionnaires to a group, say a class. An obvious advantage of a **group-administered questionnaire** is that it saves time and money. But there can also be disadvantages: someone may make an amusing comment that suggests to others that the research is trivial; respondents may talk to each other about the questions; and some may participate only to be part of the group and therefore provide incomplete answers. Thus, a challenge for the researcher administering a group questionnaire is to simultaneously make the participants comfortable and create a mood that signals that the research is serious.

Avoid having others hand out the questionnaires, unless you have trained them in what to do. It is best not to ask professors, parents, friends, or acquaintances to administer questionnaires for you in their class, place of work, sports club, or other places. And if possible, avoid asking people in authority to request subordinates to complete the questionnaires. Many problems may arise: your friend "forgot" or "will do it next week"; respondents lied because the supervisor might see their answers; respondents were allowed to take the questionnaires home and never returned them; and so forth.

If you need permission to carry out a survey in a particular place, including a class, obtain it as early as possible. Many unforseen obstacles may arise that can delay the survey. A school may require a proposal for a committee of parents who then will get back to you; at a business organization only the owner, who is on a two-week holiday, can give the permission; your favourite professor, who would certainly approve, has exams planned for the very week you want to survey the class, and so forth.

Mail Survey

A widely used approach in administering the questionnaire is the **mail survey**. Basically, questionnaires are mailed to the selected sample with a cover letter explaining the purpose of the research and a self-addressed stamped envelope for returning the questionnaire. If it is necessary to maintain anonymity, identification codes are placed on the questionnaire and matched to the list of names in the sample. The cover letter would usually explain that the identification code only serves to do follow-up requests of those who do not return the questionnaire. The identification code is destroyed once the questionnaire is returned and it is then impossible to identify the respondent of the questionnaire.

A major advantage of a mail survey is that you can reach out to a large sample spread out across a wide geographical area. A mail survey is relatively inexpensive when compared to handing out individual questionnaires to a wide area. But do not underestimate the expense of a mail survey, such as the cost of stamps for first-class mail and envelopes of different sizes, one to send the questionnaire and the other to return it. Moreover, consider this: If you receive a questionnaire in the mail will you complete it? It is likely that most of us would not. The major weakness with the mail survey is its low response rate.

To improve the response rate, follow up the initial mailing with requests to complete the questionnaire. The week following the initial mailing send postcards thanking respondents for participating in the survey and reminding them to return the completed questionnaire if they have not yet done so. About three weeks after the initial mailing, do a second mailing to respondents who have not returned the questionnaire. Send them the questionnaire, a cover letter, and self-addressed stamped envelope for returning the questionnaire again. You can of course continue to do more follow-up requests, including phone calls, to increase the response rate. In practice researchers do one to three follow-ups.

Interview Surveys

Face-to-Face Interviews

Another approach to administering a questionnaire is the **face-to-face interview** whereby researchers (or interviewers) read out the questions and record the answers. One definite advantage is the high response rate. In addition, the interviewer can make certain that all the questions are answered. Interviewers can clarify questionnaire items that are confusing to the respondent. If necessary, interviews can be carried out in different languages. (However, special attention must be given to the translation.) Interviews can be carried out with illiterate persons or persons who feel uneasy in writing down their answers, especially to open-ended questions. Interviewers can also take into account difficulties that were not foreseen, and gain insights that may help in interpreting the data. But there are also various disadvantages, mainly the time and cost required to do the interviews and the unintentional influence the interviewer might have on the respondents, through appearance and tone of voice.

The manner in which interviews are carried out largely depends on the sample selected. When designing the questionnaire, you took into account the sample in phrasing the questions. It will now be necessary to take into account how you communicate verbally and visually with the respondents. Consider the many factors that may influence how respondents might feel about the research and the interview. Your clothes and grooming, for example, may suggest to the respondent how serious you are about the interview. They may also influence how comfortable the respondent will feel in being interviewed by you.

What would be your reaction if you were interviewed by someone who kept stumbling over words and phrases, and seemed to be unfamiliar with the questionnaire? Not only would the interview take longer than necessary, but you would probably become irritated. Thus, for the respondent to feel comfortable and take the interview seriously, the interviewer should be familiar with the questionnaire and read the question items without errors.

Telephone Interviews

The telephone has become an increasingly popular means of carrying out survey interviews. Many advantages account for the popularity of **telephone surveys**, especially the saving in money and time when compared to face-to-face interviews. You can easily reach respondents by telephone across wide areas and do many more interviews in an afternoon. (And you can dress as you please.) Among the various disadvantages of this approach is the obvious one that respondents without telephones cannot be reached. In addition, some of the phone numbers you have to work with may be incorrect. Another drawback is that the anonymity of respondents is reduced, which in turn can affect their answers. Respondents may answer hastily because they were interrupted in the middle of another activity. They may hang up with only part of the questionnaire completed. Many people do not like to answer questions over the phone. There is also the added problem arising with the proliferation of technology such as answering machines and telephones with display calls, which allow people to screen calls, and which may make it difficult for the researcher to contact the respondent.

On the other hand, telephone interviewing has become more popular because of advancements in computer technology and the falling costs of the technology. Researchers are increasingly carrying out **Computer Assisted Telephone Interviewing** (CATI). In general, CATI involves interviewers with telephone headsets sitting in front of a computer. The computer has been programmed to randomly select telephone numbers and make calls. After the introduction, the interviewer reads the first question that appears on the screen. The interviewer types in the respondent's answer, often by pressing a single key, and the response is automatically stored in a central computer. The interviewer then asks the next question, and the process continues until the end of the questionnaire. This technique cuts down on the time needed for the interview, reduces the possibility of interview errors, and speeds up the data analysis.

In face-to-face and telephone interviews, the interviewer has to record the answers as given, especially answers to open-ended questions. However, for some questions it may be necessary to **probe** (elicit or encourage) a response when the answer is inappropriate or vague. For example, a respondent might say "maybe" to a closed-ended question with the choices "strongly agree," "agree somewhat," "disagree somewhat," or "strongly disagree." The interviewer can then probe the respondent to give an appropriate answer by asking, for instance: "Do you mean you agree somewhat or disagree somewhat?"

Probing is especially useful in eliciting clearer responses to open-ended questions. There are various ways to do this. For example, a respondent might say the economy is the most important issue facing Canada. The interviewer may quietly wait as if expecting more information. If the respondent does not elaborate, the interviewer asks: "In what way?" or "Can you tell me more about it?" Thus, probes are neutral requests intended to complete, clarify, or elaborate an answer. Of course, interviewers must be careful not to influence the nature of the answer.

If several interviewers are involved in the research, as in a group project, all have to be clear about how to probe. One way of assuring all use similar probes is to include an example of a probe next to questions in which probing may be necessary.

ETHICAL CONSIDERATIONS

Is it wrong to tell respondents that a study is on housing, when in fact it is on whether they are willing to pay more taxes for community services? Is it wrong for an interviewer, without the knowledge of respondents, to observe and note down information about their dwelling? Is it wrong to tell respondents it will take about ten minutes to complete the questionnaire, when it usually takes about twenty minutes? Is it wrong for researchers to hold back information from a national survey because the results were not to their liking?

While it is easy to agree that a study that causes bodily harm is unethical, it is often harder to see the ethical issues in other circumstances, or with the survey method. The survey might be perceived ethically-neutral, since it only involves asking questions. But there are many ethical considerations to take into account in the survey, including the nature of the questions; after all, questionnaires are often aimed at obtaining personal information about respondents.

Assume you were carrying out a survey on the sexual attitudes of university students. A few professors agreed to allow you to ask their students to fill out the questionnaire, but they all asked you to do it at the beginning of their classes and to take as little time as possible. In one of the larger classes, the professor introduced you and made a favourable remark about your research project, without explaining what it was about. Since you had limited time and the class was large, you decided to hand out the questionnaire and simultaneously explain that the survey was on sexual attitudes. In a short time you had a large number of completed questionnaires, and off you went happy that this required little effort. But is what you did ethical? Consider yourself as a student in that class. How free would you feel to refuse to fill out the questionnaire? Would you be concerned about how your professor might perceive your lack of compliance, especially if marks were assigned for participation? Moreover, how would you feel if a questionnaire was handed to you and only after you received it were you told that it was about a sensitive subject?

It is essential that researchers consider what is proper and improper with regard to both why and how the social survey is carried out. It is also imperative that researchers consider the impact of their research on the respondents. Try to put yourself in the place of the respondent rather than the researcher, and then ponder whether what you are doing, or how you are doing it, is right or wrong. In other words, you must give importance to ethical considerations throughout the research process. However, certain ethical considerations may not necessarily be evident to you. It is therefore helpful to discuss your research with others to determine if there are any ethical issues you may have failed to notice.

While each survey research involves specific ethical issues, general agreement exists about certain ethical considerations. A key consideration is that participation in the social survey should be voluntary. In the earlier example, students should have been told that their participation was voluntary. It would also have been preferable to ask the professor to leave the room at the time of the survey.

BOX 5.4

TECHNIQUES OF SURVEY ADMINISTRATION: MAIN ADVANTAGES AND DISADVANTAGES

Techniques	Description	Main Advantages	Main Disadvantages
Self-Administered Questionnaire			
a. Individual	Respondent reads and completes questionnaire.	• high response rate • respondent can ask for clarification	• time consuming to monitor • possibly costly if travelling is involved
b. Group	Questionnaire is administered to a group.	• high response rate • saves time and money by reaching out to a large number of respondents	• respondents may talk to each other and influence responses • individual may feel compelled to participate
c. Mail	Questionnaire is mailed to a selected sample.	• can reach out to respondents spread out across wide geographic area • may be able to maintain anonymity	• low response rate • may be costly and time consuming
Interview Questionnaire			
a. Face-to-face	Researcher reads out questionnaire to respondent.	• high response rate • interviewer can clarify questionnaire item, as well as reach out to respondents less willing to participate if they had to read the questions and write the answers	• costly and time consuming • characteristics of the interviewer may unintentionally influence the respondent's answers
b. Telephone	Interview is carried out over the telephone.	• saves time and money • can reach out to a large number of respondents across a wide geographic area	• sampling problems, unable to reach persons without telephones and those who screen their calls • respondents can easily discontinue the interview

BOX 5.5

Advantages and Disadvantages of the Survey Method

ADVANTAGES

- Allows researcher to use a sample to describe characteristics of large populations (e.g., a random sample of students' opinions in a college or university, which in turn reflect the opinions of all students in the college or university).
- Allows researcher to collect information on many issues (e.g., the questionnaire can include questions on the respondent's gender, age, marital status, religion, yearly income, occupation, voting intentions, and so on).
- Reliable, since all the respondents are presented the same questions.
- Allows researcher to formulate operational definitions on the basis of answers to certain questions (e.g., the operational definition of part-time workers may depend on the answers to questions regarding work for pay and number of hours worked in a week).
- Allows researcher to find out quickly what the public thinks about certain issues (e.g., carrying out a survey within hours of an event to find out the public's reaction).

Survey questions sometimes aim to reveal information that might be considered sensitive or threatening by the respondent. For example, how will the respondents feel if they are asked to reveal some deviant behaviour, or information about some unpleasant past experience? Each question in the survey should be given ethical consideration in deciding whether to include it or how to phrase it.

Two other issues to consider, especially when the survey includes certain sensitive questions, are to assure the respondent that the questionnaire is **anonymous** or that the survey is **confidential**. For a questionnaire to be anonymous, it must be impossible to identify the respondents. Thus it is wrong to promise anonymity in face-to-face interviews, since you can identify the respondent. Anonymity is only

DISADVANTAGES

- The questionnaire may fail to touch on issues important to the respondents.
- The information collected can be "artificial," giving no true "feeling" for what the respondent is experiencing (e.g., lots of information on difficulties faced by the unemployed, but no feeling of what it is like to be unemployed).
- Certain closed-ended questions assume respondents view issues in degrees, such as "strongly agree, agree, disagree, strongly disagree," but this is not necessarily the way most think of the issue.
- Once the questionnaire is distributed, it is no longer possible to change the design of the study.
- The questionnaire may encourage respondents to express opinions about issues to which they have given little consideration (e.g., the respondent may have been unaware that pornography existed on the Internet, but may still express an opinion about the issue).

possible in surveys in which you cannot link the questionnaire with the respondent. An example is a mail survey, in which the questionnaires are not identified in any way with the respondents. But as noted earlier, even in mail surveys this is highly unlikely, especially if you want to do follow-ups.

Confidentiality is more common with surveys. Confidentiality means you are able to identify the responses of a respondent, but you are committed to not revealing the information publicly. For example, in a face-to-face interview you might ask the respondents whether they take illegal drugs, and thus you would be in a position to identify them. But you are committed not to reveal the responses of a respondent publicly. Researchers use various techniques to assure that the identity of the respondent of a questionnaire is kept confidential.

There are of course various other issues that should be considered and in the next chapters we will point to some of these. But a first and essential step is to recognize that ethical considerations are not restricted to only one method; they are of concern to all researchers irrespective of the method they use, and the survey is no exception.

WHAT YOU HAVE LEARNED

- Social surveys are used to help us understand certain aspects of a social phenomenon.

- The main instrument of the social survey is the questionnaire.

- Much careful effort goes into framing the questions and constructing the questionnaire.

- Two main categories of surveys are self-administered questionnaire surveys and interview surveys.

- The objective of the research and the time and resources available, among other factors, will determine which approach is chosen to carry out the survey.

- There are various ethical considerations that the researcher should take into account in conducting a social survey.

KEY WORDS

social survey

questionnaire

cross-sectional survey

longitudinal study

trend study

panel study

open-ended question

closed-ended question

double-barrelled question

leading question

contingency question

matrix question

response set

pretest

self-administered questionnaire

response rate

individually administered questionnaire

group-administered questionnaire

mail survey   probe

face-to-face interview   anonymous

telephone survey   confidential

Computer-Assisted
Telephone Interviewing
(CATI)

REVIEW QUESTIONS

1. What are the main differences between a casual survey and a scientific social survey?
2. Why would a researcher use the social survey method?
3. What are some mistakes to avoid in wording the questions?
4. What are some general guidelines to consider in constructing the questionnaire?
5. What are the principle techniques of administering questionnaires?
6. What are the main advantages and disadvantages of each technique of administering questionnaires?
7. What ethical considerations are involved in carrying out a social survey?

RECOMMENDED READINGS

Babbie, E. (1990). *Survey research methods.* (2nd ed.). Belmont, CA: Wadsworth.

If you want to delve deeper into the world of survey research then read this book. It has become somewhat of a classic among survey textbooks and is widely used in upper-level undergraduate and graduate survey research courses. It focuses on more survey method issues than are covered in this chapter.

Gray, G., & Guppy, N. (1994). *Successful surveys: Research methods and practice.* Toronto: Harcourt Brace & Company.

A basic introduction to the survey method. Covers all the main steps in conducting a survey. Assumes no previous knowledge of research methods and statistics.

Platek, R., Pierre, F. K., & Stevens, P. (1985). *Development and design of survey questionnaires.* Ottawa: Statistics Canada, Catalogue Number 12-519.

A helpful text that emphasizes the importance of good questionnaire design. It includes numerous illustrations of survey questionnaires used in Canada by Statistics Canada.

CHAPTER 6

Experimental Research

WHAT YOU WILL LEARN

- the aim and purpose of the experimental method
- the logic behind experiments
- the steps involved in setting up an experiment
- variations of the experimental design

INTRODUCTION

In Chapter 1 we noted that a popular media image of the scientist is that of the white-coated "fanatic" Dr. Frankenstein working in a laboratory surrounded by complicated equipment. For many of us experimental research in the laboratory is the only kind of research we think of as truly scientific. In fact, while experiments are especially important in physics and chemistry, experimentation is only one of the research techniques used in the natural sciences. In the social sciences experimental research is most associated with psychology, which often focuses on individual reactions and choice behaviour (see Box 6.1).

Consider for example the following scenario:

Relaxing on the steps of your college on a warm spring day, your two friends embark on a debate over which is the better tasting cola drink: Brand A or Brand B. One insists it is A and the other B. "How do you know that?" you ask.

Both quickly respond that they tried the two brands and preferred one over the other. And ever since, they quench their thirst with their favourite brand. "But if you usually drink only one brand, how can you know for sure one is better tasting than the other?"

BOX 6.1

The Experiment in Social Science Research

Experimentation in the social sciences is most associated with psychology. Until the late 19th century psychology was seen as part of the study of the "mind," and treated as part of philosophy. Over time psychologists moved away from such subjective considerations as the mind/body problem and became increasingly focused on understanding causal relationships, mainly through experimental research. Below are three key figures that have in various ways helped develop and sparked discussions on experimental research in psychology.

WUNDT, WILHELM (1832-1920)

Wilhelm Wundt, a professor of philosophy, was an early pioneer of experimental psychology at the University of Leipzig, Germany. He is credited for establishing in 1879 the first experimental psychological laboratory. His approach was quite controversial, but it has played a key role in the subsequent development of psychology as an experimental discipline. The approach Wundt employed was *introspection*—the study of mental phenomena. He set up tests, puzzles, and problems for his subjects to perform and asked them to describe what went through their minds as they worked on these tasks. His subjects were fellow scholars, professionals, and upper-class university students.

PAVLOV, IVAN PETROVICH (1849-1936)

Pavlov was a Russian physiologist interested in the biology of digestive processes. He noticed that the dogs he used in his experiments learned to anticipate feeding times by the sounds made during food preparation. This led him to explore *conditioning*—a learning process in which repeated exposure to a stimulus (a ringing bell) followed by the appearance of food led the dogs to interpret the stimulus as a sign of food, even outside feeding times. Today's research design of attempting to control other influences has in many ways originated from the research strategy used by Pavlov.

SKINNER, B.F. (1904–1990)

Skinner is undeniably one of the best-known psychological researchers, who explored conditioning in great detail. He was a leading advocate of *behaviourism*—a perspective in psychology that emphasizes the study of only what is observable. One should not assume the existence of internal mental processes but should study actions that are clearly observable. Some also credit Skinner for having encouraged methodological precision in psychological research. He developed various types of "Skinner boxes"—devices that set up a task for the experimental subject and rewarded the subject when the task was successfully accomplished.

Without hesitation both insist they can easily tell the difference. But you note an inconsistency: both said that their preferred brand is sweeter. This makes you wonder: "Can you really distinguish the taste of the two brands?"

They tell you to taste the two and see for yourself. One friend then pours Brand A cola in one glass and Brand B in another. She tastes the two and tells you she can definitely tell which is her preferred brand. They now turn to you to do the same. You rarely drink cola, but try anyway. You cannot distinguish a difference in taste between the two. They suggest you should drink more cola, and that if you carried out a survey you would find that people can tell the difference. "But that would only tell me whether people think they can distinguish between the two, and not whether they can actually distinguish the taste of the two brands."

So how can you find out? You realize your friends knew which glass their preferred brand was in. Their ability to distinguish between the two brands may have been dependent on knowing which brand they were drinking. What if they did not know? You redo the test, but this time neither of your friends know which glass their preferred brand is in. Do you think the results would be the same?

Although it contains several flaws, your simple taste test would have the basic features of an **experiment**, whereby the researcher attempts to control aspects of the situation and then observes the change that results. You would first observe their ability to distinguish the taste of the two brands when they knew which glass held their brand. You would then deliberately hide this information from them and see if they could still distinguish between the two. Of course, a properly carried out experiment is more demanding, as we shall see in this chapter.

Experimental research is a technique that aims at demonstrating and specifying or clarifying cause-and-effect relationships. In the above example, the experiment would be set up to discover whether or not people's preference for a brand of cola drink resulted from, or was caused by, people's ability to distinguish the taste of the different brands. In chemistry, experimentation will determine how much a mixture will need to be heated before its component parts will react and form a new compound. You have probably undertaken physics experiments at high school, such as altering the placement of weights in order to get a lever to balance.

While the experiment is viewed as the prime technique in scientific research, the basic logic of experimental research is also very much a part of everyday problem solving. For example, on a cold, damp day your car will not start. You do not want to spend money on a tow truck so you open up the hood. You look for any loose electrical lead, you check the battery by turning on the lights, you may clean the spark plugs or dry off the distributor cap. After each problem area is checked you try to start the motor. What you are doing is eliminating alternative causes of the problem. Similarly, when we learn to cook, each meal is an "experiment." With every repetition of the meal we learn more precisely how much seasoning to use, exactly how long to cook things, and so on.

Finding out why your car or other appliances will not work and learning how to cook better-tasting food all share with the experimental method the *search for causes*. What is causing the trouble with the car or the vacuum cleaner? Why does the cake not rise or the spaghetti sauce taste funny? What causes these problems?

In scientific research a simple experiment would be one in which we manipulate a variable to assess its effect on another variable. (Refer back to the discussion in Chapter 2 if you need to refresh your memory about variables). But while experiments in certain natural sciences, such as chemistry, can be generally tidy and simple to manage, experiments in social research face various constraints.

Most importantly, social research involves human beings. As we will see later, there are ethical considerations and legal restrictions in using people in experiments. Even when people volunteer, other factors in their lives can occur over which researchers have no control, and which can influence the results of the experiment. Furthermore, human beings are likely to change their behaviour simply as a result of knowing they are part of an experiment.

Social scientists have attempted to overcome some of the obstacles researchers face in doing experiments by developing different types of experiments. One type is the **laboratory experiment,** which is an artificial situation controlled by the researchers. Another type is the **field experiment,** which is conducted in real-life settings. Researchers give up some of their controls over the situation. In both laboratory and field experiments, researchers retain some control over the situation and manipulate some variable(s). In contrast, the **natural experiment** involves no manipulation. Researchers observe changes in social behaviour as they occur after natural events such as floods or earthquakes, or social events such as plant closures or riots.

Each type of experiment is covered in this chapter. However, the focus is largely on the laboratory experiment, since the other types are seen as approximations of the laboratory experiment. In addition, an advantage of the laboratory experiment is that it is generally small scale and controlled by the researchers. Field experiments are generally large, expensive, and long lasting. Natural experiments involve waiting for a suitable event to occur. Regardless of the type of experiment, the underlying logic is the same.

THE LOGIC BEHIND EXPERIMENTS: CAUSATION

We noted in Chapter 2 that the idea of causal explanation flows from the basic premise of all science that there is order or patterning in nature and social reality. For many researchers the research process is a sequence that moves from discovering and describing patterns to explaining why and how the patterns work. In the social sciences there is some debate over the possibility and importance of causal explanation and the kinds of explanation that might be appropriate. As we saw in Chapter 2 and shall see in the next chapter there are many social science researchers who argue that the social world is so complex that adequate description is at least as important and possibly more important than causal explanation.

Experimental research is mainly explanatory. It is designed to ascertain the degree to which one thing affects or causes another. In this way the researchers aim to build knowledge about cause-and-effect relationships, or to account for why and how things happen. Suppose you tried the simple taste test on a few friends who all had a preference for one of the two brands of cola drinks. Assume the results showed they were unable to distinguish the taste of the two brands of cola. You examined the relationship between preference for a brand of cola drink and the ability to distinguish between the brands of cola. But your inquiry will probably not stop here; you would want to know why the relationship exists or does not exist. Asking why is looking for

Higher Suicide Risk for Perfectionists

Alasdair Clayre was a high achiever: brilliant enough to be compared with Sir Isaiah Berlin as a philosophy undergraduate at Oxford, a recipient of the prestigious Prize Fellowship of All Souls College, elected an Oxford Don. He also wrote a novel, performed his own songs as a folk singer and produced award-winning television programs.

And yet the day a book he had worked on for years—to accompany a television series—was to be published, Mr. Clayre ended his life by jumping into the path of a train at a subway station in North London. According to friends, he had been mortally fearful of what reviewers might say about his book.

Mr. Clayre's death was largely due to a relentless perfectionism, in the judgment of Dr. Sidney Blatt, a psychologist at Yale University. Dr. Blatt cites the suicide, along with that of figures like Vincent Foster Jr., the deputy White House counsel, who Dr. Blatt also believes was a perfectionist, as testimony to the dark side of unrelenting standards for achievement.

Dr. Blatt is among a growing group of experts who see perfectionism as both blessing and curse, prompting high achievement but making the achievers implacable self-critics, vulnerable to overreacting to what they perceive as failure, often to the point of depression.

And once a person is depressed, new data show, perfectionism increases the risk of suicide more strongly than does an attitude of hopelessness, which for years clinicians had seen as the single emotional attitude making depressed patients most prone to kill themselves.

Other studies show that perfectionists respond poorly to prevailing treatments, medication and psychotherapy that often work well for other depressed patients.

In an analysis of data from a National Institute of Mental Health study of 155 patients being treated for clinical depression, those who had the highest scores on scales of perfectionism did more poorly than other patients in treatment, whether medication or psychotherapy.

One possible reason, said Dr. Paul Pilkonis, a psychologist at the University of Pittsburgh who was a co-author of the study, may be that "these patients misinterpret even small successes as failures.

"Even if they are getting a little better, that may not be better enough to meet their standards," he said. And so they can misperceive even progress as failure.

In another recent study, Dr. Paul Hewitt, a psychologist at the University of British Columbia, and his associates compared 25 alcoholic patients who had tried to kill themselves with similar alcoholic patients who had never tried to kill themselves.

"Compared to the patients who never made an attempt, these people were very high in a particular kind of perfectionism, feeling that the people in their lives—a spouse, boss, parent—demanded a level of performance that they were unable to meet," Dr. Hewitt said. "For these people, a failure means more than an internal disappointment. It brings a feeling of alienation and loss of key connections."

Dr. Blatt and others say that harsh parental standards are a frequent source of neurotic perfectionism. Such expectations send a message to the child that whatever he or she does is never quite good enough, and that the child must be flawless in order to win approval and love.

Citing findings from the mental health institute's study of depression and other studies, Dr. Blatt says that perfectionists seem to benefit most from extended therapy rather than the shorter forms that have become the order of the day.

Among reasons why longer therapy may be more effective for perfectionists, Dr. Hewitt said, is that their sense they must seem perfect often keeps such people from seeking help until they are in extreme crisis. "They not only hide their problems, but also, once in therapy, are slower to open up about them than are other patients," he said.

Several studies concerning risk of suicide are referred to in this reading. How could they have been set up so that a causal connection between perfectionism and risk of suicide was established?

a cause. And the experimental method provides a means of searching for the cause.

However, neither nature nor social life comes ready labelled as sets of causes and effects. Consequently, the discovery and measurement of causal relationships are difficult to achieve. The search for causes, as we saw in Chapter 2 (see Box 2.1), combines logical analysis and empirical research. Here we shall focus on three conditions to establish causality: temporal order, consistent association, and the elimination of plausible alternatives.

Condition 1: Temporal Order

There must be a *clear time sequence*, such that the "cause" consistently appears before the "effect." For example, say you want to find out whether the time spent studying for an exam affects the grade obtained. Obviously, the cause (time spent studying) has to come before the effect (grade on an exam). Or, suppose you want to see the effect of a film on the dangers of smoking on a group of students who smoke. You could first give them a questionnaire to find out what they know about the dangers of smoking, then show them the film, and then give them a post-film questionnaire. The film may provide them with information that they did not know before seeing it. Obviously, the students would first have to see the film before you can determine the effect of the film on the students.

In actual research it can often be quite difficult to establish a clear temporal order of cause and effect. For example, social scientists have explored and described the way of life of some urban poor as a "culture of poverty." But research in this area has been plagued by a chicken-and-egg controversy. This culture is characterized by, among other things, negative attitudes to regular work and undisciplined work behaviour. Some researchers argue that the culture of poverty is a consequence of economic conditions. In other words, low wages and insecure jobs do not encourage people to be hard working and reliable. Thus bad working conditions (independent variable) cause a cultural pattern of negative worker attitudes and behaviour (dependent variable). Other researchers argue that the culture of poverty is learned. It is transmitted from generation to generation and moulds people so that they are incapable from the outset of fitting into stable routines and disciplining themselves. Consequently, there is a supply of willing casual workers due to a cultural tradition (independent variable), and these workers take up jobs others will avoid (dependent variable).

Thus, experimental research requires an assumption of a clear sequence that can be put to the test. But what is cause and what is effect also depends on how you analyze the situation.

Condition 2: Consistent Association

There must be a *consistent pattern of association* between cause and effect. In other words, whenever or wherever you see the effect, you will (at least in most cases) find the cause is also present. In the above example on the effect of a film about the dangers of smoking, what the students learned was presumably from the film. There was an association between the film (cause) which appeared before their change in knowledge about the dangers of smoking (effect).

However, the association is rarely perfect, and this poses problems in causal interpretation. There may have been a sharp increase in the students' knowledge on the dangers of smoking, or a very slight increase, or no increase, or even a decrease. To cope with this ambiguity, social scientists use statistical interpretation to see whether there is enough of a relationship to warrant a causal interpretation.

Condition 3: Elimination of Plausible Alternatives

Before accepting the idea that there is a causal connection, researchers have to satisfy themselves that the connection *is the best possible explanation*. They have to be able to rule out alternative explanations. For example, the students' knowledge of the dangers of smoking may not have been affected simply by the film. Students may have taken part in other events during the period between the time they saw the film and when they were given the post-film questionnaire to determine the change in their knowledge of the dangers of smoking. Or, possibly, the pre-film questionnaire got the students thinking about the dangers of smoking and this in itself increased their knowledge. (Consider how you could set up the experiment differently to avoid this possible problem. Later we will suggest how to improve the experiment.)

To rule out other possible explanations, social scientists look for alternative explanations. The experiment allows for this by isolating the variables involved so that no other possible cause is around. As we will see later in this chapter, social scientists have developed different experimental designs to help them try to eliminate other possible influences. Moreover, an experiment can be repeated many times to see if the association between possible cause and effect is consistently found.

STEPS IN EXPERIMENTAL RESEARCH: THE LABORATORY EXPERIMENT

Essentially, a laboratory experiment involves manipulating one variable while attempting to either control the influence of other variables or hold them constant. The focus is then on the effect the manipulated variable (the independent variable) has on another variable (the dependent variable). In our smoking students example, showing the film is the manipulated variable. The effect of the film is measured by comparing the responses to the questionnaire before and after seeing the film.

The laboratory experiment is considered to be the basic approach to experimentation. Other approaches are seen as approximations to the laboratory experiment. Therefore, our discussion of the major steps involved in experimental research focuses mainly on the laboratory experiment (see Box 6.2).

Step 1: Experimental Hypothesis

The point of an experiment is to expose or measure causation at work. Therefore, it follows that you have to be clear about the relationship you expect between two variables in a setting over which you have much control. For example, what did you expect to find in showing the film on the dangers of smoking to a group of students? You expected

BOX 6.2

How to Conduct an Experiment

1. Select a research topic and develop a clear causal hypothesis focused on a few key variables.

2. Operationalize:
   - Isolate the key elements of the causal connection.
   - Decide how to establish contrasting situations or treatments for the experimental group and the control group.
   - Develop valid and reliable measures for the initial conditions and the effects of the independent variable, and pretest these where necessary.

3. Design the study:
   - Review the experimental design and check alternatives to eliminate potential sources of error and ethical problems.
   - Ensure that only the independent variable can be responsible for any changes over the course of the experiment.
   - Consider running a pilot test to ensure that the experiment will run smoothly.

4. Select the subjects:
   - Consider the population the hypothesis applies to and set up a method of sampling from that population.
   - Consider how the subjects (participants) are going to be allocated to the experimental and control groups.
   - If the experiment is a long-term one, consider using larger numbers to compensate for any dropouts.

5. Consider the issues of internal and external validity:
   - Try to anticipate any threats to internal validity, such as biases in dividing subjects into experimental and control groups.
   - Do likewise for external validity, by considering problems in generalizing from your experiment(s).

6. Perform the experiment:
   - If necessary, measure the initial conditions or characteristics of both experimental and control groups (pretest).
   - Expose the experimental group to the independent variable.
   - If necessary, measure the final conditions or characteristics of both groups (post-test).

7. Debrief the participants:
   - Explain why any deception was necessary.
   - Ensure that any stress arising from the experimental experience is relieved.

8. Analyze and interpret the data, and prepare a report.

the change in their knowledge of smoking to be dependent on their viewing the film. Stated differently, viewing the film was the independent variable, or the variable that was manipulated. And the dependent variable was the change in their knowledge about the dangers of smoking after viewing the film, or the effect of the manipulated variable. Hence, the first step in an experiment is to clarify the causal connection, what are assumed to be the causal or independent variables, and the effects or the dependent variables. Without a clear hypothesis, no well-designed experiment can emerge.

An example of this process is Stanley Schachter's (1959) development of an experiment on stress and affiliation. (There is much more to the work of Schachter than is presented here, but this summary is sufficient for our purposes.) Schachter had read a number of books and articles on religious hermits, convicts, and prisoners of war who had been socially isolated for long periods of time. He noticed that all the accounts of their experiences reflected high levels of stress and anxiety. He began to wonder whether isolation from others, for whatever reason, was itself the cause of this stress. In other words, was there a causal connection between isolation and stress? This led him to consider how this connection might operate under more general conditions and led him to formulate the hypothesis that people who are not isolated turn to others as a result of stress. Notice the drastic simplification that begins at this stage. Schachter is not interested in the different kinds of stresses that religious hermits as opposed to prisoners of war may experience, just stressful experiences in general. What emerges from this review of the literature is a clear, uncomplicated hypothesis: stressful experience leads people to affiliate or turn to the company of others.

Thus, the first step in experimental research is to assert the relationship that exists between two or more variables—that is, to state your hypothesis. Your next challenge, however, will be to devise a way to measure the relationship between the variables—in the study by Schachter, to measure the relationship between stressful experience (independent variable) and affiliation (dependent variable).

Step 2: Operationalizing

An experiment requires considerable imagination and creativity. Notice that an experiment involving stress with human beings immediately raises ethical as well as practical problems. As discussed later, social researchers need to follow strict guidelines that ensure human participants in experiments are not subjected to unnecessary or excessively upsetting experiences. Such limitations have to be carefully considered when designing the experiment.

Designing experiments is also a process of simplifying "reality" so that only the key elements in the causal relationship are involved. Schachter ultimately came up with an elegant, straightforward experimental design. Two groups were to be set up: the **experimental group** was to be subjected to a disturbing experience and its reactions were to be measured; the **control group** was to be placed in an identical situation or environment as the experimental group but without being subject to the disturbance. The disturbing experience is the independent variable. If stressful experience does cause people to turn to each other (affiliation) then the two groups should be clearly different in their reactions by the end of the experiment.

In designing the experiment we also need to consider whether the procedure actually measures what it is supposed to measure. If it does this it has **validity.** We are also concerned about the extent to which the experiment would yield the same results if repeated. Experiments and other research techniques that can be consistently repeated are considered to have the desirable quality of **reliability.**

The stressful experience Schachter set up involved an assistant pretending to be a medical researcher whose task was to administer electric shocks using a formidable-looking machine. The experimental group was subjected to a clearly stressful situation. When meeting with the experimental group the assistant acted in a cold, distant way and said that the shocks would be quite uncomfortable although not physically harming. The control group was not placed in a clearly stressful situation. When meeting with the control group the assistant was friendly and informal and went out of his way to emphasize the mild nature of the shocks.

Before the shocks were supposedly to be administered, the assistant told each group that there would be a delay in the proceedings while the machinery was set up. They were then told they could wait either together or individually in different rooms. Before leaving to do so, they were asked to fill out a questionnaire. The questionnaire probed how anxious they were and whether they intended to wait in the company of others or individually. When all the questionnaires were com-

Adopted Romanians Lagging

Study Blames Early Deprivation

TORONTO—Canadians who brought back hundreds of orphans who had been warehoused in civil-war-torn Romania in the early nineties are finding the early deprivation is having lingering and unexpected effects on their adopted children, researchers say.

Studies at Toronto's Hospital for Sick Children and Vancouver's Simon Fraser University say children they have tracked tend to be at least a year behind in school, and many have not developed an appropriate reserve about strangers.

Many of the adoptive parents of the estimated 1,000 Romanian children in Canada were unprepared for these problems, or wrongly believed they could bridge any gap that existed initially, Elinor Ames, a developmental psychologist at SFU, told a national adoption conference in Toronto yesterday.

When Dr. Ames started her study of 46 Romanian orphans and their adoptive families in 1990, she asked the parents what their worries were. Fifty-seven per cent mentioned health or medical problems, and only 39 per cent thought developmental delay might be a problem.

"Do parents really think you can keep a child in a crib 20 out of 24 hours in a day and they will still meet their developmental milestones on time?" Dr. Ames asked.

In the group of Romanian children she studied, all of whom had spent at least eight months in an orphanage, the average IQ five years later was 90, 10 points below average; the range was between 69 and 127.

For those children adopted as two- or three-year-olds, who had spent a couple of years in the institutions, she found the average IQ was 69, the range 52 to 98.

At the high end of the ranges are those the researchers know were kept clean, those who had been given a toy to play with, and those who were a favourite of any orphanage staff member.

Researchers at the Hospital for Sick Children have found a similar lag in cognitive ability in 56 adopted Romanians they have studied since 1990, and the amount of delay in cognitive development is tied directly to the length of time spent in an institution. They also found more social, communication and behaviour problems in children who had been in orphanages longer than six months.

Dr. Susan Goldberg, a developmental psychologist at the hospital, also came up with a finding she says could alter theories about parent-child attachment.

In experiments involving Romanian-born and Canadian-born four-year-olds, she found a tenfold difference in the tendency of the Romanian-born children to be indiscriminately friendly.

"They would walk up to a stranger and behave affectionately with no hesitation and without checking with their mother."

This kind of unguarded behaviour normally is thought to result from the lack of a secure bond with a parent, she said, but the Romanian children observed did have good bonds with their adoptive parents.

"Preschoolers who go up to strangers and behave affec- tionately cannot be said to be well protected," she said. "We have to clue in parents that being sociable and friendly isn't always a positive thing."

Indiscriminate affection is a good survival skill in an orphanage—it can win the child attention from busy staff—but even children who have been in an adoptive family for several years con- tinue to show this behaviour, Dr. Ames agreed.

In this reading, psychologists have carried out a natural experiment to apply experimen- tal logic and causal analysis. How did they arrive at their conclusions?

Source: Jane Gadd, "Adopted Romanians Lagging: Study Blames Early Deprivation," *The Globe and Mail* (24 May 1996), p. A5. Reprinted with permission.

pleted both groups were then told the experiment was at an end and that no shocks were to be given.

Clearly the two groups experienced very different situations: the experimental group experienced high stress (being threatened with severe shocks), and the control group experienced low stress (being threatened with mild shocks). As very few of us are masochistic, the threat of physical discomfort is almost universally stressful. In this sense the experimental or independent variable has validity—i.e., it is a true or real stressor for most people. It also has reliability, for the threat of physical discomfort will produce stress in most people most of the time and so can be used when the experiment is repeated with different groups by different experimenters. (The questionnaire used in the study was previously shown to be reliable and valid; it was pre- viously used over a wide range of applications.)

Step 3: Designing the Study

In setting up the experiment one attempts to rule out possible expla- nations other than the one intended. Schachter, for example, selected two samples that were as similar as possible and created situations in which he could measure the changes. The experimental group was treated to a stressful situation and then compared to the control group that did not face the stressful situation. The use of a control group is common in the experimental design.

However, other experimental designs exist. Sometimes there is no control group in the experiment; one compares a pre-intervention con- dition with a post-intervention condition. This is the design of the ear- lier example on the effect of a film on the knowledge of the dangers of smoking. The design of this experiment aimed to measure the effect of the film on a single group. But, as we noted earlier, the pre-film questionnaire in itself may have encouraged students to think about the dangers of smoking and influenced their knowledge irrespective of the film. Is it possible we could improve this experimental design?

One approach is to combine the two mentioned designs. There are an experimental group and a control group. Each is given the same prefilm questionnaire. However, only the experimental group is shown the film. After a delay, possibly the time it takes to view the film, the experimental group and the control group are given the post-film questionnaire. Then the knowledge on the dangers of smoking of the two groups is compared. Presumably, if the experimental group shows a sharp change in knowledge, it was due to the film.

Exhibit 6.1 illustrates these three possible designs for testing the effect of the film. As you move from the simple to the more complicated design consider how each design improves on the previous one. Ultimately the only limit to the number of designs is the ingenuity of the researchers. What is important to note is that social scientists design experiments to arrive at trustworthy conclusions about a cause for the change in social behaviour.

Step 4: Selecting Subjects

The key to a successful experiment, such as the one by Schachter, is that any differences between the experimental and control groups are a result of the experimental manipulation—the introduction of the independent variable into the situation—and not the result of other factors. It is important to ensure that both groups are identical and that the only difference between the two groups is that one experiences the experimental stimulus while the other does not. Thus, the room in which the experiment occurs, the apparatus, and the person presenting the experiment to the group are identical in Schachter's experiment. The only difference is the way the experiment is presented to the two groups.

To ensure that the experimental and control groups are identical, the researchers assign the subjects (the participants in the experiment), to each group in a manner that ensures that the subjects are as equal as possible in terms of relevant characteristics. The most common technique is that of **random assignment,** whereby the subjects are randomly allocated into two subgroups. It uses the same basic mechanism and assumptions as the selection of random samples discussed in Chapter 4: every subject should have an equal chance to be placed in one group or another (see Exhibit 6.2). Thus, subjects could be randomly assigned to the different groups by numbering the list of

EXHIBIT 6.1

Experimental Designs

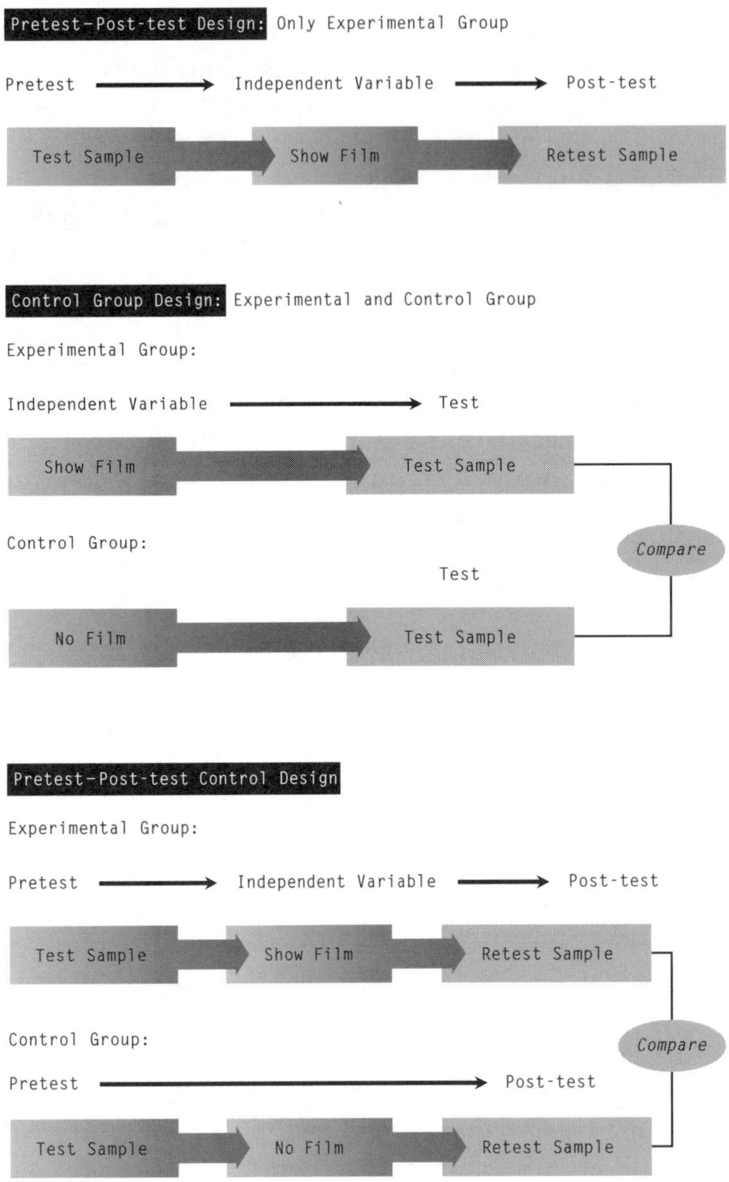

Pretest–Post-test Design: Only Experimental Group

Pretest   ⟶   Independent Variable   ⟶   Post-test

| Test Sample | Show Film | Retest Sample |

Control Group Design: Experimental and Control Group

Experimental Group:

Independent Variable   ⟶   Test

| Show Film | Test Sample |

Control Group:

Test

| No Film | Test Sample |

Compare

Pretest–Post-test Control Design

Experimental Group:

Pretest   ⟶   Independent Variable   ⟶   Post-test

| Test Sample | Show Film | Retest Sample |

Control Group:

Pretest   ⟶   Post-test

| Test Sample | No Film | Retest Sample |

Compare

subjects and selecting numbers by means of a random number table. The first name drawn would go into the experimental group, the next into the control group, and so on. However, take note that unlike

EXHIBIT 6.2

Random Assignment

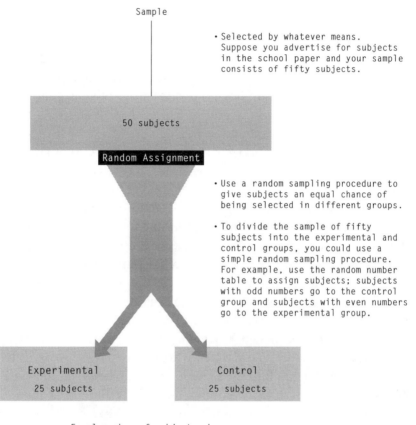

Sample

- Selected by whatever means. Suppose you advertise for subjects in the school paper and your sample consists of fifty subjects.

50 subjects

Random Assignment

- Use a random sampling procedure to give subjects an equal chance of being selected in different groups.

- To divide the sample of fifty subjects into the experimental and control groups, you could use a simple random sampling procedure. For example, use the random number table to assign subjects; subjects with odd numbers go to the control group and subjects with even numbers go to the experimental group.

Experimental
25 subjects

Control
25 subjects

- Equal number of subjects who are reasonably similar in terms of relevant characteristics in each group.

random sampling, which determines who takes part in your research, random assignment determines whether a subject will be in the control group or the experimental group.

Step 5: Internal and External Validity

The purpose of random assignment is to make certain that all subjects have an equal chance of being selected to either group. Their ultimate placement into the two groups is not dependent on a choice made by either the researchers or the subjects. If researchers could choose, then their conscious or unconscious desire to see the experiment succeed might lead them to stack the experimental group with certain kinds of people. For example, it could lead them to place friendly, sociable people in the experimental group, so the group would be made up mainly of subjects who would be more likely to seek the company of others. In a study on stress, the personality characteristics of those in the experimental group, and not the stressful situation, could account for their reactions in the experiment.

A similar problem might occur if the participants were permitted to choose for themselves which of the two groups they could go into. Perhaps the more nervous individuals would volunteer to be part of the control group to try to avoid stress. Again any reactions on the part of the experimental group could now be interpreted as being a result of the types of people in the groups, rather than of anything that was controlled in the experiment.

Thus in assigning the subjects randomly to the different groups, and controlling other factors of the experiment, the aim is to design the experiment in such a way that changes are due to the independent factor. If one is confident that the experimental results (the measured or observed differences between the experimental and control groups at the end of the experiment) are due to the experimental or independent variable then the experiment is said to have **internal validity**. Internal validity means that alternative reasons for the results have been eliminated by the way the experiment was organized and carried out.

Another important consideration in checking the experiment's design is to consider its **generalizability**. If this experimental set-up or procedure is repeated many times with different groups by different researchers, will it still find the same relationship between the variables involved? If an experiment is supposed to tell us something about people in general, as was Schachter's experiment, then we shall have to check it out with men and women, different age groups, and so on. If experimental conclusions can be generalized to a broad range of human populations then the experiment has **external validity.** Schachter's first experiments, for example, were initially conducted in England with young female students. But one could repeat the experiment elsewhere with samples of other population groups randomly assigned to experimental and control groups and expect the same results.

FIELD EXPERIMENTS

Until now our discussion has focused on the laboratory experiment. Its advantage is that researchers have much control over the situation for discovering and measuring cause-and-effect relationships. They artificially isolate a limited range of variables and focus as precisely as possible on the key variables in a causal relationship. By controlling the way the variables interact they may be able to measure the impact or the degree of causation involved. A disadvantage of such experiments is that they do not create a real-life setting. Indeed, many real-life situations are difficult, if not impossible, to create artificially. Social life involves complex, interrelated systems of elements, not discrete, easily separable components of independent and dependent variables. Moreover, as we noted and will say more about later, the use of experiments in social science raises considerable practical and ethical problems. Consequently, researchers have often been forced to compromise and look for research designs that provide some of the advantages of the laboratory experiment without incorporating all its features.

Unlike the laboratory experiment, the field experiment is conducted in a real-life social situation, such as a subway or a library. Suppose your study involved finding out whether students were willing to help a drunk student. You might set up a situation in which an apparently drunk student sits near the entrance of the library and shows signs of needing help standing up. You could then record whether he received help, who came to his assistance, and how much time it took. An advantage of such an experiment is that it studies social behaviour in a more realistic situation than in a laboratory. But you would have far less control over the factors that may interfere with the situation. Possibly certain students did not approach the drunk student because they expected a nearby professor to help him. Since you are unable to control the many possible factors that could have interfered, it is difficult to establish a clear causal relationship. Thus, a challenge in setting up a field experiment is to have as much control as possible while manipulating the key causal factor.

An interesting example of a field experiment is Henry and Ginzberg's (1985) test to see if racial discrimination existed in Toronto's labour market. The researchers attempted to discover if there were differences in the number of job offers obtained by equally qualified white and black applicants. They also wanted to see if applicants from different racial and ethnic backgrounds were treated differently in job interviews.

Two field-experimental procedures were used. First, similarly qualified black and white applicants applied in person for the same job. Second, applicants using five different ethnic accents (white-majority Canadian, Slavic, Italian, Pakistani, and Jamaican) made phone enquiries about advertised job openings. In both cases employers were confronted with apparently normal people searching for jobs in the regular fashion. In fact, while one set of applicants—those for semiskilled and unskilled jobs—were high-school and university students who would normally be seeking these as temporary work, another set applying for more skilled work were professional actors trained to participate plausibly in the more demanding job interviews involved for this level of work. By matching applicants in terms of their qualifications, applying for the same jobs, and applying by phone and in person, many real-life variables were successfully controlled for, and the results are convincing because of the realistic nature of the experiment. What do you think the results showed?

An important difference between field experiments and laboratory experiments is that the former are often used in applied research. Field experiments are undertaken to examine social policies and institutions such as schools, welfare organizations, government training programs, and the like. When changes in policy are being considered government agencies often introduce pilot studies or test cases where the new arrangement is introduced on a small scale and the results compared with the old ways of doing things. Such studies have the advantage of uncovering problems with the new policies before the government has gone to the expense of changing the entire system.

Since the 1970s there has been increasing debate over "welfare payments" to very poor, chronically unemployed people in our society. In the United States this debate has been accompanied by a number of evaluation experiments—field experiments aimed at discovering whether welfare payments discourage people from searching for work or not, whether guaranteed sums are better than amounts that fluctuate according to your job search activities, whether payments tied to training are better incentives to seeking work than no-strings-attached payments, and so on. Such experiments have generally taken the form of taking a random sample of very poor welfare families, assigning some to a special treatment such as payments tied to work training or a guaranteed minimum payment (the experimental group), and assigning the rest to continue with the existing arrangement.

The two groups are then followed up regularly through interviews and reports that keep track of their family incomes, expenditures, job search activities, and perhaps other aspects of their lives, such as marital stability. Contrary to popular opinion, these studies find that no welfare-payment schemes are clear disincentives to seeking work.

This research technique has all the components of a laboratory experiment except that society itself becomes the laboratory. Because the experiment occurs in the field, the researchers have no control over factors that might affect the situation but have not been considered in the research hypothesis. For example, surges of economic growth encourage the long-term unemployed to seek work, while economic recessions discourage people without skills from actively looking for jobs.

The researcher also may not fully control the application of an independent variable in a study set up by a government agency. For example, the government agency might insist on screening recipients instead of randomly assigning them into a treatment group, or it might severely limit the length of time permitted for the study. As well, selecting and dividing groups or areas into those who get the new policy applied and those who remain with the old may be influenced by political or administrative concerns, which could undermine the validity of the outcome. However, the major advantage of this and other kinds of field experiments are that they involve real issues in realistic settings.

NATURAL EXPERIMENTS

Researchers are able to maintain some control in field experiments, but sometimes we want to examine a possible causal relationship that we cannot control or manipulate. For example, consider the impact that natural disasters such as floods, fires, and earthquakes, or negative social events such as plant closures and accidents, can have on social behaviour. These phenomena cannot be manipulated as if they were independent variables. Instead, researchers interested in the influence of these phenomena on social life would carry out a natural experiment.

For example, say you want to study the personal recovery of flood victims. Obviously you can only carry out the experiment after the flood has occurred. It is also likely that you neither anticipated the flood nor considered the study before the flood happened. Therefore, you would have no baseline information on the victims before the event. You cannot be sure whether the changes among the victims were due to the flood or to other factors, or if they would have occurred without the flood. The information gained by your study, however, can provide important insights and even suggest ways of helping flood victims. Since it is difficult to test a cause-and-effect relationship, a natural experiment often serves as a source of hypotheses that need further evidence.

Clearly, a natural experiment is at times the only way to test experimentally some complex and interesting real-life situations. A classic example in social psychology was Hadley Cantril's (1940) study of panic.

In 1938 a Boston radio station broadcast a dramatization of H.G. Wells' science fiction novel *War of the Worlds*. The radio drama began unannounced, with what sounded like an official government emergency newscast announcing the invasion of New England by Martians and the efforts of the United States armed forces to contain the invasion. The play was enjoyed by many thousands of listeners, but a significant minority fled for the hills on hearing the news bulletin. Cantril interviewed a sample of those who had panicked and those who had remained at home. He then compared the two groups. What do you think he discovered?

In a more recent work Charles Perrow (1984) built on knowledge arising from his appointment to a special commission investigating the accident at the Three Mile Island nuclear power station in Pennsylvania. As commissioner, he read many reports of accidents, near accidents, and engineering problems in the nuclear power industry. This enabled him to understand the vulnerabilities in nuclear power technology, and to see many of the human problems associated with working with very complex and sensitive technologies. This led him to hypothesize that the complexity of the technology itself created an environment in which "human error" would flourish.

After finishing his work with the commission Perrow embarked on a research project that compared highly complex technologies such as nuclear power, aviation, space exploration, and chemical refining with other accident-prone but simpler technologies such as mining and dam construction. By accumulating detailed case studies of accidents in these industries he was able to identify a range of conditions that seemed to be consistently associated with large-scale accidents. Each case study was, in a sense, treated as an experiment and the results compared with the other case studies. Despite being an entirely qualitative and largely descriptive study, the logic of causal analysis, strongly expressed in experimental research, clearly comes through in Perrow's work.

METHODOLOGICAL PROBLEMS IN EXPERIMENTATION

Experiments are most successful where the researcher has the most control over all the elements involved. But in social research such control is constrained by ethical considerations and undermined by the very nature of the material being experimented on. In addition, when human beings know they are part of an experiment, they are likely to behave differently than they usually would. This is known as the **Hawthorne effect.** Studies carried out at the Hawthorne plant of the

TABLE 6.1

ADVANTAGES AND DISADVANTAGES OF EXPERIMENTAL RESEARCH TECHNIQUES

	Advantages	Disadvantages
Laboratory Experiments	Allow for much control over the situation Possible to manipulate one variable while controlling or keeping constant the influence of other variables Strong at measuring cause-effect relationships	Artificial (i.e., one has little confidence that the results of the experiments would be the same in real life) Many aspects of human behaviour are difficult to examine in the laboratory (such as intimate dating relationships or family violence)
Field Experiments	Allow manipulation of variables in real-life situations Subjects are likely to behave as they normally would in such a situation Often useful in applied research, such as measuring the effect of a government policy	Difficulty in measuring cause-effect relationships Researchers lack some control over the situation Unexpected developments can influence the situation Generally longer lasting and thus more expensive and difficult to conduct than laboratory experiments
Natural Experiments	Studies social behaviour in its natural setting May be beneficial in suggesting how agencies might help people affected by natural disasters, such as floods, and by negative social events, such as riots	Weak in providing proof of cause-effect relationships No control over independent variable May have to wait for the event to occur

Western Electric Company in the late 1920s and early 1930s found that whether physical conditions were improved or made worse, the workers being studied increased their productivity. Later, researchers concluded that the unintended influence had been the workers' response to the interest shown in them. According to these researchers, the workers ignored the changes in physical conditions and produced more *because* they were part of the experiment.

Social scientists have since discovered that their experimental "subjects" are not passive, reacting only to the instructions and conditions consciously set up by the experimenter; they are "participants," bringing their full range of sensibilities and social abilities to the experiment. As participants they actively cooperate by trying to guess the purpose of the experiment and then "helping" the researcher by modifying their behaviours to achieve that purpose. They pick up subtle, unintended cues from experimenters and react to these even though they may be irrelevant or counter to the purposes of the experiment.

Experiments in social science often take lengthy periods of time during which the participants are released and returned to the laboratory several times. During this time the participants may encounter other participants and share their experiences. This may produce group dynamics, such as deliberate helping with the experiment. Should the encounter be between individuals who are in different groups in the experiment (experimental versus control groups), an awareness of the differences in treatment or experience may develop and lead to rivalry or resentment between the groups.

Even if these communication processes do not take place, because of the lengthy time period many other things may affect the lives of the participants that may undermine the internal validity of the experiment. People, especially young people, grow and change over time. The experimental experience may reinforce or interact with these growth or maturation processes. The passage of time permits the occurrence of events that may have an effect on the experiment. For example, if an experiment is focused on prejudice, then political events, an outburst of ethnic rivalry, or a newspaper story may affect the participants' attitudes and interact with the experimental conditions in ways that are difficult to identify.

If the experiment involves repeated testing, such as performing skills tests, quizzes, or problem-solving tasks, the sheer repetition of testing will lead to improvement regardless of any experimental manipulation. Further, the longer the time taken up by the experiment, the more likely it is that fatigue and boredom will contaminate people's responses. In the case of very lengthy experiments, there may be dropouts, and researchers will have to check that the number of dropouts does not significantly change the balance between the experimental and the control groups.

ETHICAL CONSIDERATIONS

Experiments in social science raise serious ethical questions. Many psychological or social psychological experiments involve some degree of *deception*—as was the case with Schachter's experiment, in which the purpose and the procedure of the experiment were misrepresented to the participants. The false pattern is itself the independent variable. In field experiments professional actors are often hired to simulate muggings, to break social conventions, or to pretend to need help in some public location. Often these deceptions are harmless in the sense that no physical threat is involved, but very often some element of stress is created as an unavoidable part of the deceptive experimental procedure. In some cases this stress may be quite severe, as was the case with the notorious obedience experiments by Stanley Milgram (1974).

Milgram set up situations in which naive subjects were urged to give successively more intense electric shocks to a victim (in reality a collaborator with the researcher) whenever he made mistakes in reading. Despite the fact that the task involved shocking the victim to an apparently dangerous level and despite the realistic pleadings and screams of the victims, about two-thirds of the naive subjects followed the directions of the researcher.

The publication of Milgram's experimental research ushered in a period of intense debate among social scientists, especially psychologists, over the nature, appropriateness, and ethical problems of experiments. The results of that debate have been a tightening of ethical regulation of human research across the social sciences and the introduction of a new procedure in human experimentation: **debriefing.** The term originated in the armed forces, where it meant a review of a military operation after it was carried out in order to learn all that could be useful for future operations. In psychology it was used by Milgram as a synonym for what he called "dehoaxing"—to make clear to the participants of an experiment that they had been hoodwinked and to explain why. In Milgram's case it was also found necessary to counsel some of the participants who had been seriously distressed at the thought of inflicting physical harm on others. Since Milgram's experiments psychologists have generally tried to avoid intensely stressful forms of experimentation, which had been a distinct trend in the 1950s.

WHAT YOU HAVE LEARNED

- The experiment is a technique designed to uncover causal relationships.

- Causal interpretation involves showing a clear time sequence, ensuring consistent association, and eliminating alternative explanations.

- Laboratory experiments allow researchers much control over the situation; require the use of carefully developed measures; and may require the random assignment of participants into experimental and control groups.

- Field experiments are conducted in real-life situations, but researchers give up some control over the situation.

- Natural experiments are carried out in real-life situations to study natural and social events, but researchers have no control over the independent variable or other influences.

- Experiments have been valuable in social research, but they face serious challenges in terms of internal and external validity.

- Experiments with human participants often involve deception and stress, which raises difficult ethical issues.

KEY WORDS

experiment	reliability
laboratory experiment	random assignment
field experiment	internal validity
natural experiment	generalizability
experimental group	external validity
control group	Hawthorne effect
validity	debriefing

REVIEW QUESTIONS

1. Identify the characteristics of a classical laboratory experiment.
2. What distinguishes a control group from an experimental group?

3. Why would researchers assign subjects randomly to the experimental and control groups?
4. What distinguishes a laboratory experiment from a field experiment?
5. What distinguishes a laboratory experiment from a natural experiment?
6. What are the advantages and disadvantages of field and natural experiments?
7. How are validity and reliability obtained in experiments?
8. Why is debriefing an essential part of experiments with human participants?
9. Explain the difference between internal and external validity.
10. What are some factors to consider in attempting to generalize from the results of laboratory experiments?
11. Obtain a copy of the Henry and Ginzberg experiment on discrimination (or a social psychology experiment selected by your instructor) and analyze it by

    a) identifying the elements of experimental design within it (i.e., the hypothesis, variables, pretest and post-test measures, etc.);
    b) identifying the elements of control in the design;
    c) identifying any weaknesses in control; and
    d) assessing the external validity of the experiment.

RECOMMENDED READINGS

Cook, T. D., & Campbell, D. T. (1979). *Quasi-experimentation: Design and analysis issues for field settings*. Chicago: Rand McNally.

An analysis of the logic of experimental research in relation to non-laboratory research.

Festinger, L., Reicken, H. W., & Schachter, S. (1956). *When prophecy fails*. New York: Harper & Row.

A fascinating study of a natural experiment that resulted from a chance reading of a news story about a bizarre flying saucer cult.

Martin, D. W. (1991). *Doing psychology experiments*. Monterey, CA: Brooks/Cole.

A humorous work, which thoroughly covers the logic behind experiments and their design. Discusses such issues as getting ideas for experiments and reviewing the literature.

Field Research

WHAT YOU WILL LEARN

- the purpose of field research
- how to conduct nonparticipant observation research
- how to conduct semiparticipant and participant observation research
- the ethical issues associated with field research

INTRODUCTION

One day, several weeks after the semester has started, you walk into class to find a fellow student sitting at the desk you normally occupy. How would you feel? Until this disruption occurred you had not noticed that it was "your" desk. But you and your classmates quickly establish your territories in every classroom with very little thought. Some of you habitually seek the back seats, others the front, or seats by a window, and so on. Once seated you mark your territory by various signs of ownership—relaxing your body posture, perhaps even stretching and sprawling out; putting your bag and coat on the desk; scattering pens, paper, and folders around, and so on.

Of course, in addition to such territorial activities, a lot of other social processes occur in the classroom. Social connections from outside are brought in, as indicated by groups of friends sitting together. Social connections are also made in the classroom as gangs, cliques, and partnerships form over the course of the term. As well, some of your fellow students may remain outside of these networks. As the course proceeds you and your classmates will perform different roles in the class. You may be a "keener," cooperating with the teacher by responding to questions and actively engaging in discussions. Or you may be a "class clown," mocking the lectures and discussions by pretending to be extremely stupid or making off-the-wall comments. Other roles you may recognize (or even play at) are the aloof, disconnected, silent type, or the disruptive, don't-give-a-damn type.

There are a variety of types of teachers as well: the very strict sergeant major types who bully a class into submission; the magnetic personalities who can charm and beguile; the jokers; the storytellers; and the aging hippies. Finally, there is the very complicated process of classroom dynamics. How do the students and teachers play out their roles, act out their moves? How do these plays and actions change as the term wears on?

You probably recognize a lot of your own classroom experience in the above descriptions. Thinking about it will probably lead to modifications and extensions of these ideas, and soon your classroom experience will never be the same again! It will no longer be a comfortable, semiconscious set of taken-for-granted routine activities, but something that when analyzed shows a lot of complicated social activity. It is the aim of most field work to describe social activities in depth so that these complications can be appreciated and understood.

When you begin to think about the social organization and actions in a classroom it quickly becomes apparent that there is a great deal going on. Observing all this is no simple task. It takes time and concentration. Observing a class while being in class will probably lead your attention away from what you are supposed to be studying! Being a student may be the only way to get inside the class, but observing at the same time as acting out the student role will be very challenging.

Field research requires researchers to go to the groups they wish to study. Instead of bringing human subjects to specially prepared experimental settings or taking carefully developed and pretested questionnaires to a select sample of respondents, the researcher goes into the field and observes the flow of social life as it naturally takes place. Unlike the field experiments discussed in Chapter 6, the field research we discuss here does not try to provoke reactions in order to test hypotheses. On the contrary, field researchers try to minimize the impact of their presence on those they observe and let hypotheses or interpretations develop from their observations. Field research involves a wide range of research techniques, including observing individual and group behaviour; interviewing people; collecting documents and artifacts; and photographing, sketching, and mapping physical aspects of group life. (For the history of field research see Box 7.1.)

Field research has many applications. One use of this method is to study social behaviour so familiar that it consists of unconscious

BOX 7.1

History of Field Research

THE PRESCIENTIFIC ERA

Explorers, travellers, missionaries, and conquerors describe the foreign lands they travel to. For example, *Thucydides*, a Greek general in the 5th century B.C., described the Persians and other peoples in the lands where his army fought; *Marco Polo* described his travels to China in the 14th century. The aim of these writings was mixed: to inform, to entertain, and often to draw moral conclusions about appropriate and inappropriate ways of living.

THE ENLIGHTENMENT ERA

The scientific revolution in 17th-century Europe led to the belief that social problems could be solved by actions based on truthful information. For example, *John Howard* travelled through Europe to study conditions in the prisons in the late 18th century. His work led to the foundation of the John Howard Society, which was dedicated to the humane treatment of the jailed. *Charles Booth* lived with the London poor as part of a study of the lives of working people in the late 19th century. The aim of these writers was to apply the knowledge they obtained to the solution of pressing social problems.

THE ERA OF SOCIAL SCIENTIFIC FIELD RESEARCH

By the turn of the century the social sciences had emerged as academic disciplines; that is, they became concerned with knowledge for its own sake rather than for its ability to solve moral and social issues. This was reflected by individuals who promoted field research as a set of procedures for gaining knowledge. *Bronislaw Malinowski* was the first anthropologist to live with a group of people for a long period of time in order to study them. His work established the British school of "social anthropology." *Franz Boas* was an American anthropologist concerned with the disappearance of native people's culture resulting from the settlement and industrialization of North America. He trained his students in native languages so that they could interview native informants in order to build up a picture of their culture prior to the coming of white society. At the same time, the *Chicago School of Sociology* developed under the leadership of *Robert Park*. Park was trained as a journalist as well as a sociologist. He urged his students to go out into the streets and neighbourhoods and write about social life based on direct observation and investigation. There was little systematic attention to the methods of field research. This changed in the 1950s when other social researchers developed strong arguments for the use of surveys and experimental logic. In response, those influenced by the Chicago School began to lay out their ideas in a more systematic way—a perspective that became known as *symbolic interactionism*. This approach emphasized the importance of understanding social activities and social settings in terms of the meanings they have for the participants. This approach continued the Chicago tradition of descriptive, qualitative studies of neighbourhoods, marginal occupations, deviants, and social movements.

From the 1960s on, qualitative research became increasingly popular and controversial. Historians developed "oral history" techniques such as in-depth interviews of survivors of significant recent events, and became increasingly sensitive to the elite bias of much historical documentation. Anthropologists were now studying non-European societies, which were urbanizing rapidly, and turned to sociological writings on fieldwork in urban settings to guide them. But symbolic interactionism came under increasing criticism from feminists and others for being too concerned with defending itself from the scientific emphasis of other social researchers and too little concerned with developing a systematic, qualitative sociology that could include an understanding of the importance of the emotional and irrational aspects of social life.

routines and activities. Another use of fieldwork is to study small-scale, intimate social settings such as bars, community groups, and gangs. The social organization of the classroom is an example where both of these applications come together.

The Aims of Field Research

Field research can vary considerably in both its focus and its aims (see Box 7.2). Social anthropologists attempt to describe the way of life of

What Do Field Researchers Do?

THE AIMS OF FIELD RESEARCH

1. To discover and describe patterns of social life as it occurs naturally.
2. To understand a group member's own point of view.
3. To get a complete picture of a group's way of life, beliefs, customs, etc.

THE FIELD RESEARCH PROCESS

1. To be "on the spot" recording social life as it occurs.
2. To be sufficiently involved with the group to be an eyewitness and/or to directly experience group life.
3. To observe group life without upsetting or disturbing it.
4. To understand the insider's point of view without losing the analytic perspective of an outsider.
5. To notice both explicit (recognized, conscious, spoken) and tacit (unacknowledged, implicit, unspoken) aspects of culture.
6. To notice both ordinary and unusual events and activities.
7. To see activities, events, and relationships as parts of a complete whole, not as unrelated items.
8. To use a variety of techniques and social skills in a flexible manner as the situation demands.
9. To produce data in the form of extensive written notes, maps, diagrams, and pictures, and where appropriate to record and collect data in the form of photos, video and audiotapes, and artifacts of group life.

an entire group of people; to do so in terms of the people's own understanding, experience, and values; and to capture the way of life as a complete whole. Sociologists do likewise when they try to study an entire community, such as a small town, an ethnic group, or a neighbourhood in a big city.

Other social researchers focus on a smaller field of study, such as a bar, a workplace, or a youth gang. As well, they often study a specific kind of experience or activity, such as a visit to a tattoo parlour or a day in the life of an addict, and focus on the details of social interaction and communication that create and organize these "micro" social worlds.

As we pointed out in Chapter 2, there is a division within social research concerning the appropriate philosophy and general approach to social analysis. Many field researchers argue that the explanation of social behaviour has to be sought in the reasons and motives people operate with when they interact socially. Reasons and motives are culturally and historically determined, passed on through socialization, and modified through social interaction and experience. Consequently, understanding social life requires an understanding of underlying values and perspectives and observation of the ways these are carried through and modified in social situations. This requires careful and systematic description of the social life of a group with the aim of understanding that way of life from the viewpoints of group members. When combined with a systematic description of physical and techno-logical aspects of life, this approach is called **ethnography**—"ethno" meaning people or folk, and "graphy" meaning to describe or study.

Field research is not only used to study many different social phenomena, it is also not limited to any one specific technique or research tool like the experiment or the questionnaire-based survey. The key to field research is its flexibility in making use of whatever techniques are most appropriate and fruitful given the characteristics of the research setting or field.

The Varieties of Field Research

Most field research is the work of a single researcher, although some team investigations have occasionally been done. This limits the scope of the research to intimate and small-scale institutions and groupings that have some clear separation or boundary in relation to the larger society. Social anthropologists typically study small-scale tribal soci-eties or peasant communities that are geographically concentrated as well as partly isolated from other groups. Sociologists study small-scale groups such as gangs, cults, occupations, or neighbourhoods; or places where people come together repeatedly such as workplaces, bars, hospital wards, schools, jails, or shopping malls. Historians study groups of people with some experience in common such as a war, an economic depression, or a political event.

In addition, social researchers study events such as riots, social movements, or accidents in a "field research style," bringing together eyewitness accounts and experiences to discover the overall pattern or meaning of what was often a rapidly changing complex of events. As you can see, field research can be used to study an immense variety of social groups and situations.

There are three basic patterns of or approaches to fieldwork, each defined by a specific type of relationship between the observer and the observed.

In **nonparticipant observation** the observer goes "where the action is" and observes without interacting with the group under observation. The observer tries to blend into the background, watch, and eavesdrop on those around her who carry on their actions unaware that they are being observed.

The anthropologist Edward Hall (1959) carried out such observations in Asia and the Middle East and noticed how social status is expressed by behaviour. He found that in family walks there is a clear order of public walking. In the Middle East husbands are preceded by their wives and children, whereas in the Far East husbands walk ahead. Both patterns separate husbands from the rest of the family and clearly establish the wives' duty of looking after the children.

In North America these kinds of observational studies have looked at the "highway code" underlying pedestrian movement on city sidewalks, behaviour in subways, and the hidden rules of sociable touching. In each of these studies direct observation of large numbers of naturally acting citizens, unaware that they were being observed, showed consistent, repeated patterns of behaviour. From these patterns the researchers inferred cultural rules and values that organized the behaviour. For many fieldwork researchers this is a major problem with nonparticipant observation. How can you be sure the observers' interpretation of cultural rules makes sense to the people whose behaviour is observed? Nonparticipant observation gets at people's *behaviour* but it does not get at people's experience and understanding—the *meaning* of the behaviour in the social group where it occurs.

In order to get at the meaning of social life, field researchers argue that it is necessary to *participate* as well as to observe, although one may try to limit one's participation and be a "hanger on." This is referred to as **semiparticipant observation:** the researchers join in social activities as a way of establishing trust but generally maintain some distance between themselves and the group.

A classic example of this approach was Erving Goffman's *Asylums* (1962), a study of mental hospitals and other closed institutions. Goffman realized that being too closely connected with one of the groups in an asylum would limit his access to the other groups. If he came in as a patient he could not easily mingle with the medical staff, the orderlies, or the nonprofessional staff. As a make-believe medic he would not be totally trusted by patients and nonmedical staff would probably treat him with reserve. To solve this problem he obtained the hospital administration's agreement to create an entirely fictitious position whose responsibilities were so vague that he was not identified with any of the key subgroups in the mental hospital. Consequently he was able to be everywhere and anywhere and speak to anyone at any time.

Other situations where semiparticipant observation is necessary include those where sex, age, or ethnicity clearly identify the observer as an outsider. Most anthropological studies are of this type, because the researcher is so clearly from another society. But the outsider status also applies to studies of youth by adults, of the handicapped by the non-handicapped, of slum dwellers by middle-class academics, and so on. This is the most common type of field research. Of course, semiparticipant observation does involve some loss of information, because some parts of the social group or subculture remain closed off to the researcher, an outsider.

To overcome such access problems a few researchers have become full-fledged participants in the groups they have observed. A dramatic example of this **participant observation** approach comes from the world of journalism rather than social science. John Howard Griffin, a white journalist, decided to explore American society as it was experienced by blacks in the early sixties. He did this by undergoing a painful series of skin coloration treatments (he later died of skin cancer as a result of these treatments), which enabled him to pass as an Afro-American. He published a book about his often harrowing and painful experiences as a black in an often hostile white society—*Black Like Me* (1976). This book had a big impact on popular opinion because it provided white Americans with a sense of what it was like to be black in America.

These three varieties of field research can be used alone or in combination with each other and with other research techniques. Each one has particular advantages and applications as well as certain limitations, so let us look at each one separately.

NONPARTICIPANT OBSERVATION RESEARCH

Why Use Nonparticipant Observation?

Anthropologists, sociologists, and psychologists say that human beings are largely products of socialization into a culture. Not only are our values, beliefs, and attitudes shaped by learning how to think, believe, and act in social groups, but our emotions and physical responses are socially learned. Much of this learning takes place at a very early age and we become so well trained that our conformity to social requirements becomes a habit and takes the form of routines that we are unaware of. It is only when we move into other social groups or see others with different rules and routines that we may notice the many rules we follow.

Because we are unaware of so many of our cultural rules it is difficult to discover them through interviews. The interview could be confusing and uncomfortable and might possibly lead to some resentment or be broken off by the subject before it was finished. Observation, which does not require conversation, is a better way to discover the everyday, commonplace, nonverbal behaviours by which we unconsciously express cultural rules. Observation is also useful in studying young children who may be operating according to cultural rules but who are not able to explain what these rules are. Researchers also depend a great deal on observation in the early stages of conducting fieldwork in unfamiliar settings in order to pick up nonverbal clues to help them identify regular patterns of interaction and to distinguish the important from the unimportant in the flow of social life. Thus, observation is both a technique essential for the study of phenomena that are difficult to get at in other ways, and an exploratory technique that prepares the way for, and may accompany, other techniques.

Choosing a Question

As with all research, the first step in an observational study is deciding what to study. For instance, social life is full of unconscious, nonverbal routines. Some are simply not open to study through observation by outsiders because they occur in private settings: undressing and dressing routines at bedtime or waking, for example, or nonverbal patterns in sexual seduction. However, there is a vast array of nonverbal action taking place in accessible public places such as parks, shopping malls, sidewalks, bars, cafés, schoolyards, public transit vehicles, and so on. These locations and their associated social behaviour patterns offer many interesting possibilities for observational research. For example:

> How do people avoid collisions or unintended intrusions?
> How do people preserve spheres of privacy in the midst of crowds?
> What are the differences between men and women in their public gestures?

Steps in Nonparticipant Observation Research

1. Choosing a research question: an appropriate topic of study using this technique.
2. Identifying the location: where the actions of interest are likely to be seen.
3. Preparing to make observations: exploring the field, selecting sites, checking appropriate times.
4. Developing observational skills.
5. Doing a trial run.
6. Observing: watching, listening, collecting, and recording data.
7. Reanalyzing data and writing the research report.

What happens when there are breakdowns of social orderliness?
What adjustments to behaviour are made when places become crowded or when crowds thin out?
Do people change their behaviour when certain other groups appear, such as a group of nuns, or a detachment of police or security guards, or a gang of children or teens?

Any of these questions, or others like them, would be an appropriate focus for an observational study.

Defining the Location

Defining the focus will determine *where* the observations should take place. At one extreme, defining the study as an exploration of the rules of elevator behaviour will lead to a focus on a single type of setting: elevators. At the other extreme, investigating how people maintain their identity as loners in public places would require a very broad range of locations: in bars, on the sidewalk, in malls, in parks, and so on.

Preparing to Make Observations

Observation depends on being at the right place at the right time in an appropriate state of readiness. All this requires some preparation; you cannot just turn up and do it. How long can you stay in one spot without arousing people's suspicions? Are there police or security checks that might turn out to be a problem? Since observation takes time you have to consider some basic comforts and supports. Can you get to food and drink easily without interrupting the observation for too long? Where are the washrooms? Are there places you can go to write up field notes quickly if the field is far from your home or place of study?

Clearly, locations have to be checked out to identify the best places for people-watching. Where can you place yourself so that you are not conspicuous (and therefore likely to interfere with what is going on) but you can see quite easily the kinds of behaviour you want to observe? Several careful inspections of the observation sites are necessary, then, to find out about these basic features.

Such explorations are also required for other reasons. Most public places have a rhythm of activity, which has to be discovered in order to get the best results. Cafés near warehouses and truck terminals may be intense hives of activity when most of us are asleep or just dragging ourselves out of bed. Bars and clubs may be really jumping only long after parents have turned in. Shopping malls are quiet in the mornings, populated by young mothers and senior citizens, become crowded with all sorts of people during the midday lunch period, then quieten down only to become more populated again as children and teenagers come out of school and people leave their places of work. Public places are populated by different types of people depending on the hour of the day, the day of the week, or—as in the case of parks, amusement parks, and public beaches—the season of the year. It is essential to know or to discover these cycles of activity before you draw any conclusions from your observations.

Getting a sense of the type of people who will populate the place or places where you are observing is also essential to finding out how you have to be dressed and behave in order to blend in and not attract attention.

Developing Observational Skills

Another important reason for checking observation locations is the need to experience the difficulties and requirements of observation—in short, to train yourself to overcome the pitfalls and develop your observational skills. Even sparsely populated parks, malls, or school playgrounds can be full of distractions—people, behaviour, and events that are interesting but irrelevant to your study. Nothing much may happen for long periods of time and then along comes a flood of interesting activities. You may find yourself feeling very self-conscious, possibly even embarrassed, like an intruder who should not be there. These feelings can easily become a preoccupation and draw your attention away from the actions of others. You may be asked for directions, approached by a panhandler, or eyed by an attractive member of the opposite sex. Any of these events can take your mind off the task at hand. Experiencing these diversions and discomforts before you begin your real period of observation is useful.

You should include in these trial runs some training of your ability to observe with ease and alertness. Do not try to push yourself to the limits if you feel tired. Your observations will be less reliable and the quality of your study reduced. Learn to pace yourself and take breaks. Breaks can be used to bring your notes up to date, or to review them to make sure they are legible, understandable, and do not leave out some important items that may still be fresh in your memory.

Develop your observational capacities during these pretests. Look for characteristic, repetitive, commonplace behaviours and populations; listen to the characteristic sounds of the setting, the levels and modes of communication (shouts, relaxed talk, formal talk, hushed whispers, nonverbal gestures, grimaces, etc.); get a sense of the *ambience* of the place or places (friendly or not, relaxed or not, casual or businesslike and formal, etc.). Through all these observational acts build up a picture of the settings or environment, the populations, and the actions and interactions of these populations.

Taking Notes

Finally, the trial observations will bring you face-to-face with the major problem of observation, namely, *recording your observations*. Scribbling notes in public places often marks you off from the bulk of the people there. Maybe you are a struggling writer at work on the next Great Canadian Novel. Perhaps you are a journalist or a police officer. Possibly you are a student working on some essay notes, or someone writing out a shopping list to replace the one left at home. Some of these identities (journalist or policeman) are likely to be disruptive of people's behaviour; others (student or forgetful writer of lists) are innocuous. You have to judge for yourself how open you can be in combining watching with recording.

She's Not Heavy, She's My Sister

"Models look weird to me," says Amanda Odei, a 15-year-old African-Canadian who lives in Toronto. "When they give their measurements I borrow my mother's tape measure and I can't believe it. It's not real. My doctor told me that at 5-foot-10 I should weigh 200 pounds."

Ms. Odei, who swims and plays squash, soccer, basketball, volleyball and tennis, has no time to diet. Sure, Janet Jackson's washboard stomach is her model, but strong is her goal. "Thick," she calls it.

"I was taught that if you were skinny, you don't look good; you're not sexy. You have to have some thickness."

There is growing evidence that black and white girls view their bodies in dramatically different ways. "In white culture," says anthropologist Mimi Nichter, co-author of a landmark study done at the University of Arizona in 1995, "the window of beauty is so small."

Her study shows that black girls benefit from a much more liberal interpretation of beauty. Two-thirds of black teens who participated in the study defined beauty as "having the right attitude," and said that women grow more beautiful as they age. Seventy per cent were satisfied with their bodies, and 65 per cent believed it is better to be a little overweight than underweight.

White teen-agers who participated in the study defined beauty as being 5-foot-7 and 110 pounds (Kate Moss's vital statistics). Not surprisingly, 90 per cent were dissatisfied with their bodies. Some even admitted to wanting to hurt or kill any "perfect" rival who invades their territory.

In the same vein, a group of white girls at Warwick Academy in Bermuda say that if a perfect girl (a Cindy Crawford look-alike) turned up, all the boys would love her and all the girls would hate her and look for flaws until they found one. "She would be called a bitch," according to one girl.

In stark contrast, African-American teens describe themselves as being supportive of one another. Sixty per cent of those in the University of Arizona study said they'd tell a friend she was "looking good." Just 11 per cent admitted they would be jealous of her.

They defined a perfect black girl as someone who has a good sense of humour, is easy to talk to, smart, friendly and fun. She doesn't have to be pretty, though "well kept" is important. She should also "have it goin' on," which entails making whatever she's got—be it long nails, pretty eyes, big lips, nice thighs or a big butt—work for her.

"I don't have an ideal woman," Amanda Odei says. "All people look good in their own way."

Her friend, who attends a mixed-race school, says she went through years of teasing before she "realized that black people are built differently. Black people are thick. Black girls have muscles; they are strong. Strong is a good thing, uh huh."

Both girls nod vigorously.

In white society, thinness has become the ideal. As a result, many white girls try to attain perfection through pathogenic dieting. Frequently, they are merely following their mothers' lead.

Indeed, in a recent study of Canadian women, 80 per cent of participants whose weight was in a normal range said they want to lose weight. Merryl Bayer, head of the National Eating Disorder Centre at the Toronto General Hospital, explains the pressure many white girls face: "The white teen's parents are probably dieting or talking about it; her mother's peers are talking about it, and their fathers and sons may be denigrating fat women." Ms. Bayer adds that medical workers often find that infants who fail to thrive (grow and flourish) are being malnourished by mothers who are afraid their babies will grow up fat.

Underlying the differences between black girls' and white girls' attitudes towards beauty are 200 years of cultural differences. In white, middle-class America, says anthropologist Nichter, part of the dream of making it is making yourself over. People in the black community realize that they won't be able to move up the ladder as easily as whites, she says. Black girls can't afford to think about themselves in a negative way because it will hold them back.

"In non-white families like mine, it's really important to raise kids who feel good about themselves, who feel strong and proud, in order to survive," confirms Carla Ribeiro, a 26-year-old African-Canadian graduate student at York University in Toronto. "I was taught from early adolescence, 'This is how you are. You work with that and maximize what is good.' It's really a sense of acceptance of your body and who you are, to increase your sense of your own strength."

A black teen in the University of Arizona study said that "African-American girls have inner beauty that they carry with them: their sense of pride." This pride is described as something the girls inherit from their mothers.

Indeed, Ms. Odei, who is the youngest of five children, wants to look like her mother. "When she was on the beach in Jamaica all the guys were on her," Ms. Odei says. "Same with my grandmother. Last time I saw her she was dancing."

White girls in the University of Arizona study said things like, "My mother is okay for a mother," or "She must have been beautiful when she was young." They

regarded aging as something to be avoided at all costs.

A strong cultural identity immunizes the black girl against excessive food and weight preoccupation, as well as fear of aging. A group of black 15-year-olds at a private school in Bermuda say that when they see large women on the bus (women who take two seats), they think of the women as self-confident and able to stand up for themselves.

Patrice Carter, a dynamic 26-year-old African-Bermudian meteorologist, became anorexic when she was sent to a white boarding school in the United States. "I ended up in the hospital," she says. "When I was sent home, my mother and aunts jumped on me and said, 'Girl, why are you trying to kill yourself?'

"I realized not only was I sick, I looked like hell. I needed some thickness. They saved my life."

Asked why she listened to her elders, when most anorexics ignore their families' concerns, Ms. Carter says, "Hey, I had to listen, how could I not?

"In our culture, women are the power. Often the woman is the sole parent, who holds down two jobs, takes care of the house, raises the children, works in the church. And power means being large in every way. Big is healthy, strong.

"What women hold power in your culture?" Ms. Carter demands. "Supermodels who barter their thin bodies for money. And when they lose it, what then?"

Amanda Odei visited a modelling agency with a friend, and was told that she would be able to get work because of her height. "Only I had to lose weight," says Ms. Odei. "The woman wanted me to be a size 6, or 4. I'm a 14 or 16."

Ms. Odei laughs and rolls her eyes. The money from a modelling career would be nice, but she's not in any rush.

This reading refers to an anthropologist's study of contrasting cultural definitions of beauty. Which kind of field-work would you undertake for such a study? What type of observations might you make?

Source: Liz Nickson, from "She's Not Heavy, She's My Sister" in *The Globe and Mail* (13 April 1996), p. D3. Used by permission of the author.

You will find that recording can take away from watching and that it is often better to break up observation by retreating to a convenient café to write up your notes in the field in a full, clear, legible way while the details are still fresh in your mind. Not only do you give yourself a break from the pressures of observation but writing up your observations can focus your mind on what to look for when you return to observe.

PROBLEMS WITH NONPARTICIPANT OBSERVATION

Time and Effort

Unless you decide to videotape behaviour in public places (potentially a much more intrusive technique of observation) observation is inexpensive but very time consuming. To get good results considerable preparation—checking out locations and pretesting and developing observational skills—is necessary. Even then you may end up spending a long time with little to show for it. Unpleasant weather keeps people at home, an economic depression empties the bars, malls, and pleasure parks. Observation also makes great demands on the observer. We all differ considerably in our ability to keep focused in crowded, active situations; to be alert to subtle nuances of behaviour and action; to remain sensitive to visual and other stimuli; to witness and recall; and to act unobtrusively.

Reliability

Observation and related techniques (such as participant observation and case study analysis) are research methods where the *personal equation* (see Chapter 2) is very significant. Because observation depends on the observer's ability, checks on the **reliability** of the observations are necessary. Several observers in the same location can have their data carefully compared. During the training or trial observation period, observation can be done in tandem with another or several other more experienced observers. Ultimately, the **replication** of observation studies is an important check on the reliability of each study.

Validity and Sampling

A single observer, or even a small team of observers, is also limited in ways that raise questions concerning the **validity** of observations. Observation is time consuming and energy draining for those who do it. Consequently the amount of first-hand observation is quite limited and has to be concentrated on a few carefully chosen locations. Previewing sites before this selection is made is also probably restricted to places near the researcher's home or place of study. There is no random sampling from a carefully developed sampling frame. Locations are chosen for their suitability and accessibility, resulting in a **convenience sample.** As a result, observation studies may be uncertain bases for generalization.

The Kind of Data Collected

A final problem associated with observation studies, one they share with qualitative techniques in general, arises from the kind of data they produce. All three variants of observation—nonparticipant, semiparticipant, and participant—produce what anthropologist Clifford Geertz (1973) has termed "thick description." Thick description is description that conveys the depth, richness, or complexity of social life. Thick description is lengthy, elaborate, and "literary" rather than concise and summarizing (as statistical description is). Even observers who do not necessarily follow Geertz' prescription will tend to end up with a mass of detailed descriptions of settings, behaviours, gestures, spatial positioning, and so on. Such material is difficult to break down into typologies or to code. As a result, data analysis is often complicated and time consuming.

BOX 7.4

Steps in Semiparticipant and Fully Participant Observation Research

1.   Choosing a research question: an appropriate group or organization to study using these techniques.
2.   Preparing to observe: learning as much as possible about the people and places you are going to be involved with.
3.   Entering the field: adopting an identity, establishing relations with the group, learning their social rules.
4.   Learning to observe while participating.
5.   Recording the data and analyzing it to guide further observation.
6.   Leaving the field.
7.   Reanalyzing data and writing the research report.

SEMIPARTICIPANT AND PARTICIPANT OBSERVATION

A participant observer "gathers data by participating in the daily life of the group or organization he studies" (Becker, 1958, p. 652). How much participation the observer engages in varies greatly, depending on the nature of the group and the commitment, perhaps even the foolhardiness or bravery of the observer. John Howard Griffin's act of changing his physical appearance is probably the most extreme case of becoming as far as possible indistinguishable from those you study.

The boundary between semiparticipant and participant observation is not a very clear one. Even fully participant observers are always partly outside the group because of their concern to describe and analyze what is going on as it is happening. While ordinary people just get on with ordinary life the observers continually pull back to take notes, to remember, to probe more deeply, so that they are always, however slightly, mentally hanging back from full participation.

In contrast to pure or nonparticipant observation, a participant observer speaks to the people being observed. By interviewing and conversing with the subjects of observation the researcher tries to discover the group's own interpretations and experiences of their activities, to find out the history of the group, and to understand aspects of group life that may not be accessible to direct observation. Yet many of the techniques of direct observation will still be essential in participant observation.

A participant observer tries to gather whatever kinds of information are available in the situation, including observing behaviour directly; looking at written records, letters, diaries, etc.; or taking note of physical aspects of the group (buildings, tools, clothes, arts, environment, and resources, etc.). These different items of information often require diverse research techniques to record and analyze. Consequently participant observation is much more complicated to describe and to undertake than nonparticipant observation. The participant observer is gathering varied types of data and is caught up in the life of the group at the same time. He is interpreting what is witnessed and spoken about, and continuously making decisions about what events or actions have to be followed up, who to speak to next, and so on. This requires a great deal of social alertness and the ability to be flexible and to improvise in the field of study.

Fieldwork is not easy to describe because field situations vary enormously and are apt to change from day to day as the researchers encounter new aspects of group life, make new contacts, and so on. Not only do the groups studied vary and change during the fieldwork but fieldworkers also differ in their styles of involvement and in their data-gathering observational techniques. Some people are more gregarious and at ease mixing in with the flow of interaction, talking to and questioning the people they meet. Others may be very good at self-effacement, less obtrusive ways of tagging along for the ride, and eavesdropping. Both approaches can get good results even though they are built on very different personal approaches to social interaction. In this respect fieldwork research is more like a craft or an art than a science. But this does not mean that "anything goes," as the following discussion of fieldwork procedures should make clear.

Defining the Focus

Participant or semiparticipant observation research is essentially a learning experience. Field researchers will go into the field with a general sense of what they are looking for but very often questions, issues for analysis, or hypotheses emerge as the fieldwork progresses, rather than being defined at the outset.

The first step in a participant observation study is the selection of a subsociety or subculture which is of interest and to which you can gain access. Potential subjects might be deviant or unconventional groups such as delinquents or cult members; culturally distinct groups such as ethnic and religious minorities; geographically limited locations where intense, repeated social activity occurs such as bars or factory shopfloors; or ongoing subcultures whose members share common concerns, values, and perspectives without definable territories such as Trekkies or computer hackers. The key characteristic of all such groups is their distinctiveness, which sets them apart from wider society. This may set up barriers and accessibility problems, which you will have to deal with both in preparing and in setting up your research and often in conducting the fieldwork itself.

Preparing for the Study

A good field study requires a great deal of careful preparation. It requires good relations between the observer and the observed, and depends on extensive access to the group in general and to individuals willing to act as guides, interpreters, and informers. The broader the range of cultural events, artifacts, records, and perspectives you have access to, the deeper will be your understanding of the subculture. Participant observation is therefore a wide-ranging, time-consuming process. Because of the time and the "people skills" involved participant observation makes great demands on the abilities of the researcher to be open and flexible. The researcher must make the best use of new opportunities for observation as they arise from the flow of life, and must cope with times when group life becomes less hospitable to outsiders.

The more you have studied the group and prepared the way for the field research—by carefully approaching potential informants or people with appropriate connections and by reviewing what is known about the group—the smoother your entrance into the group and the more at ease you will be once in the field. The more background you obtained before entering the field, the less time you will take becoming familiar with the setting. At the same time, you have to retain an open mind about the group and not let this background information colour or bias your experiences and observations in the field.

Such background preparation is also necessary in order to decide the probable role that you will adopt in the field. The advantages and disadvantages of various types of participation during fieldwork are laid out in Table 7.1. In some groups you will have no choice but to participate fully or almost fully. Studies of outlaw motorcycle gangs and unconventional religious cults would be examples. In many other cases you have some choice in your degree of participation. Are you

TABLE 7.1

ADVANTAGES AND DISADVANTAGES OF FIELD RESEARCH TECHNIQUES

	Advantages	Disadvantages
Nonparticipant Observation	Limits chance of observer disturbing normal behaviour	Access to behaviour patterns only
	Non-involvement of observer encourages objectivity	Problems interpreting what is happening without other data
	Good for studying everyday behaviour in public places	
Semiparticipant Observation	Necessary where researcher is obvious outsider	Observer's presence may alter group activities
	Gives researcher direct access to group, and thus to members' beliefs and ideas	Some aspects of group life may still be inaccessible
	May be useful to be an outsider if group is divided by conflicts	
	Outsider role reinforces objectivity	
Participant Observation	Necessary for the study of "closed groups" such as cults and criminal groups	Very psychologically demanding
	Greater involvement of researcher leads to empathy and understanding of group	May involve personal danger or participation in illegal acts
	Greater involvement opens up range of group life to observation	Researcher may be trapped in a particular role
		Requires a long period of preparation
		Researcher may lose objectivity

going to participate as fully as you can or just tag along? How do you intend to identify yourself to the people you are going to study? Are you an independent researcher or identified with a specific project, institution, or sponsor?

The more fully you participate, the greater the range of observations and experiences you can take in. But your involvement might itself influence the group. Extensive participation also increases the risk of becoming trapped on one side of social divisions existing within the group. Extensive participation also influences the researcher. The more involved in the group you become the greater the risk of losing your objectivity and seeing things exclusively from the group's viewpoint.

In general it is easier to be open about who you are and what you are doing than to conceal your identity and your research aims. The greater the gap between your account of yourself and reality, the greater the potential embarrassment and damage accidental disclosure will bring. Going in openly as an observer makes interviewing informants, asking questions or being generally inquisitive, and recording data much easier. Recording observations in the field will be especially difficult if everything has to be noted while you are away from the events and persons themselves. By being open about observing you allow yourself some leeway to take the occasional note, perhaps even photos and videos, and to ask questions about things as they happen.

Entering the Field

As with nonparticipant observation, it can be extremely useful to visit the site of your field research before the research really begins. This allows you to become familiar with the sights, sounds, social activities, and other basic characteristics of the scene and gives you a sense of what to expect. You also become a familiar part of the scene yourself the more you visit it, so that you are partly established there when your fieldwork proper begins. These visits and the process of gradually fitting in may also be useful in making contacts. In fact this technique may be the only way to make contact if you are studying very loosely organized, highly informal groups such as youth gangs, addicts, prostitutes, or regulars at a bar.

Field research in more organized settings such as communities, hospitals, and workplaces are simpler to gain entry into. One may join a community organization, or get a job or position at a workplace, or do volunteer work in hospitals, jails, homes for the elderly, etc. Being a researcher here is an extension of being a somewhat inquisitive joiner, volunteer, or new employee.

The major problem in the loosely organized field settings is, perhaps, the suspicion that such groups have of outsiders and the slow and sensitive process of working your way in and establishing trust. The major problem with the "organized" field is that of getting trapped by a particular role at a specific level of the organization that limits your access to other people and parts of the field. Of course, entry into the field or group you have chosen to study is no guarantee of access to information. Trusting relations have to be set up and maintained throughout the fieldwork. Field researchers have to be on their toes and alert to keep up this trust.

Doing Fieldwork

The initial period of fieldwork is spent getting used to the processes of observing and participating—learning how to fit into the group. While you should take a lot of notes, quickly learn how to "interview on the run" and observe as much as you can, many of your early observations will need to be reinterpreted as you learn more about the group's life. Angry and aggressive gestures that at first seem to indicate tension and conflict may later be revealed as just a style of "coming on." Conversely, pleasant or polite behaviour may mask a lot of hostility and politeness itself may be a very subtle way of expressing anger and resentment. As you participate more you will observe new behaviours that will lead you to reinterpret what you have already seen as well as repetitions of events that firm up some conclusions or interpretations you have already arrived at.

As for recording what you see, note taking is the least intrusive technique—much less obvious than tape recording and videotaping. Both the latter require accompanying written description and presentation in a final report anyway. The best recording technique is to jot down the essentials in a small pocket-sized notepad and develop the ability to recall what people said, who was there, how they looked and acted, and where the incident took place.

Field interviews often have to be very brief, occurring in lulls between periods of activity. Field researchers often have to interview and observe the setting simultaneously, which poses great difficulties if you have to take notes on the interview as well. Abbreviating the notes by writing down the topics of the conversation as they take place allows you to observe at the same time. The details of the conversation can be filled in later.

Whatever notes you have been able to take in the field should be written up in full every evening or in breaks during fieldwork. Because only brief notes are possible in the field itself, field researchers have to rely on memorizing what they see and hear in the field. The longer the period between the initial encounter and the full writing up the more unreliable the record because of probable lapses of memory. Since the emphasis of fieldwork is to understand the way of life of a group from the group's own perspective it is particularly important to accurately report conversations, recreating people's statements *verbatim* and preserving their terminology and speech patterns as closely as possible.

Collecting and Analyzing the Data

In addition to writing up their notes on a daily basis, field researchers soon find it necessary to review these notes; earlier misunderstandings can be cleared up in light of later knowledge. Sort through the accumulating record to look for repeated patterns of events, activities, communications, and interrelationships that may provide working hypotheses and a frame of reference for further observations in the field. What connections between events and people do there seem to be? Are there alliances and conflicts that repeat themselves (or shift) from one situation to another? Do there appear to be hidden lines of communication, alliance, or relationships that explain otherwise puzzling actions and events? Do you need to look for some specific items of activity, or see events, people, or individuals you have not yet concentrated on? Are areas of observation still confused or do you have ideas that have too little support?

This process of sorting, sifting, and analyzing your field notes means that **data analysis** and **data collection** become much more closely connected than is the case with other research methods. Elsewhere you collect your data first, and *then* you analyze it. In field research the movement back and forth between data analysis and data collection can sometimes make it difficult to distinguish between what actually happened or what something means to the group under observation; your best recollection and description of what happened or its meaning to the group; your selective interpretation of the event or meaning as you recorded it in your field notes on location; your shifts in understanding or perception as you later transcribed, reanalyzed, and reinterpreted your field notes; and finally, the rewritten presentation of data in your final report.

Although there is no absolute or perfect resolution of these problems some precautions may be taken that allow the initial researchers and others to check on possible sources of unreliability.

1. The initial field notes (on table napkins or backs of envelopes, or in torn, crumpled, and dirty pocket notebooks) should be kept

until the full report has been written and accepted by the appropriate reviewing groups.

2. The write-ups from these field notes should be kept and clearly identified as write-ups.
3. All notes should be clearly dated.
4. Field note reviews, analyses, and interpretations should either be written separately from the field note write-ups or clearly identified as secondary material. Writing these interpretations is best done in a clearly labelled, separate notebook with appropriate dating of all entries.
5. It is often worth the effort of keeping a **personal journal** to document your own feelings, anxieties, perceptions, and responses to day-to-day events as the fieldwork occurs. This too should be carefully dated and reviewed regularly to check for possible sources of bias, negative or positive emotional responses, blindspots, etc.

The procedures of data analysis in fieldwork are covered in Chapter 9.

Leaving the Field

As the fieldwork phase approaches completion, ethnographic researchers need to consider the process of leaving the field. Have you already made clear through your introduction to or involvement with the group that you will be moving on? If not, some thought needs to be given on how to leave. Fieldwork is an intimate research technique that involves building close personal ties between observer and observed. Many fieldworkers report feelings of guilt as the time for leaving approaches. Sometimes the group has used the fieldworker or has expected the researcher to provide some service or benefit and a bargain or implicit contract has been set up. "We'll tell you about our lives if you stand up for us in the courts" (in studies of deviants), or "publicize the injustices committed against us" (in studies of ethnic and religious minorities). Have the researchers delivered on their end of the bargain? Are they planning to?

If you are leaving with boxes full of field notes and other data you are clearly indebted to the community or network you have studied! At the very least you owe the group a courteous farewell by thanking everyone and acknowledging this debt. Apart from being good manners, leaving the field "in good standing" may allow you to keep contacts and do some follow-up observation and interviewing that might improve your study or add to it at a later date.

THE ADVANTAGES AND DISADVANTAGES OF FIELDWORK

Advantages

Supporters of field research argue that it has four major advantages over any other kind of research technique: *holism, depth, appreciation of complexity*, and *meaningful understanding of subjects*. The importance attached to these advantages depends on the aim and focus of the researchers.

Social anthropologists often stress the first advantage, *holism*, which means that researchers can see the way of life of a group as a whole and see how its various parts fit together. One can see how attitudes and actions fit or do not fit, how public and private spheres of life are separated and how people pass from one to another, how different parts of a group interrelate, and so on.

Depth refers to the fieldworker's ability to get behind the scenes, to penetrate the public face of organizations and groups, the stereotypes we have of deviants, the private and informal levels of social actions, and so on. Fieldwork makes possible access to parts of life that are not normally open to outsiders. In modern societies with their great variety of ethnic and religious groups, subcultures and countercultures, this special access to their inner life is very important. These societies are also permeated by stereotypes generated by the mass media, which makes it more important to develop techniques of social research that go beyond public opinion.

By *complexity* field researchers mean that there is always more than meets the eye in social life. Social relationships are often ambiguous and ambivalent. Groups who are in long-term conflict tend to work out patterns of interdependence and tacit understandings that set limits to the conflicts. Teachers, for example, have techniques for handling or controlling class clowns. However, they may, on occasion, welcome the class clown as someone who breaks up normal routines, and introduces an element of liveliness and alertness into the classroom. In addition, the class clown momentarily takes the spotlight away from the teacher and provides some comic relief for everyone in the class.

Researchers who focus on very specific and limited elements of social interactions—greetings, joke telling, being waited on at a bar, and so on—find that these involve many little rules, patterns, cues, and signs. These very commonplace, everyday pieces of social behaviour have great depth and complexity, which are best revealed by some ethnographic technique. As well, there are rhythms, cycles, or seasons to social life that occur over long time periods and are sometimes not easily seen even by participant observers because of their limited stay in the field. But ethnographers argue that these things have even less chance of being grasped by surveys, experiments, and limited forms of direct observation techniques.

Perhaps the most important advantage of fieldwork for many researchers is that it is a way of studying *how people understand their own lives*. Fieldwork is very much aimed at understanding the point of view of the people studied. What do their lives *mean* to them? What are their *reasons* for the way they do things? Getting at the meaning of a way of life is a crucial step beyond mere description: to understand meaning is to understand *why* people act the way they do. In this qualitative approach to social research, then, to understand meaning is to *explain* a way of life in its appropriate, human terms.

Disadvantages

The field researcher has to deal with four major problems. First the very presence of an observer, however participatory you are, may alter the way the group operates. All field research requires a settling in period during which the observer becomes accepted as a member of the group or as just part of the scene. Only after the group has accepted your presence will it settle back into its normal ways of behaving.

The second concern is that not only does the group have to get used to you, but you have to get used to the group. You will have to abandon your own culture and learn the group's ways of believing, thinking, and acting. If this resocialization does not occur, you risk **ethnocentrism,** imposing your own cultural interpretations on the life you are observing.

The third concern is to ensure that the methods used to reveal social life do not distort or create false pictures of that life. Interviews, however in-depth, may reveal how people think about their lives, but they do not necessarily show how they *act*. Dependence upon interviews and conversations may produce a picture of ideals, beliefs, and thoughts but will leave out many other aspects of group life. In addition to talking, researchers have to see how people actually behave, communicate with each other, express their emotions, break rules, and so on. Consequently a variety of research techniques, each of which will reveal some part of social activity, have to be used. The information from each method can be used as a cross-check on the other data to provide a more reliable picture of the entire group's way of life or an in-depth look at a particular segment of life.

Finally, fieldwork is often very dependent on special relations with specific individuals within a group or social scene. You will most likely have made contact with one or more of the group members prior to going into the field. These individuals will pave your way into the group and will probably continue to be important guides and **informants** as the fieldwork proceeds. It is very important, then, that these contacts are indeed well informed and knowledgeable about the group and its culture. If they are low in the "pecking order" or are marginal or deviant in relation to the group, their information will have certain biases, which you need to take into account.

Field research can be a demanding and time-consuming process whose success in many ways hinges on the personal abilities of the field researcher. This renders fieldwork one of the least *replicable* techniques of study. The long period of preparation and the time taken to properly prepare for and pursue the fieldwork means that repeated observations on the same community tend to be separated by very long time periods. Even replications using different communities involve considerable time lags. Because of these long time lapses so much is likely to have changed anyway that later researchers are no longer really repeating the study but are investigating a much different group. As a result it is difficult to tell the degree to which differences between earlier and later studies are due to different interpretations, researcher bias, etc., and how much is due to real social change. Consequently, many social scientists argue that fieldwork is valuable as the first stage of a longer research program that should move from pure description toward more focused data gathering designed to test hypotheses.

Lack of replicability means that we are dependent on one researcher or one research team's interpretation of group life. In the few cases where repeat studies have been done we are confronted with different interpretations of the group. For example, Oscar Lewis (1951) restudied a peasant village in Mexico forty years after Robert Redfield, and Derek Freeman (1983) studied Samoa about thirty years after Margaret Mead. Both follow-up studies came to drastically different conclusions about the communities observed and argued that the earlier studies were biased misinterpretations. Unfortunately it is very difficult to sort out how far the differences of perspective arise from the inevitable social changes occurring over decades, and how far they are the result of differences in theoretical viewpoints.

ETHICAL CONSIDERATIONS

In fieldwork-based studies two ethical issues are particularly marked: *invasion of privacy* and *deception*.

Is the observation of your classmates and teachers an invasion of privacy? The case could be made that because you are looking at behaviour in public places, rather than intimate or private activities, it is not. However, your teachers and classmates do not know that they are being watched. They have not been given a choice to accept or reject becoming subjects of your research. In this sense a basic ethical principle of all social research—**informed consent**—has been violated. Of course, asking for permission to observe classroom processes and revealing your intention to observe the behaviour of students and teachers may well lead to modifications of those behaviour patterns. You will no longer see the social dynamics of the classroom in their natural state and the validity of your observations may be suspect.

Does the researcher's right to do research, then, override the general public's right to privacy and informed consent? There is no clear, rigid rule here. Responsible research involves weighing the balance of rights and responsibilities very carefully.

Field research often places researchers in positions where difficult ethical choices must be made. Your observations of teachers and students might reveal some negative features of classroom life. Some students may have developed a very effective technique for cheating on tests. A teacher may slant lessons in ways suggesting bigotry and prejudice against some ethnic or religious minority group. Do you take your findings to the student newspaper? Do you confront the cheating students or challenge the teacher? Do you go to a dean or academic ombudsperson? Or do you accept the unsavoury findings, submit them in your course essay, and leave your research methods teacher with these moral dilemmas? Once again there is no easy, standard answer to these kinds of questions.

The issue of deception is an equally complex one. Certain social groups, such as religious cults or extremist political sects, require **covert observation**. Covert observation occurs when researchers join or observe a group without revealing their true identities or purposes. Such concealed participant observation is a very controversial technique in anthropology and sociology, the two disciplines most dependent on ethnographic research. Most researchers see covert observation as a last resort, to be used only when open observation is impossible and in situations where significant new knowledge might be obtained.

Because participant-observation research involves a high level of contact between the researchers and their research subjects, the issues of **confidentiality** and **anonymity,** or of protecting the research subjects from harms arising from publication of research results, are also important. Superficial changes of informants' names or place names are often insufficient to protect the anonymity of the group and its members. The very depth, richness, and holism of fieldwork studies often make it easy to work out which particular community and individuals are being described. Even if the researchers do their best to maintain anonymity, readers, reviewers, and journalists are often able to work out where the study occurred and who some of the subjects are. In the case of deviant groups such breaches of anonymity or confidentiality may be especially damaging.

The exact nature of the ethical problems associated with fieldwork will vary from study to study. Studies involving deviant groups, or penetrating behind public appearances into private life; studies of cults or other groups requiring covert observation techniques; and studies of controversial and divisive aspects of social life such as abortion or racism are likely to involve the greatest difficulties. There are no easy answers to the ethical problems associated with research. You will have to answer these basic ethical questions to your own satisfaction at every stage of the research process.

WHAT YOU HAVE LEARNED

- Field research is an approach to social research that attempts to discover patterns in social life through careful observation of social activities in their normal or natural settings.

- There are three basic types of field research: observation, semiparticipant observation, and participant observation. Each has its own advantages and limitations.

- Field research often combines the three types of observation with each other and with other research techniques such as documentary research, or in-depth interviews.

- Field research involves qualitative data analysis techniques similar to those used in historical research, but rather different from the data analysis in most experimental and survey research.

- Certain kinds of fieldwork, especially covert observation, raise difficult ethical questions.

KEY WORDS

ethnography

nonparticipant observation

semiparticipant observation

participant observation

reliability

replication

validity

convenience sample

field interviews

data analysis

data collection

personal journal

ethnocentrism

informant

informed consent

covert observation

confidentiality

anonymity

REVIEW QUESTIONS

1. What are the aims of field research? How does field research differ from survey and experimental research?
2. Why is nonparticipant observation useful? What kinds of social phenomena is it best suited to study?
3. Why are reliability and validity significant problems in field research?
4. Why is semiparticipant observation necessary?
5. What are the advantages of openness in fieldwork?
6. Why is replication a significant issue in field research?
7. What special ethical problems are associated with fieldwork?

RECOMMENDED READINGS

Burman, P. (1988). *Killing time, losing ground: Experiences of unemployment.* Toronto: Wells & Thompson.

A study of the experiences of seventy-five unemployed men and women, using in-depth interview techniques by a sociologist who helped set up a community support centre.

Reiter, E. (1991). *Making fast food: From the frying pan into the fryer.* Montreal: McGill-Queens Press.

A study of work and workers in the Burger King chain. The author had to be persistent and clever in order to overcome the reluctance of the industry to be studied and the difficulties of relating to a young labour force with a high turnover rate.

Wolf, D. (1991). *The rebels: A brotherhood of outlaw bikers.* Toronto: University of Toronto Press.

A description of the way of life of motorcycle gangs based upon the author's experiences of riding, drinking, and fighting as a member of an outlaw motorcycle club in Edmonton, Alberta.

CHAPTER 8

Indirect or Nonreactive Methods

WHAT YOU WILL LEARN

- why indirect research methods are necessary
- when and how to use unobtrusive measures
- when and how to use content analysis
- when and how to use secondary data analysis

INTRODUCTION

Suppose you have become interested in your fellow students' level of health awareness and health-related lifestyles. You may have developed a questionnaire that included a number of questions on dietary or eating habits. On pretesting the questionnaire you find that there is an apparently high level of awareness of healthy eating. Intuitively this does not seem quite right to you. You are aware that you and your friends consume large amounts of soft drinks, fries, and chips in the cafeteria. The responses to some of your open-ended questions seem too pat, sounding like the lectures on healthy living you got at high school. Around the same time this was on your mind your grandmother asks what you are doing at college and you tell her about your survey on diet. She is not very impressed with the "health craze" and says that in her youth people had so little choice they felt lucky to get three square meals a day and "no one worried about fat and fibre." This sets you wondering not only about your questionnaire but about the history of dieting and modern-day obsessions with health.

Thinking about your study further you begin to see that there are different ways of checking up on student eating habits apart from directly asking questions in a survey. You could become an observer in the cafeteria, or work with others and try to record the variety of food and drinks consumed. Perhaps you could persuade the cafeteria management to show you their sales records to find out which foods are most popular. If you have a really strong stomach (and some good work gloves) you could even go through the cafeteria trash to get a sense of food consumption patterns from the leftovers in the garbage!

Your rethinking might also lead you to become interested in the influence of high-school education on health awareness. You begin to dig out your old high-school folders and discover quite a lot of material in the form of classroom handouts, pamphlets, and the like. But you now realize you would have to read and analyze this material and carefully compare it with the statements in your survey if you are going to show the influence of schooling on health attitudes.

Your grandmother's comments have also sparked your curiosity and you have now begun to pick up old paperbacks on diet and health from garage sales. These are both plentiful and cheap and you begin to realize your grandmother was right: there is a "health craze." You begin to think that perhaps it would be interesting to put current dietary thinking in the context of this longer-term ebb and flow of diet fashions.

Your research has now grown more ambitious and probably more interesting. It has also grown more complicated. You are moving away from relying solely on the direct research method of the survey. You have now added the three main **nonreactive** or **indirect** methods of getting information on the topic that interests you:

1. Using physical evidence of human activity (sorting through the cafeteria trash) is known as **unobtrusive measurement** of behaviour. It has long been used in archaeology but has only recently come to be used as a technique by anthropologists, historians, and sociologists interested in contemporary social life and culture.
2. Analysis of ideas, themes, and topics in documents (school class materials, teachers' guides, etc.) is known as **content analysis** and has been used most prominently by political scientists.
3. Tracing changes in human behaviour and ideas by reading available documents (old paperbacks from garage sales) is also, of course, the primary method in historical research.

The research methods we looked at in Chapters 5, 6, and 7 are **direct methods**. With the exception of nonparticipant observation, the subjects of these methods of research are aware that they are being studied. When researchers set up an experimental situation and recruit participants to be tested in some way, or interview or mail questionnaires to selected respondents, or observe and perhaps participate in a group, participants, respondents, or actors will become aware that they are being studied. As we have seen this sometimes creates difficulties for the researchers. Experimental subjects try to work out the purpose of the experiment and "help" the experiment by gearing their responses to what they think the researchers want. Survey researchers have to be extremely careful that their questions do not imply a "correct answer" or carry undertones of approval or disapproval of certain responses. Field researchers have to blend into the background if they are nonparticipant observers, or become accepted as part of the group if they participate. In either case, field researchers have to avoid changing the social activities they wish to observe. However, several research methods avoid responses from the people being studied by using indirect or nonreactive means of gathering data.

The various indirect methods of research may be used in relation to either quantitative data—data expressed in numbers and organized and interpreted statistically—or qualitative data—data expressed in words or symbols and interpreted the same way. In addition, we shall discuss secondary data analysis, the reanalysis of data that has been collected and organized for another purpose but can be of use to your own research.

UNOBTRUSIVE MEASURES

Why Do We Need Unobtrusive Measures?

Unobtrusive measurement uses the physical evidence or traces left behind by human activities. Archaeologists and physical anthropologists depend entirely on physical traces, which are the only evidence available from long-dead civilizations and ways of life. Human bones and possessions in old graves, flint chippings, arrowheads, burnt bones from leftover meals, and broken pottery as well as the remains of castles, pyramids, and palaces are all important in helping us build a picture of a human group that leaves no or few documents for us to interpret.

Social researchers studying contemporary societies can speak to people or observe them directly in action. Consequently unobtrusive measurement has not been widely used. After all, direct observation and questioning is easier and more reliable. Observations can be repeated and checked by others; questions can be pretested before being used in case study interviews or a survey. Guessing or inferring human actions and beliefs only from the traces left by human actions is extremely difficult and not highly reliable. You do not see people in action; you do not discover their attitudes or beliefs directly through questioning or speaking to them. Why use a more difficult and less reliable method when direct methods are available?

As we have seen in our student diet example, there are circumstances when a direct method of research may not be reliable. When this is the case, other methods may be substituted or used as checks on the less reliable aspects of the direct-research technique. This is the case with our example where people are "paying lip service" or trying to live up to a social norm that has wide appeal, such as healthy eating. Of course, some students may honestly believe they are eating well. Some students may be right, but others are not, perhaps because they are unaware of their habit of snacking between meals. Habitual activities that we are unaware of can be investigated using nonparticipant observational methods, as discussed in Chapter 7. Where habits also leave physical traces such as soft drink cans, chip bags, and candy wrappers, then it is possible also to use unobtrusive measures as a way to demonstrate that these habits exist and perhaps to estimate their importance or to infer connections with other aspects of social life. In one such case, urban researchers have looked at paths worn into the areas outside apartment complexes to map networks of interaction and sociability among apartment dwellers and between them and the surrounding neighbourhood.

A second area where unobtrusive measures might be useful is in the study of inarticulate groups. For example, child psychologists might visit day cares and examine toys looking for patterns of wear as a way of discovering patterns of play among infants of different ages. Such researchers might also adopt the technique of urban researchers and look for paths worn in playground areas and parks to see how children use the spaces provided for them.

A third area where unobtrusive measures could be useful is one where activities are socially disapproved of or where direct research would arouse hostility and deception. Studies of urban youth gangs might be examples here. Such studies are difficult because of the gangs' distrust of outsiders, and researchers are too old to become participant observers. Police and juvenile authorities or social workers may provide some useful information but their major concerns are the control or deterrence of gang activities, and this may bias their reports. Consequently some researchers have used indirect methods such as the analysis of graffiti to keep track of gang activity. Each gang has a turf it defines with graffiti, which have specific style and content. The graffiti operate as boundary markers, expressions of gang identity and solidarity; and the imagery reflects values and concerns of the time.

Toilet-wall graffiti have been studied by social psychologists and psychologists in an attempt to trace beliefs and attitudes that are socially disapproved of or are viewed as private and not for public expression or display. As you might expect, researchers have found sexual fantasies and obsessions, infantile preoccupations with excrement and body parts, extreme political views, racism, and bigotry are recurring themes.

Finally, perhaps the most extensive application of unobtrusive measures to the study of modern social life is in the field of industrial archaeology—a discipline that has grown rapidly since the 1960s. Unobtrusive measures are appropriate for studying human technological activities where "traces" (the wastes created by mining or manufacturing, for example), "erosions" (physical changes in the landscape created by uses such as building roads, railways, or canals, or quarrying and mining, logging, farming, etc.), or "accretions" (leftover buildings, disused machinery and tools, etc.) are left behind as the result of using the technology. Since the industrial revolution in the 18th century, technology has become an increasingly dominant part of our lives, and has changed at an increasingly rapid pace. Keeping track of these changes has become an important part of social research and more and more social research has become focused on technological change.

In industrial archaeology, looking for evidence of different technologies in such forms as disused mines, railways, or factory buildings and fragments of machinery and materials involves the use of different methods and data. Direct fieldwork and careful observation of the physical evidence (unobtrusive measures) is impossible without preliminary work with documents such as local historical records, old maps, and so on. These are needed in order to identify areas where the technology is likely to be found and to pinpoint the possible locations of surviving physical evidence. Once discovered, physical remains need to be analyzed and interpreted and again documentary and even interview-based research is necessary. Government and business records, catalogues of bankruptcy sales, postcards, and other documents are used to identify the physical items discovered. Surviving workers and their relatives (if the research is on the fairly recent past) may be interviewed to get details of day-to-day work routines and a more precise understanding of how things worked.

Advantages and Disadvantages of Unobtrusive Measures

Unobtrusive measures developed primarily as techniques for studying human behaviour without arousing reactions on the part of those being studied. The approach was developed by psychologists and social psychologists who "rediscovered" the approach used by archaeologists, physical anthropologists, and historians studying extinct societies.

Unobtrusive measures may extend the range of social phenomena that may be researched or they may provide additional data in a study that also uses direct methods of research. Such measures have the advantage of being nonreactive. Consequently where problems of interviewer effect, demand characteristics, or access to a group are likely to occur, using unobtrusive measures has considerable advantages.

However, there are several disadvantages or limitations associated with unobtrusive measures:

1. Sifting through physical traces in garbage cans, touring neighbourhoods in search of wall graffiti, and visiting such sites as parks or apartment complexes are very time consuming. This is especially true if you attempt to develop a sampling procedure in order to use statistical techniques.
2. Unobtrusive measures are similar to covert observation in the sense that you are "going behind people's backs" as a deliberate research strategy. Therefore important ethical issues concerning rights of consent and privacy are raised by this kind of research.
3. Unobtrusive measures are perhaps best used in conjunction with other methods. As archaeologists know, physical evidence by itself is very limited. The meanings and motivations, thoughts and beliefs that make up the social and cultural context of the physical traces cannot be easily or reliably inferred without additional data.

CONTENT ANALYSIS

In introducing this chapter we suggested that responses to surveys might reflect conformity to popular ideas rather than genuinely personal responses. Looking for the sources of these ideas and understanding why these ideas are so widespread would require a different research technique. Where do these ideas come from? How are they transmitted on a large scale? How are the ideas presented? What form of communication is involved? These kinds of questions lead to research into the social organization of communication; mass media;

and analysis of communicated messages, their senders and receivers or targets.

Content analysis is the systematic examination of communications or messages. Much content analysis is done on mass media such as newspapers, radio, and television programs. Because of the sheer amount of such material available, content analysis has often been identified as a quantitative technique that breaks down communications or messages into standardized units and organizes and interprets the resulting data statistically.

Content analysis can also be applied to documents other than those produced by the mass media. This has a long history; in the 17th and 18th centuries the Swedish Lutheran Church counted certain words in hymns and sermons in order to search out heretical ideas. Content analysis can also be applied not only to text but also to works of art, film, photographs, music, and even to body language. In addition content analysis is not always quantitative. Both quantitative and qualitative content analysis are concerned with discovering repeated or consistent themes and meanings in the messages that are analyzed.

In searching for themes in messages, content analysts may be looking for clues to the intentions of the broadcaster, writer, or promoter of the communication; the kind of audience the message is being aimed at; the unconscious or semiconscious influence of culture; the kinds of issues or concerns that people are focused on; or social changes and trends. To explain this more clearly let us return to our example of research on students and their diets.

An Example of Content Analysis

You have dug out your old lectures and class handouts. Perhaps you find references to books and pamphlets, and even to a video or two as well. What could you do with this material? You could read the written material and obtain and watch the videos and get an overall impression of the ideas they contain. Perhaps you could summarize these ideas to your own satisfaction and even provide some "representative" quotes in a paragraph or two in your research essay. But this summary could be easily challenged. What is the evidence? Are the quotes really representative or are they atypical? Are the quotes accurate or is their meaning distorted by being taken out of context?

In response you could tell your teacher to look at the material herself, but it is doubtful whether this would be accepted as a legitimate defence of your summary! What is required is some systematic, reliable, and objective procedure for establishing and summarizing the main ideas contained in the pamphlets, handouts, and videos. Here is where content analysis comes in. Content analysis requires repeated, careful reading or viewing so that you can break down the content into message components or units of meaning, themes, images, keywords, etc.; and if possible provide some measures of the weight or importance of these components.

Units of Meaning

To break down the material into units of meaning researchers look for items of text and images that occur repeatedly. In our example, we may find that certain foods are likely to be positively endorsed and others referred to negatively. This should be simple to identify. A second simple message might be the way diet is connected to a healthy lifestyle or health in general. In other words, what are the specific benefits that are presented as the results of healthy eating? A third fairly direct aspect of the communication could be the way health is explained. Is there a lot of jargon? Are scientific reasons or studies referred to? Are authorities on the subject—doctors, medical and biological researchers, dieticians—quoted or referred to or featured in some way?

So far the content analysis is quite straightforward, dealing with very explicit ways the messages are presented. A somewhat more complex analysis might look at the way messages are presented rather than at their direct content. Are there, for example, different ways of directing the information to male and female students? This may include differences in the language of the message, such as an emphasis on slimness and being attractive for females, as opposed to an emphasis on strength and athletic abilities where males and diet are discussed. This difference might appear in the videos as images showing males and females in clearly different activities.

Other aspects of the way messages are presented might be the use of humour and of "horror stories." What rhetorical or cinematic techniques are used? How does the text or video presentation try to be "cool" and non-adult?

Coding

Systematically breaking down documents, programs, etc. into meaningful units requires a **coding system.** A coding system is a set of rules that tells you how to distinguish the content from the medium—i.e., the meaning from the text and images. These rules are clearly laid out so that anyone following them will get identical or nearly identical results.

Once you have defined what messages or units of meaning you are looking for, you need to organize a coding sheet listing these units. As you read through the pamphlets or look at the videos you check off the messages specified on the coding sheet as they appear. You will use an identical coding sheet for every pamphlet or video, which will give you a consistent framework for identifying repeated ideas, themes, and images.

Examples of coding sheets—one for pamphlets and one for videos—are provided in Table 8.1. Both sheets concern what benefits of healthy eating are mentioned. The pamphlet coding sheet codes the number of times these benefits are mentioned. The video coding sheet also directs you to look for the way males and females in the audience are targeted and adds a new message unit to be coded: the way males and females are presented.

Many rules in a coding system may be quite simple, such as those for counting the frequency of a single word, a phrase, an image, or the space taken up by an idea or theme. Although the rules for counting may be simple there are problems with this simple type of content analysis. Do very brief appearances or mentions get counted? Is the absence of a theme or image important as a sign of a bias?

Measures

Identifying the various message components is often seen as just the first step in content analysis. You have shown that a particular message or way of presenting a message exists in a document, broadcast, video, etc., but you have not really established *how important* the message or way of presenting it is. Most content analysis attempts to show the importance of a message by quantifying the analysis. This may be done in several different ways. The number of times a message, theme, or idea is stated within a medium is the simplest. The amount of time or space taken up by a particular idea or image within the total document, broadcast, etc. is another simple measure. Identifying key words and counting the number of times they appear is yet another simple measure of importance or salience. In mass media items the importance of a message may be reflected by positioning, such as a front page location in a newspaper or prime-time broadcasting on radio or television.

The two coding sheets in Table 8.1 have columns for the number of appearances or mentions of a specific idea and columns for the relative importance of appearances or mentions. In the pamphlets, the relative importance of an idea might be measured by the amount of text

TABLE 8.1

CONTENT ANALYSIS CODING SHEETS

I. HEALTH LITERATURE

Theme	Number of mentions	Style: humorous/ serious	Target: male/female reader
Importance of a good diet			
Specific health benefits			
Athletic benefits			
Physical/social attractiveness payoffs			

II. HEALTH VIDEOS AND GENDER IMAGES

Theme	Number of minutes	Style: humorous/ serious
Social attractiveness for females		
Athleticism for females		
Other benefits for females		
Social attractiveness for males		
Athleticism for males		
Other benefits for males		

devoted to the idea as a proportion of the entire text; in videos, the measure might be the time devoted to specific images as a proportion of the length of the whole video.

Sampling

Content analysis is most often used to analyze large amounts of written, broadcast, or visual material such as newspaper reports, advertisements, films, records, and radio and television broadcasts. The only practical way of analyzing so much material is to analyze samples. In the case we have discussed, sampling may not be practical or even necessary. There may be only a few standard educational pamphlets and videos used in a region, and getting access to out-of-province materials may be very difficult. Getting access to mass-media publications or broadcasts is another matter entirely. The sheer volume of the material often forces sampling on you.

Sampling for content analysis may be a tricky matter because the units you sample and the units of observation (what you analyze) are not necessarily the same. For example, you may be interested in the way conservative versus liberal newspapers report large-scale strikes. To study this you have to select some newspapers of each political leaning, identify some major industrial strikes in a given period, and read the editorials and leading articles dealing with the strikes. You have selected a sample of issues of two types of newspapers, perhaps you have selected two or more newspapers as representing political types. Here you are sampling newspapers. What you look at and analyze with the aid of coding procedures will be editorials and articles.

Similarly, in analyzing ethnic or gender stereotyping in magazine advertising you will sample magazines but only analyze advertisements. In television studies researchers often sample types of programs but study the types of commercials in, or the sponsors of, those programs.

The method of content analysis we have explored so far is a quantitative approach. In order to analyze your findings you will need to become familiar with the techniques of quantitative data analysis outlined in Chapter 9. There is also much scope for qualitative analysis of communications images and this is what we shall now turn to.

Qualitative Content Analysis

In the course of doing your research on students' health awareness and diet, perhaps you noticed certain images in the school videos on health. All of the students appearing in these videos, male and female, were very healthy, attractive, tanned individuals who obviously worked out regularly. While very pleasing to look at they were definitely an unrepresentative sample of the students you know. It occurs to you that something is going on here that is not adequately presented in your measurement of units of meaning. The videos were presenting cultural ideals—desirable norms that are rarely achieved in real life. You begin to wonder about these ideals of physical appearance. Where do they come from? Have they changed over time?

It also occurs to you that visual images are very powerful and that in earlier times when few people read, such images would be very important. This leads you to search your textbooks in sociology, history, and anthropology for references to body images in different societies and at different times in history. These preliminary literature searches might lead you to discover historical works that use medieval paintings as sources of information on childhood and the family; that explore the ways paintings distort the human body in conformity with popular stereotypes; and that examine the persistence of images and stereotypes found in classical mythology in pre-modern art and modern advertising.

Inspired by these social interpretations of art, you decide to visit the nearest museum of fine art and try your hand at qualitative analysis of visual images. But what do you look for? You are aware that the kinds of people represented in European paintings until fairly recently were mainly religious figures or the rich and powerful. You suspect that, like contemporary fashion photographers who spend time making up their models prior to photographing them, artists were very careful in portraying their religious subjects and very flattering to the rich and powerful. But this should mean that the paintings really did show ideal images rather than realistic ones, and it is the ideal that you are searching for.

So, what do these paintings (and perhaps sculptures as well) tell you about ideals of physical beauty? What are the overall body types that are presented (thin or fat, short or tall, well muscled or soft)? What complexions and skin tones seem to be favoured? What are the textures of flesh like? Are these qualities the same for males and females? Do they change over time? What kinds of poses, activities, and settings predominate in these paintings and how do these change over time? Do you see continuities as well as changes over time? Are there continuities and parallels between images in art and contemporary advertising?

And how would you write out your findings? Would you use verbal, descriptive techniques or would you try to quantify the information? How would you measure flesh textures, or poses, or settings? Look back to the references you have found and you will find that historical writing is largely qualitative even though most historians analyze textual communications or records rather than visual images such as paintings.

Perhaps the most famous example of such historical analysis is Max Weber's *Protestant Ethic and the Spirit of Capitalism* (1958), which looks at the sermons, writings, and teachings of notable Protestant leaders to make the argument that Protestantism was a source of cultural values allowing and promoting the rise of capitalism. Weber looks at moral values, and especially the things that were identified as "evil" or "sinful" in Protestant teachings, to build up a picture of the cultural world of the different Protestant groups emerging during the Reformation. This analysis was not based on word counting or on using coding sheets. Instead, Weber used a method he called **"verstehen,"** or **interpretive understanding**. That is, he immersed himself in the writings of the Protestants in order to empathize, to experience the world as they saw it, and to explain their actions in terms of their experiences and their world view.

A similar piece of historical research is E.P. Thompson's *The Making of the English Working Class* (1963). In contrast to Weber's study, which had the advantage of looking at a literate elite (Protestant reformers, churchmen, and other leaders), Thompson was studying an underclass whose members were largely illiterate and left little documentary evidence of their own making for the historian to analyze.

Thompson wanted to discover the roots of English working-class culture and political traditions. He argued that these roots were found in their initial reactions to the new types of work being forced on them by the rise of industrial factory employment, and in criticisms of industrialism that circulated in the wider society. Thompson looked at the elite newspapers, pamphlets, letters, and other documents that complained about the difficulties of getting cooperation from the new factory workers, their lack of discipline, and their unwillingness to abandon habits of pre-factory life. For Thompson, these complaints were valuable as clues to the ways working people reacted and felt about the rise of industrial work.

At the same time radical ideas had spread to England from the French Revolution and found a sympathetic audience among craftsmen and small business people negatively affected by the rise of the new industrial system. Many of these people were literate and their pamphlets, petitions, and other documents provided Thompson with clues to an emerging political culture of opposition to and criticism of the new industrial economy.

Both Weber and Thompson used documentary sources and analyzed the content of these documents. But the techniques are qualitative, not quantitative. While there is some overlap between the two approaches (Weber looks for repeated themes or images expressing certain values or identifying certain actions as evil or sinful; Thompson looks for consistent references to factory workers' behaviour or criticisms of industrialism in middle-class pamphlets), the aims of the analyses are rather different.

Quantitative analysis aims at showing the existence of certain ideas and themes in newspapers, broadcasts, and other media and establishing how much of a presence or weight these ideas and themes have. It does this by showing how often words, phrases, or images occur, how much space or time is devoted to them, etc. Qualitative content analysis tries to show how ideas and images are interrelated into a complex meaningful whole, which in turn organizes the experiences, perceptions, and actions of individuals or groups in a particular time and place. In quantitative content analysis the emphasis is on establishing the existence and weight of units of meaning. In qualitative content analysis, breaking down and identifying units of meaning is one step in the process of interrelating these meanings into a larger, more complex whole.

Advantages and Disadvantages of Content Analysis

Content analysis can be applied to all forms of human communication. It is a method with enormous scope and can focus on very important aspects of contemporary life because of the importance of mass media in today's society. The data is all around us and is, for the most part, easily accessible. The technique is nonreactive and consequently avoids the problems of reactions to interviewers and questions found in interview-based surveys and case studies; the attempts by participants to understand and cooperate with researchers and other problems arising in experiments; and the reactions of groups subjected to observation in fieldwork.

Content analysis is an inexpensive technique, requiring patience and care rather than complex equipment or lengthy training. It is also a flexible technique in that it can be undertaken by a single researcher or by a team. The technique is flexible, as well, in another sense: it can be used as the sole or main technique or it can be used in conjunction with other research techniques. For example, content analysis is often used to code the responses to open-ended questions in surveys.

As with all research methods, content analysis requires careful preparation. The themes, ideas, or units of meaning have to be clearly identified and operationalized ahead of time. The sampling process has to be carefully thought through. What books, newspapers, magazines, and films will be selected for analysis and why? What is going to be focused on in these materials? How is the coding sheet set up? Is it clear, logical, and unambiguous? The reliability of coding is a major issue in content analysis. Does the coding sheet give consistent results? Can two different coders come up with nearly identical results using the same coding procedure?

Finally, while content analysis has developed mainly as a quantitative technique, questions of interpretation are often a major problem. Human communication is very complex. Messages may contain several layers of meaning; meanings that are ambiguous or contradictory; meanings that are deliberately or unconsciously hidden. Counting key words or phrases or visual images can be done fairly *reliably* but may not *validly* reflect the meaning of the messages.

SECONDARY DATA ANALYSIS

The indirect methods we have discussed so far work with **primary data.** That is, they either gather the data (for example by sorting and categorizing cafeteria garbage); or they use social products such as documents, videos, and television programs as data for analysis. Another very important area of nonreactive research is the use of the data already gathered by governments, corporations, and other organizations, such as censuses, financial statements, and the like. In social research such records are known as **available data;** the reorganization, analysis, and reinterpretation of such data are known as **secondary data analysis.** Secondary data analysis is also widely used to check on and often to reinterpret the published findings of other social scientists.

A study shows that there is a rise in divorce rates among couples who were under twenty-five years of age at the time of their divorce. The study considered whether the couples had children and concludes that childless couples are more likely to divorce. But you note that although the researchers provide information on how many years the couples had been married, they failed to consider this factor in their analysis. So you analyze the data these other researchers collected and take into account how long the marriage lasted. You find that most divorces occurred in the first years of marriage. Consequently, you rearranged and reanalyzed the data that other researchers collected, and arrived at another explanation: most divorces occurred in the early years of marriage when couples were more likely to be childless.

The media report that last month 44 000 new jobs were created. No mention is made of the type of jobs. You wonder whether many were part-time jobs. The source of the information is the Statistics Canada Labour Force Survey. So you decide to look up the data in the monthly publication on the labour force available in the library. As you look up the information, other questions come to mind. Has there been in the last decade a rise in the proportion of the labour force that works part time? Has there been a rise in the proportion of part-time workers who would prefer full-time work? Do youths account for an increasing proportion of part-time workers? To answer your questions you realize that you would have to analyze data from the last decade. You need not only to look up the information compiled by Statistics Canada, but to carry out further analysis of the existing data.

Carrying out an analysis on existing data involves much more than simply reporting the data. You need to arrange and analyze the data others have gathered and arrive at your own interpretations. For example, say your study is on crime in major cities of Canada. To carry out your analysis you will probably have to rely on crime statistics compiled by government and nongovernment agencies. Such data would have already been examined by researchers of these agencies. In other words you would not be the first to analyze the data. But you would use the same information to carry out some other analysis.

Studies analyzing data that already exist are quite common in the social sciences. Consider for example the economist who relies on published government data for a study on the rise in foreign direct investments in Canada; the political scientist who reanalyzes various Quebec referendum polls to contrast the voting behaviour of francophone and nonfrancophone youths; the sociologist who uses existing hospital data to determine changes in the length of time newborn babies are kept in the hospital; the psychologist who relies on official data on suicide to analyze trends among different age groups; the historian who uses 1881 and 1891 census data to establish the settlement pattern of ethnic groups in the Prairies, and so on.

Why Use Existing Data?

There are at least three reasons why social scientists analyze data gathered by others. A major reason is that the data are available, and it may be costly and possibly require enormous resources and time to re-collect the data. This is especially true in carrying out national sample surveys. Many such surveys are undertaken by or for government agencies, such as Statistics Canada. An example is the monthly Labour Force Survey, which uses a complicated sampling procedure. (For more on the Labour Force Survey see Box 5.3.) The survey's data are organized and published on a regular basis, are readily available, and could be used to carry out various analyses, such as examining changing trends in women's employment or youth unemployment.

Another reason for using existing data is to contest the interpretation the original researchers made of their data. For example, say researchers did a study on the time students spend on school work. The researchers conclude students spend very little time on homework. But you question this interpretation since the study was carried out in the third week of the semester. Students have fewer assignments and this could affect the results. You reanalyze the same data and note that most students had no written assignments. Moreover, students who did have written assignments spent more time on their homework than students who did not have such assignments. Your reanalysis of the data others gathered suggests a different interpretation of the findings.

A third reason for relying on existing data is to analyze a different issue from that studied by the original researchers. Suppose for the

Hooked on Digging into Family Lore

How's this for romantic: Ann Ward and her husband Dale, genealogy buffs both, couldn't resist digging into the National Archives on their honeymoon in 1991, where they unearthed Mrs. Ward's sixth great-grandfather from land petitions of early Ontario farm settlers.

Their hotel was only three blocks away from the archives, Mrs. Ward, a 45-year-old public health nurse and president of the Ontario Genealogical Society, recalled with a laugh.

Once the sleuthing grounds for dusty historians and academics, the National Archives have become a new frontier for Canadians in search of their ancestry.

The surge in interest is so great that genealogy now accounts for 30 to 40 per cent of the 130,000 annual inquiries to the federal archives, a substantial increase over the past decade, said Carol White, chief of genealogy and personnel records.

Genealogy how-to courses on university campuses and community colleges are thriving, while genealogical societies from British Columbia to Ontario enjoy record growth.

The Ontario genealogical Society has seen its membership climb to 6,000, including 625 new members in the past year. British Columbia's Genealogical Society has about 750 members, probably its highest membership, said president Peter Claydon, a Vancouver engineer who himself earmarks one week a year of vacation time for his own research. And Joy Doyle of the Alberta Genealogical Society said membership has grown 10 per cent this year to 900.

"It's not just getting your pedigree chart filled in," Ms. White said in an interview in her office near the Parliament Buildings. Genealogy is wanting to know "how did people live."

With its high ceilings and bright, airy rooms, the genealogy floor of the National Archives attracts beginners and hounds alike. Indeed, the lure and the lore of family history are a seductive mix. "Hooked" is how genealogists often describe themselves, and addicts in pursuit of a lead won't hesitate to phone total strangers across town or across the country—or to track tips down in cyberspace, now that the national agency has its own web site.

January and February are the boom months for genealogy inquiries to the National Archives, suggesting that trading stories at family gatherings over Christmas piques the curiosity of those who want to delve deeper into their roots.

Family historians demand everything from immigration and settlement records to passenger lists of ships that carried newcomers to Canadian shores.

If there are skeletons in the closet, justice files with court transcripts of capital cases before Canada's last hanging in 1961—complete with photographs of the crime scene—are also accessible.

Military personnel records are among the most frequently requested. They were once used almost exclusively to assess veterans' benefits and pensions, but at least 30 per cent of requests to see them now come from family members. They're curious, say, about the action grandfather saw in the First World War. His file would show where he was assigned and to which unit—and knowing the unit's name is the route to its war diaries.

While many files at the National Archives are open and available, some do carry restrictions. For example, personnel records from the Second World War and more recently are governed by federal privacy law. Release of their information requires either the subject's permission or a 20-year interval since the individual's death.

As well, census records after 1901 are off limits to the public, something the genealogical community wants changed, Ms. White said.

But census records that pre-date the turn of the century can be a valuable source, because they document medical information such as blindness, deafness and mental incompetency. And the 1901 census is particularly useful because, unlike its predecessors, it includes the year of immigration and date of birth for every individual.

"I know lots of older people who say 'I'm doing it for my grandchildren,'" noted Lorraine St-Louis Harrison, the genealogy unit's supervisor. Her own research traced her lineage to the marriage of a native Indian princess and a coureur de bois in Oka, Que., eight generations ago.

Interest in the archives is not limited to Canadians. Americans who think they may have a claim on Revolutionary history, and United Empire Loyalist blood, correspond with Ottawa seeking information.

Scott Wright, a 36-year-old Minneapolis lawyer who traced some of his descendants to Amherst Island near Kingston, learned that the Ottawa archives have a late-19th-century diary written by his great-great-grandfather.

Mr. Wright learned of the diary's existence from area locals during a trip to Amherst with his family. How the diary came into the archives' possession is a mystery, but Mr. Wright, who has a copy, said he was moved to tears by its account of the illness and death of the 11-year-old sister of his great-grandfather, who later emigrated to the United States.

Genealogists like Kathleen Eveleigh are only too happy

to swap information with distant relatives embarking on their own ancestral digs.

"It becomes addictive," said the 59-year-old Ms. Eveleigh, who lives near Cornwall, Ont. "When I started out I had no intention of doing all I had done." Like others, she relies on a variety of sources including marriage, birth and baptism dates, which can often be traced back several generations from meticulously kept church records or from notations in family bibles.

Ms. Eveleigh got her first taste of the National Archives while on a tour last fall with the genealogy class from a community college. And she's returning to the archives this month to lay the groundwork for a summer project that will take her back to her native Newfoundland to research her father's side of the family.

Like many genealogists when they start out, Ms. Eveleigh took some training—specifically, a "tracing your family history" course at Memorial University in St. John's, run through an Elderhostel program. Offered every summer, the course is a how-to guide on recording and storing data, where to find information and how to use public archives.

The course has become so popular of late that it's had a waiting list, said co-ordinator Elaine Healey. "It's nice to leave to your kids a legacy of who you are and where you are from," she said.

The Elderhostel program at Memorial attracts not only Canadians but Americans too. The July course will include residents of Ontario, Quebec, Nova Scotia, New Jersey and North Carolina.

Not only do genealogists document family trees, but they often want to confirm whether certain family stories are true. Mr. Claydon wanted to know about the death of a young relative in England in 1879, who, family lore had it, had been killed by a horse startled by a clap of thunder.

For the past eight years, the 54-year-old Vancouver genealogist has spent a week's holiday doing searches in the basement of the world-famous family-history library of the Mormons in Salt Lake City, Utah.

His sleuthing paid off. Using parish death records, he was able to find a newspaper account of an inquest into the relative's death. As it turned out, it was not thunder but the sound of a gun that startled the horse, and

the boy was killed when the horse cart loaded with coal rolled over him.

Family Viewing

Genealogy is like a piece of detective work: You start with yourself and work backwards. Experts recommend choosing the side of the family that is of the most interest—maternal or paternal—and sticking with it.

There is a limit to how far back you can go, and it varies from country to country depending on how many years back record keeping extended. Ancestors from England, for example, can be traced back a few hundred years; those from Spain, even longer.

The National Archives in Ottawa is the best place to start. With the exception of certain records governed by privacy and access-to-information legislation, most files are open. Among the documents available:

• Land petitions. These are especially useful for genealogists tracing any connection to United Empire Loyalists. The land petitions themselves may contain diary-like accounts of settlers' lives.

• The LI-RA-MA collection. These are documents created by the imperial Russian consular offices in

Canada from 1898 to 1922. The passport-identity papers series has more than 11,000 files on Russian and East European immigrants who immigrated to Canada in the first 20 years of this century. The files include passport applications and background questionnaires. However, many of the records are in Russian.

• Census records. These are in high demand, but only the census of 1901 and before are available to the public. The 1901 data, unlike those of previous years, show immigration and specific birth dates.

• Passenger lists of ships.

• Land-ownership maps.

• Early immigration files, which can have photographs.

• Certain military-personnel records.

In addition, genealogists work from birth, death, marriage and baptism records, either from public archives or church records. Family bibles can also be a source of these dates, since some contained sections to document these significant dates.

Wills are another important source and once probated are a matter of public record, according to Peter Claydon of the B.C. Genealogical Society. People rarely past decade local high schools gathered data on the destinations of their graduates. You can make use of this existing data to analyze and compare, say, the trends of female and male students who pursue post-secondary education.

Problems with Existing Data

Data you gather become meaningful only after you arrange, analyze, and interpret them. This is also true with data gathered by others. However, the existing data were gathered on the basis of assumptions and concepts of the original researchers. And while you may prefer some other information, you can do nothing about it. You have to accept the existing data as given, and, obviously, cannot change how the original researchers carried out the study. Therefore you need to put much effort into finding the shortcomings and weaknesses of the existing data and original research. And a good deal of your effort in analyzing the data is likely to rely on statistical procedures. (We cover some basic statistical techniques in Chapter 9.)

Thus, in using existing data it is essential to understand the aim and purpose of the original research. How were the data collected? What was the target population? What was the sample and how was it selected? What were the operational definitions of key variables? What were the limitations of the original research and the data collected? For example, if you were to use the published unemployment data from the Labour Force Survey, it would be crucial for you to know how the survey was carried out and the survey's operational definitions of "labour force" and "unemployment" (see Box 5.3). Although you might prefer another definition, or to ask other questions, you have no choice but to accept the unemployment data as collected by the original survey.

Part of your time in the research design will be spent finding out whether the data you need are available. Once you have found a source, you will have to familiarize yourself with the data as collected and compiled by the original researchers. Moreover, you may have to pay a fee to obtain the information you need from the agency that carried out the study. Fortunately there are numerous published sources of data on a broad spectrum of topics that may interest you and that are readily available for free. These sources can also be useful in providing background information or sources for your literature review. Suppose your study was an observation of students employed part time in a fast-food restaurant. You may want to find out whether data exist on the proportion of students who work part time, the proportion of part-time workers that are students, and the industries in which they are employed. If it exists you can use it as background information for your research.

Searching for Existing Data

Where you search for existing sources of data will depend on what kind of data you are looking for. One useful place with data on an array of topics is the government documents section of the library (see Chapter 3). Governments at all levels, as well as international agencies such as the United Nations, put out publications that include data.

Perhaps one of the most used sources of existing data in Canada is Statistics Canada, the nation's central statistical agency. It collects data on population, health, education, culture, labour force, income, economy, trade, tourism, energy, and much more. Some of its widely known programs are the Census of Population, the Labour Force Survey, the Consumer Price Index, the Gross Domestic Product, and the International Balance of Payments. No other organization, and certainly no individual, has the resources to obtain and collect much of the data compiled by Statistics Canada. It has about 100 ongoing surveys and issues nearly 700 titles a year. But one can easily find out what is available from Statistics Canada (and in the process even from other government agencies).

A valuable source is the annual *Statistics Canada Catalogue*, found in most libraries. It lists Statistics Canada publications by titles and subjects, together with a brief description of the content. Also included is the catalogue number of the publication, which you may need to locate the publication in the library (see Chapter 3). You can also examine the list of Statistics Canada publications and more on the Internet at the Statistics Canada Web site (see Box 8.1).

If you prefer to see examples of the type of data published by Statistics Canada, as well as other government agencies, look up the *Canada Year Book*, also available on CD-ROM. It contains articles on numerous topics, all accompanied by data. If the data are too limited for your needs, you can obtain more information by looking up the

BOX 8.1

Net Sites

Internet popularity has exploded in recent years. In consequence, government and nongovernment agencies are increasingly making existing data available on the Internet.

CANADA AND THE UNITED STATES

Below are two widely used government sites. However, for more information on Canada, the provinces, and municipalities, as well as for more information on the United States, see also the sites listed in Box 3.3.

Statistics Canada
http://www.statcan.ca/
Here you will find a list of Statistics Canada publications, the current and previous issues of *The Daily*, information on CANSIM, summary data on social trends and the economy, research papers, and more. There are also links to "statistical sites" of foreign governments and international agencies.

U.S. Bureau of the Census
http://www.census.gov/
The site includes population and other data on the United States as well as on state and local governments. There are also links to other U.S. government sites.

INTERNATIONAL ORGANIZATIONS

The sites listed below belong to international organizations whose data are often consulted by social scientists. The sites either provide some data or give information on where to obtain the data. Each site also has links to other relevant documents or sites.

International Labour Organization
http://www.unicc.org/ilo/

```
International Monetary Fund
gopher://gopher.imf.org/

Organization of Economic Co-operation and
Development
http://www.oecd.org/

United Nations Educational, Scientific and
Cultural Organization
http://www.unesco.org/

United Nations Headquarters
http://www.un.org/

United Nations Industrial Development
Organization
http://www.unido.org/

World Bank
http://www.worldbank.org/

The World Health Organization
http://www.who.ch./

World Trade Organization
http://www.unecc.org/wto/Welcome.html/
```

publication(s) cited. Most of the data are from Statistics Canada publications, but some are from other government agencies. For example, if you are looking for data on housing in Canada, the *Year Book* may cite data from the Canada Mortgage and Housing Corporation (CMHC) publication, *Canadian Housing Statistics*. You could search for the cited publication in the library to find out more about its content, as well as looking up other CMHC publications.

Also useful are the quarterly publications *Canadian Social Trends* (Catalogue Number 11-008), *Perspectives on Labour and Income* (Catalogue Number 75-001), and the monthly *Canadian Economic Observer* (Catalogue Number 11-010). The first two contain brief articles on some facet of Canadian society and are accompanied by ample data, mainly from Statistics Canada. The articles are helpful in finding out about what kind of data are available, as well as in illustrating how researchers carry out some simple analyses of the existing data. The *Canadian Economic Observer* is a valuable publication on data that are especially essential for economic analyses.

Census Questions

Over the next four years, Statistics Canada will shape numbers from roughly 12.4 million completed 1996 census forms into a socioeconomic portrait of Canada, identifying trends that drive everything from how provinces share $25-billion in transfer payments to what items appear on neighbourhood supermarket shelves. The glut of information that comes out of the census (the 1991 census produced 256 written and electronic reports) is distributed to other government departments, sold to the private sector and provided free of charge to about 700 libraries in the country.

What follows is a selected breakdown of [two] census questions out of the approximately 70 asked in the long form sent to one-fifth of Canadian households.

Question 5:

Marital Status

Who wants the question asked: Eight federal agencies and departments, including Health, Justice and Status of Women; all provinces and territories; the Canada Assistance Plan, Canada Pension Plan and National Advisory Council on Aging; Canadian Human Rights Commission; Statistics Canada advisory committees on demographic and health studies; Canadian Ethnocultural Council; three university sociology and family-studies departments and the cities of Calgary, Edmonton, Laval, Montreal and Richmond, among others.

Who they are trying to find out about: Who is single, married, divorced, widowed or separated. Seniors and single-parent families are of particular interest to analysts.

What they do with the information: It is used to prepare population, family and household estimates and track trends in those areas. Family data help create the Statistics Canada "Profiles" series, among the most widely studied materials produced by the agency. All communities with more than 250 people are profiled as part of provincial and regional studies in terms of labour-force activity, housing costs, ethnic origins, language and income. The detailed cross-sections are essential planning tools for municipalities, marketers, health-care providers and educators.

Question 6:

Is this person living with a common-law partner?

Who wants the question asked: Ten federal agencies and departments, including Canadian Heritage, Environment Canada, the Royal Commission on Aboriginal Peoples, and Veterans Affairs Canada; all provinces and territories; the Canada Assistance Plan; Canada Pension Plan; Canadian Human Rights Commission; Law Reform Commission of Canada; Population, Household and Family Estimates Program; National Advisory Council on Aging; Statistics Canada advisory committees on demographic and health statistics; the cities of Calgary, Edmonton, Laval, Montreal, Richmond and Vancouver;

four university sociology and family-studies departments; the Greek Orthodox Diocese of Canada and the Vanier Institute of the Family, among others.

Who are they trying to find out about: Those in common-law relationships, as well as seniors and single-parent families.

What they do with the information: The changing structure of the family is one of the most highly charged issues today, and is of keen interest to planners of social policy.

The Ottawa-based Vanier Institute of the Family, for example, uses family-related census data to fuel reports about family trends, child care, new reproductive technologies and family benefits. The institute, which advocates improving health, education and financial support for families, finds the census to be "the biggest, most expensive and most important instrument for us," said Bob Glossop, the Institute's executive director of programs.

Source: Sean Silcoff, excerpted from "Census Feeds Passion for Data," *The Globe and Mail* (11 May 1996) p. A6. Reprinted with permission.

Newly released data and a list of StatsCan's most recent publications are found in *The Daily*, published from Monday to Friday each week. *The Daily* has been published since 1932, but is now only available on the Internet (see Box 8.1). Issues are accessible for at least the previous six months and it has a key word search feature. If you want to find out if data exists on homicides in Canada, you can use "homicide" as a key word. You will then get a list of back issues of *The Daily* in which the word appears. (If you do not have access to the Internet you may want to look up the *Infomat*, Catalogue Number 11-002, a weekly publication that highlights the major reports and publications released during the week.)

Various **databases** are available that provide an enormous amount of information about Canada. Here we note three, all of which are available on CD-ROM. A popular and relatively easy-to-use database is E-STAT, which was developed mainly for students and teachers in secondary schools. It provides economic and social data (selected from CANSIM; more on this database shortly), and census data. The latest edition also includes data from a World Health Organization international survey on 11-, 13-, and 15-year-olds, 1991 Census of Agriculture profiles, and data from the 1991 Aboriginal People's survey at the provincial level. Like *The Daily*, this database has a key word function which enables the user to quickly search for data. The data can be rearranged and displayed in tabular, graphic, and map form.

The 1991 Census Profiles on CD-ROM contains demographic, housing, family, and economic data for Canada, the provinces, and subprovincial areas taken from the census. It is easy to learn how to use, and as with the other databases, the data can be displayed and manipulated or downloaded into a user-owned spreadsheet program. The census data are also available in print. The advantage of the CD-ROM version is largely the fact that all the data is available on a single disk.

CANSIM stands for Canadian Socioeconomic Information Management System. It contains about 665 000 variables of current and historical socioeconomic data collected by Statistics Canada and other agencies, such as the Bank of Canada. CANSIM is available in various forms, but the most accessible is the CD-ROM version. It is less user-friendly than E-STAT, and may initially be overwhelming because of the amount of information available. Therefore, you may need to spend some time becoming familiar with the search process. However, the process is simplified by the key word and topic search capability. The data can be rearranged and displayed in tabular or graphic form. Or, you can download and export the data into your own spreadsheet program. The CD-ROM version of CANSIM also contains information on the surveys carried out by Statistics Canada and the list of publications in the Statistics Canada Catalogue. (For more information on data available in CANSIM see the Statistics Canada Web site.)

WHAT YOU HAVE LEARNED

- Special techniques have been developed to help overcome the problem of human reactions to being observed, surveyed, or experimented with.

- Unobtrusive measures are useful for studying habitual actions, inarticulate or hostile groups, socially disapproved attitudes and emotions, and technological, architectural, and material traces of human life.

- Content analysis focuses on human communications and can be used in combination with both quantitative and qualitative data analysis.

- Available data use takes advantage of existing data generated for other purposes or for previous research and can be used to settle research disputes, to present alternative interpretations of other research data, or as the basis for an entirely different approach to the data.

- Computer technology is increasing the range of data available and making it easier to search for data.

KEY WORDS

nonreactive (indirect)
research methods

unobtrusive measurement

content analysis

direct research methods

coding system

verstehen (interpretive
understanding)

primary data

available data

secondary data analysis

database

REVIEW QUESTIONS

1. Why have indirect and nonreactive methods of studying social phenomena been developed?
2. When are unobtrusive research methods useful? What is the major difficulty with such techniques?
3. Why have unobtrusive measures become increasingly used in the study of modern industrial societies?
4. What kinds of questions can be answered through the technique of content analysis?
5. What is a "unit of meaning"? Try to think of examples drawn from different kinds of communications media.
6. What is coding? How would coding procedures apply to the different kinds of media referred to in the preceding question?
7. What sampling processes and problems might emerge in analyzing the different kinds of media referred to in questions 5 and 6?
8. How does measurement apply to the different kinds of media in the preceding questions?
9. What are some important difficulties associated with content analysis?
10. Why do social scientists analyze data gathered by others?
11. In order to use existing data, what do you need to understand or find out about that data?

RECOMMENDED READINGS

Goldman, R. (1992). *Reading ads socially*. New York: Routledge.

Systematically analyzes the ways women are portrayed and the appeals advertisers make to youth.

Webb, E. T., Campbell, D. T., Schwartz, R. D., Sechrest, L., & Grove, J. B. (1981). *Nonreactive measures in the social sciences*. Boston: Houghton Mifflin.

An extensive presentation of the great variety of unobtrusive measures that are possible. Presents a well-balanced discussion of the limitations of these measures as well as the ethical problems associated with their use.

Weber, R. P. (1985). *Basic content analysis*. Beverly Hills, CA: Sage.

A beginner's guide to content analysis which identifies the kinds of topics and data suitable for the approach and presents the techniques that may be used.

McKie, C. & Thompson, K. (Eds.). (1990). *Canadian social trends*. Toronto: Thompson Educational Publishing.

Canadian social trends: A Canadian studies reader (Vol. 2). (1994). Toronto: Thompson Educational Publishing.

These two volumes contain short articles, mainly from the Statistics Canada quarterly *Canadian Social Trends*, published since 1986. The articles are largely based on Statistics Canada data and are written for the general public. Aside from the wealth of information on Canada, these articles provide an insight into the kind of secondary data research one can carry out with Statistics Canada data.

CHAPTER 9

What Are the Results?

WHAT YOU WILL LEARN

- how to code primary data
- how to organize and analyze quantitative data
- how to organize and analyze qualitative data

Once you have finished collecting the data, you are faced with the challenge of making sense of it and of answering your research question or determining if there is support for your hypothesis. This chapter explores how to summarize and present your data and briefly covers some basic statistical concepts. The chapter is divided into two main sections, the first is concerned with the analysis of quantitative data and the second with qualitative data.

ANALYZING QUANTITATIVE DATA

The preceding chapters have introduced you to several important research methods. These methods are techniques for discovering or producing factual information of good quality—i.e., information that is accurate, objective, reliable, and open to others for inspection, critical evaluation, and replication. However, facts do not speak for themselves; they are clear only when they are summarized and analyzed.

Research designs are so efficient at producing information that the sheer quantity of data can overwhelm researchers unless care is taken with organization and analysis. A small survey of 100 people using a twenty-five-question questionnaire will have at least 2500 "bits" of information. This is too much to look at casually and find patterns and relationships among the bits at a glance. Laboratory experiments normally involve measuring responses of dozens of subjects, which produces hundreds of pieces of data. Using available data, such as the census or Labour Force Survey, brings you face to face with an immense accumulation of facts and figures, often extending back into the last century. These **raw data** (figures and information that have not yet been summarized or interpreted) need to be organized, condensed, and presented so that overall patterns in the data (along with any striking exceptions and puzzling deviations) are brought out clearly from the mass of details.

Coding

The first step in data analysis is to code or translate the primary data from its raw forms into more conveniently analyzable and manageable forms. Nowadays this usually involves reorganizing the raw data into a form that is easy to analyze using computers. Coding involves using a set of rules to regroup the data into categories identified by numbers. The codes lead to consistency and a standardized way of allocating each bit of raw data into its appropriate numbered category.

In some instances the coding process is relatively straightforward. For example, survey researchers often **precode** many of the questions in their questionnaires. The code categories are included in the questionnaire before collecting the data. The checkoff boxes of the answers would be numbered, as in the following question:

```
What sex are you?
     Male        □ 1
     Female      □ 2
```

Males are coded as 1 and females as 2. Thus, precoding can save time when it comes to summarizing the data. It is not always possible to precode, and in such instances researchers will have to **postcode**, or create a coding system after the data are collected.

Regardless of when researchers develop the coding system, coding involves classifying responses into categories and assigning each a code. Let us say that you have information on the marital status of those who took part in your study. You first need to decide which categories to use. Will you include separate categories or a single category for divorced and separated? Will you include a separate category for cohabiting? And so on. Once you have decided on the categories they are then coded. For example, you may decide to use the following categories and codes:

```
1 = single, never married
2 = cohabiting
3 = married, living with spouse
```

```
4 = separated
5 = divorced
6 = widowed
9 = no answer
```

Thus, an individual who is divorced, for instance, is coded as 5 with regard to marital status. It is possible that you have no information on the individual's marital status. In such a case use a number or combination of numbers that cannot be confused with other codes. In the above categories, 9 is used to indicate no response.

Deciding on categories and assigning codes can be a simple process. But for some social science research coding can be more difficult. It may not be possible to precode "verbiage" or textual information, such as answers to open-ended questions on a questionnaire. Laboratory notes describing reactions of individuals in solving tasks under competitive versus cooperative conditions may involve detailed descriptions of behaviour and interactions which require a lot of interpretation. In such cases coding may involve identifying common patterns across sentences, phrases, and paragraphs. Coding responses to open-ended questions usually involves classifying a wide variety of individual statements into a narrow range of categories. This kind of coding is identical to content analysis, discussed in Chapter 8.

Consider an open-ended survey question such as "What type of music do you most enjoy listening to?" Respondents might identify their favourite group, artist, or recording, or they might describe the type of music they like. There could be almost as many different answers as respondents. Let us say that you want to identify a pattern between the music respondents enjoy listening to and the amount they spend on buying CDs. You therefore need to develop a reliable way of combining responses into categories of music. You decide what these categories will be. Let us say you are specifically interested in comparing the spending habits of those who enjoy listening to rock, jazz, classical, and country. You may therefore decide to use the following categories and codes:

```
1 = rock
2 = jazz
3 = classical
4 = country
5 = other
9 = no answer
```

You now face the task of reading the answers to the open-ended question and deciding in which category to code the music the respondent most enjoys listening to. If the respondent lists a group, an artist, or a recording, it is your task to determine which category the response belongs in. Suppose a respondent enjoys listening to worldbeat or tango, then the category would be "other," number 5. But what if the respondent gives as an answer the CDs of Pavarotti and friends, which include Bryan Adams and other artists whom you would categorize under rock? You may have to read the answers to the question first, and then reconsider your categories. For example, you may decide to include another category, called "mixed."

Coding, then, involves processing raw data using a standardized set of codes to classify the data into numerically labelled categories. The coding scheme should be organized in terms of the specific focus of the research. There is also one other basic rule of coding: always leave the data in a more detailed state than you need for your analysis. The data can always be simplified at a later stage. For example, if you find few differences between separated and divorced respondents in a survey of family life as you analyze your data, you may decide to combine them into a "separated or divorced" category. But had you coded this group together at the outset and then found that there seemed to be differences between them you would have to scrap your analysis and return to the initial coding stage.

Data Summary

Now that you have determined the categories and coded the data, you are ready to summarize the data. There are various ways to do this. One possibility is to use a computer spreadsheet program (see Box 9.1). For example, suppose you were doing a data summary of the three questions above. Assume question one establishes the sex of the respondent, question two the marital status, and question three the type of music the respondent enjoys listening to. Your data summary sheet might look like this:

Respondent No.	Sex	Marital Status	Music	etc ...
01	2	3	1	
02	1	5	4	
03	2	1	1	
etc ...				

Thus, respondent number 01 (row 01), is coded 2 for sex (column A) and is therefore female, is coded 3 for marital status (column B) and is therefore married and living with spouse, and is coded 1 for music (column C) and therefore enjoys listening to rock. What could you say about the second and third respondents? (As you may have noted the summary sheet we are using is similar in design to a computer spreadsheet. See Box 9.1.)

BOX 9.1

The Spreadsheet

The computer has become a basic tool in organizing, summarizing, and analyzing data. Various powerful statistical software programs exist for data analysis, including the Statistical Package for Social Sciences (SPSS). However, for less sophisticated statistical analysis, a **spreadsheet** program may be sufficient, such as Lotus 1-2-3, QuattroPro, or Excel. Next to word processing, the spreadsheet is the most widely used computer tool.

The spreadsheet allows you to place the data in rows and columns. As illustrated below the rows are numbered from one on, and the columns are labelled with letters from A on. The number of rows and columns available will depend on the program, but most have hundreds of rows and columns, far more than you are likely to need.

	A	B	C	D	E	F	G
1							
2							
3							
4							
5							

CELL D2

The place in which you store information is known as a **cell.** It is identified by the position of the column and row. For example, D2 is column D, row 2.

The information included in the cell can be numbers, labels, or formulas. The numbers can be whole numbers or decimals. The labels can be symbols or words. For example, in a particular cell you may want to include the heading of a series of numbers in either a column or a row. One of the main advantages of the spreadsheet is its ability to provide a formula that will display the calculation of the values contained in the cells. For example, you can total the numbers in a column by simply providing the formula in a cell and indicating which cells to add up. The program rapidly adds the values in the other cells and displays the sum in the cell in which you stated the formula.

Spreadsheets have powerful capabilities that allow for quick organization and calculation of the numeric data. They have a variety of summary statistics that, for example, enable you to easily find the mean, the standard deviation, and more. In addition, spreadsheets allow you to create line graphs, bar charts, and pie charts.

Thus, the spreadsheet can simplify the task of organizing, calculating, and presenting your data. But you still need to be clear about how you are organizing the data, why you are carrying out certain calculations, and whether the data are clearly presented.

The next challenge is to organize the data. Assume you want to summarize the information on one variable, say the music respondents enjoy listening to. When summarizing and analyzing data derived from one variable we are carrying out a **univariate analysis.** You can simply add up the number of respondents for each category and present what is called a **frequency distribution**. (The symbol for frequency is the small letter *f.*) However, rather than present the raw data, you may also prefer to summarize the information as a percentage distribution. For example, assume we have eighty-three respondents in our sample and thirty-one enjoy listening to rock music. You could turn the raw data (31) into a percentage ($31/83 \times 100 = 37.3$). The distributions are illustrated in Table 9.1.

Note that the table is numbered (Table 9.1), titled, and the units of measurements stated (f = frequency and % = percent). Consider how you were able to organize the data in such a way that it facilitates what you will say about the results. At a glance, for instance, you can say that 12 percent of respondents enjoy listening to jazz.

TABLE 9.1

FREQUENCY DISTRIBUTION OF TYPE OF MUSIC ENJOYED

Type of Music	f	%
Rock	31	37.3
Jazz	10	12.0
Classical	9	10.8
Country	8	9.6
Other	20	24.1
No answer	5	6.0
Total	83	100

With such data as type of music, which are simply labelled, it may not matter in which order the information is listed in the table. However, some categories have to be presented from lowest to highest, or from highest to lowest, such as grades, income, or levels of education. There may be many scores, and these may be widely spread out. In such instances a simple frequency distribution would be quite difficult to read. Instead you would want to present a cumulative frequency distribution. For more information see Box 9.2.

Levels of Measurement

The data collected for our research are not all measured in the same way. In addition to the already noted variables on sex, marital status, and type of music, you may have information on age, how much is spent on CDs, the respondents' preferred radio stations, their occupations, incomes, and so on. Clearly, an individual is either male or female, but one can be older or younger by so many years than another individual, or earn thousands of dollars more or less than someone else. These data (sex, age, income, etc.) differ in terms of their levels of measurement. *Measurement* refers to sorting out or making distinctions between observations in terms of differences in some specific characteristic(s). Levels of measurement differ depending on the amount and kind of information they provide (see Exhibit 9.1).

With a variable such as music preference, respondents answer in words: "rock," "jazz," and so on. The musical preference variable, then, is measured by being sorted and labelled by these words—a process of

BOX 9.2

Cumulative Frequency Distribution

Suppose you had the grade distribution of students in a class. (We will assume they all scored over 50 percent.) If you wanted to provide a simple frequency distribution, you would make the following table:

TABLE A

FREQUENCY DISTRIBUTION OF GRADES
(35 STUDENTS)

Grades	f	Grades	f	Grades	f	Grades	f	Grades	f
100	0	90	0	80	1	70	0	60	0
99	0	89	0	79	0	69	0	59	0
98	0	88	0	78	2	68	2	58	0
97	1	87	1	77	1	67	2	57	0
96	0	86	2	76	1	66	1	56	1
95	1	85	1	75	2	65	1	55	1
94	0	84	0	74	1	64	0	54	1
93	1	83	2	73	1	63	3	53	0
92	0	82	0	72	2	62	1	52	0
91	0	81	0	71	0	61	1	51	1

As you can see, this table is quite lengthy with many scores having no frequency. If it is not necessary to show the exact score of each student in your table, then you could make it more presentable by condensing the scores into small groups of scores. For example, you could group the data into smaller equal groups, such as the number of scores that fall between 91 and 100, 81 and 90, and so on. In this way you could construct a grouped frequency distribution, as in Table B below. (What would be the grouped frequency distribution if the groups were 96 to 100, 91 to 95, 86 to 90, and so on?)

TABLE B

GROUPED FREQUENCY DISTRIBUTION OF GRADES (35 STUDENTS)

Grade	f	%
91–100	3	8.6
81–90	6	17.1
71–80	11	31.4
61–70	11	31.4
51–60	4	11.4
Total	35	100

The frequency is indicated for each group. For example, three students had scores that were between 91 and 100. As with the simple frequency distribution it might be more appropriate to also present the percentage distribution, especially if you were making a comparison between two or more sets of scores. The percentage distribution is shown in column three. (Note that the total percentage of the numbers displayed in the table is 99.9 percent. However, we write 100 percent since the difference of 0.1 percent was lost in the rounding.)

Often it may be more useful to present the frequencies in a cumulative way. For example, you could present the distributions to show how many students scored above or below a certain score. A **cumulative frequency distribution** (cf) allows you to locate the proportion of observations above or below a given point very easily (see Table C). As you move up from the lowest score to the next lowest you add the number of students who obtained each score. To illustrate, we will continue to use the scores in the above grouped frequency distribution table. The cumulative frequency for a group is obtained by adding up the scores in that group with the scores of all the other groups below it. For example, four students scored from 51 to 60 and since no other group of scores exists below this group then 4 is its frequency distribution. The number of students who scored from 61 to 70 is 11. The cumulative frequency for this group is therefore 15—that is, 11 for the group plus the 4 of the group below it. Consequently, we can tell that 15 students scored 70 percent or lower. (How many students scored 80 percent or lower?)

TABLE C

CUMULATIVE FREQUENCY DISTRIBUTION OF GRADES (35 STUDENTS)

Grade	f	%	cf	c%
91–100	3	8.6	35	100.0
81–90	6	17.1	32	91.4
71–80	11	31.4	26	74.3
61–70	11	31.4	15	42.9
51–60	4	11.4	4	11.4
Total	35	100		

We can also construct the cumulative percentage (c%) of the distribution. Instead of showing the number of students we can show the percentage of students who had a certain score or lower. To determine the c% we calculate the percentage of the cf. For example, the grouped frequency distribution of the scores 51 to 60 is 4. Therefore, we determine what is the percentage of 4 over the total 35 ($100 \times 4/35 = 11.4$). The group frequency distribution of the scores from 61 to 70 is 15 and we calculate the percentage of 15 over the total 35, which gives us 42.9 ($100 \times 15/35 = 42.9$). Consequently, we can say that about 43 percent of the students scored 70 percent or lower. (What can we say about the other groups of scores?)

classification. This is measuring data at a **nominal level of measurement;** respondents are identified by their main musical preference and each is put into their appropriate musical preference category. Similarly, when you ask for the sex of respondents in a questionnaire, you divide the responses into male and female. Nominal measurement organizes the data into groups or categories that are mutually exclusive (either rock, jazz, or classical). It allows the researcher to count the numbers in each group, as was done in Table 9.1, for example. Hence, simple counting and percentages can be applied to variables at the nominal level of measurement.

Now suppose you have information on whether individuals strongly agree, agree, disagree, or strongly disagree with banning a CD that has a violent message. You are able to count how many are in each

EXHIBIT 9.1
Levels of Measurement

Nominal Scale Example: "Type of Music Listened To"

Jazz   Rock   Classical

Ordinal Scale Example: Musical preference

First choice   Second choice   Third choice

Interval Scale Example: Temperature

-5°C   5°C   15°C   25°C

Ratio Scale Example: Income

0    $10 000 $20 000 $30 000 $40 000 $50 000

category, but you are also able to rank the categories in terms of a range of agreement/disagreement. Some strongly agree while others agree, and so on. This allows you not only to divide people into groups, as with nominal measurement, but also to make a "more or less" comparison between the groups in terms of the specific characteristic agreement or disagreement. Whereas nominal measurement provides you with one piece of information—the different groups—the ordinal measure provides you with two pieces of information—the different groups and their ranking along a specific dimension. As with nominal measures you can count the numbers of respondents in each group and calculate a percentage of these numbers. This is an **ordinal level of measurement.** It allows you to count how many are in each category and rank the categories. However, it does not allow you to say how much of a difference there is between the categories. For instance, we do not know whether the difference between "strongly agree" and "agree" is the same as the difference between "strongly disagree" and "disagree."

The **interval level of measurement** permits you to indicate how much of a difference exists between one group and another. It allows you to rank observations or data on a scale with regular intervals, and to identify differences with greater precision. Interval measurement provides you with three items of information: a difference or distinction, a "more or less than" comparison, and a quantitative measurement of how much more or less.

However, there is one thing that an interval measure cannot do, and that is express one score as a proportion or ratio of another. We cannot say that Tuesday was twice as warm as Monday or that Ian, whose IQ score is 100, is only 80 percent as intelligent as Ellen, whose IQ score is 125. Conventional temperature scales and IQ measures have no **true zero.** Many days in the year have below-zero temperatures; and anyone who can read and write can take an intelligence test and will get some points on it, so a true zero is impossible to establish. Where a true zero can exist we can use a **ratio level of measurement,** which specifies both the difference in rank and the ratio numerically. For example, if John spent $25 on CDs and Mary spent $50, we can say that Mary spent $25 more than John and also that she spent twice as much. Or again, if Ellen has had fourteen years of formal education while Ian has had only seven, we can say both that Ellen has seven more years of education than Ian and that Ian has had half the education that Ellen has. The characteristics of different levels of measurement are summarized in Table 9.2.

Why do we need to be concerned with the levels of measurement of variables? The level of measurement affects how we organize and

TABLE 9.2

CHARACTERISTICS OF DIFFERENT LEVELS OF MEASUREMENT

Characteristics	Levels of Measurement			
	Nominal	Ordinal	Interval	Ratio
Classifying into mutually exclusive categories	X	X	X	X
Rank ordering		X	X	X
Equal and measured spacing			X	X
Comparing scores as ratios of each other				X

analyze the data. As we shall see, certain statistical techniques require variables that meet certain minimum levels of measurement. For example, we noted earlier that the variable, "type of music respondents preferred listening to" is a variable at the nominal level of measurement. Look at the frequency distribution in Table 9.1. Can you say what type of music on average the respondents enjoy listening to? Or, is it more appropriate to ask which music *most* respondents enjoy listening to? What if instead you asked the same question about the amount of money they spent on CDs? To understand this further, let us consider measures of central tendency.

Measures of Central Tendency

At times researchers may want to have a single number that summarizes certain information. One such number is known as a measure of **central tendency,** since it is usually located toward the centre around a value where most of the data are concentrated. An example would be the class average on an exam—a single number that summarizes all the grades in the class. In everyday conversation the term "average" is used loosely to compare things. We get a sense of how our friends performed on a class test in order to judge whether our own performance was above or below average. We may compare a new pizza service with our old favourite and say it's "about average." Used this way the term average may mean "like," or "similar to," "not very exciting," or "disappointing." Researchers require more precise terms and in fact use several different kinds of measures of central tendency, or average, which can differ in value for the same set of data. The three best-known measures of central tendency are the mode, the median, and the mean.

The Mode

The **mode** is the most frequent value in a distribution. For example, in the frequency distribution in Table 9.1 more respondents listened to rock music than to any of the other types of music. For another illustration suppose you had the following information on the daily number of hours persons who enjoy country music listen to the radio: 1, 1, 5, 6, 1, 5, 2. The mode is 1, since it occurs more often than any other score.

The mode can be used with nominal, ordinal, interval, and ratio levels of measurements. It is the only measure of central tendency available for nominal level variables such as the "type of music respondents enjoy listening to," sex of respondents (male, female), or marital status (single, widowed, divorced, etc.).

However, the mode is a rough measure of central tendency. In some instances there may be no mode, or there may be more than one mode; in such a case all of them need to be noted.

The Median

The **median** is the middle point in a frequency distribution. It is the point at which half the cases or scores are above and half are below. Again let us take the following distribution of daily number of hours a set of persons listen to the radio: 1, 1, 5, 6, 1, 5, 2. Which would be the median score? To determine the median, first rank the scores from the lowest to the highest: 1, 1, 1, 2, 5, 5, 6. Next, locate the score that is in the middle, that splits the distribution into two equal parts. In the total seven scores, two is the median since there are three scores below it and three above.

But what if there is an even number of cases, say eight scores? Again the median separates the scores down the middle; find the two middle values and calculate their average. To illustrate, say we have the following eight scores: 1, 1, 1, 2, 5, 5, 6, 7. The two middle values are two and five. The median is their average—that is: $(2 + 5) \div 2 = 3.5$.

The median can be used to measure ordinal, interval, or ratio data, such as age, how much respondents spend on CDs, or how many hours they listen to the radio. It is especially useful when you need to know what the representative middle number is of a distribution.

What's Wrong with These Numbers?

We tend to invest statistics with tremendous authority. But like any other information, how useful they are depends on how and why they are collected.

These numbers were compiled from records collected and distributed every day to the media by the Metropolitan Toronto Police. *Globe and Mail* reporter Gay Abbate sifted through each day's records for 1992 and 1993 and picked out robberies and attempted robberies and the victim's description of each robber. She then sorted the suspected robbers into groups according to the race the police had recorded for each. (Toronto police are not allowed to compile such data themselves.)

The Globe and Mail attempted this exercise to show the difficulties in collecting statistics by race. While the chart conveys some information, the overwhelming number of caveats shows how unreliable such numbers can be.

Many people think any attempt to link crime with the skin colour of a suspect is spurious. Others believe that if the method of collecting them were improved, they could say a great deal about discrimination against a particular group.

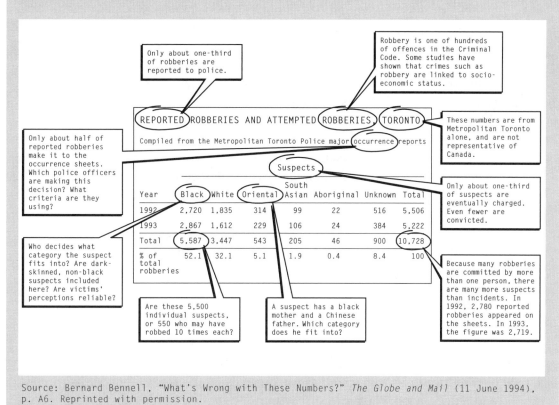

Only about one-third of robberies are reported to police.

Robbery is one of hundreds of offences in the Criminal Code. Some studies have shown that crimes such as robbery are linked to socio-economic status.

Only about half of reported robberies make it to the occurrence sheets. Which police officers are making this decision? What criteria are they using?

These numbers are from Metropolitan Toronto alone, and are not representative of Canada.

Only about one-third of suspects are eventually charged. Even fewer are convicted.

Who decides what category the suspect fits into? Are dark-skinned, non-black suspects included here? Are victims' perceptions reliable?

Are these 5,500 individual suspects, or 550 who may have robbed 10 times each?

A suspect has a black mother and a Chinese father. Which category does he fit into?

Because many robberies are committed by more than one person, there are many more suspects than incidents. In 1992, 2,780 reported robberies appeared on the sheets. In 1993, the figure was 2,719.

REPORTED ROBBERIES AND ATTEMPTED ROBBERIES TORONTO

Compiled from the Metropolitan Toronto Police major occurrence reports

Suspects

Year	Black	White	Oriental	South Asian	Aboriginal	Unknown	Total
1992	2,720	1,835	314	99	22	516	5,506
1993	2,867	1,612	229	106	24	384	5,222
Total	5,587	3,447	543	205	46	900	10,728
% of total robberies	52.1	32.1	5.1	1.9	0.4	8.4	100

Source: Bernard Bennell, "What's Wrong with These Numbers?" *The Globe and Mail* (11 June 1994), p. A6. Reprinted with permission.

The Mean

A popular measure of central tendency is the arithmetic **mean,** which is commonly known as the average. The mean is calculated by adding up the values of the distribution and then dividing by the total number of values. The mean of the earlier distribution of daily hours persons listen to the radio is:

$$\frac{1 + 1 + 5 + 6 + 1 + 5 + 2}{7} = 3$$

The calculation of the mean can be summarized by the following formula:

$$\overline{X} = \frac{\Sigma X}{N}$$

$\overline{X}$ = the symbol for the mean, pronounced "X bar"

Σ = the Greek capital letter "sigma" or the "sum of," which indicates that we must add up the values that follow

X = the raw score in the set of scores

N = the total number of scores

In other words, the arithmetic mean (X, or 3) is equal to the sum of (Σ) raw scores (X_1, X_2, X_3, and so on, or 1, 1, 5 and so on) divided by the total number of scores (N, or 7).

Although the mean is widely used, in certain instances it may not be particularly helpful. For example, suppose you wanted to calculate the mean amount of money respondents who enjoy country music spend on CDs in a month. Your eight respondents each spend the following (expressed in dollars): 10, 15, 20, 20, 10, 10, 15, 300. What is the mean? The answer is $50, but does this appropriately reflect the distribution? One respondent spent $300, far more than the other seven added together. If we omitted the extreme score of $300 the mean for the remaining seven would be $14.29, a figure that seems much more representative. In other words, the mean can be affected by extremely large or small scores.

Comparing the Mode, Median, and Mean

Which measure social scientists use depends on the research objective and especially on which measure is appropriate. The mode can be used with nominal, ordinal, interval, and ratio levels of measurement. For example, you would want to use the mode to determine the preferred radio station of the largest number of respondents. The median requires that we rank the categories from lowest to highest and therefore cannot be used for nominal data, but can be used for ordinal, interval, and ratio data. For example, you can determine the median income of respondents, but it would be impossible to give a median of nominal data such as sex, preferred radio station, or type of music. The mean is used with interval and ratio data. For example, it makes sense to compute the mean age of the respondents, but it would be meaningless to compute the mean sex of the respondents.

When the mode, median, and mean are equal then the scores have a **normal distribution**—that is, they follow a bell-shaped curve (see Exhibit 9.2). Many physical and psychological characteristics are normally distributed. Few of us are very small (for our age) or extremely large, or very obtuse or very smart. Most of us are "around the average" for common physical and psychological characteristics.

Many social characteristics, however, are not symmetrical in their distribution patterns. More people live in poverty than are very rich; the proportions of the population in different age groups or with different levels of education are not symmetrical. In such cases the mode, median, and mean are quite different. If such features of social life were to be represented graphically, the results would be asymmetrical, or skewed. (see Exhibit 9.2). Some scores pile up in one direction giving the curve a pronounced "bulge" and an equally marked tail. A **negatively skewed distribution** pattern has a much larger tail on the left. This distribution might represent our aging population, with a very small proportion of infants and children, and the aging baby boomers prominently showing up off-centre to the right. A **positive skew** is the reverse, with a clear tail on the right and the bulk of scores on the left. This would probably be the shape of income distribution in our society, showing the tiny numbers of the very rich, and the bulk of the population in the middle and lower income groups.

Measures of Dispersion

Although the mode, median, and mean can be useful summaries of the data, they do not tell us how widely spread the values are.

To illustrate the usefulness of knowing the spread of values, calculate the means of these two sets of scores:

```
Set A:  10, 10, 14, 16, 17, 20, 25
Set B:  12, 13, 14, 16, 18, 19, 20
```

EXHIBIT 9.2
Normal and Skewed Distributions

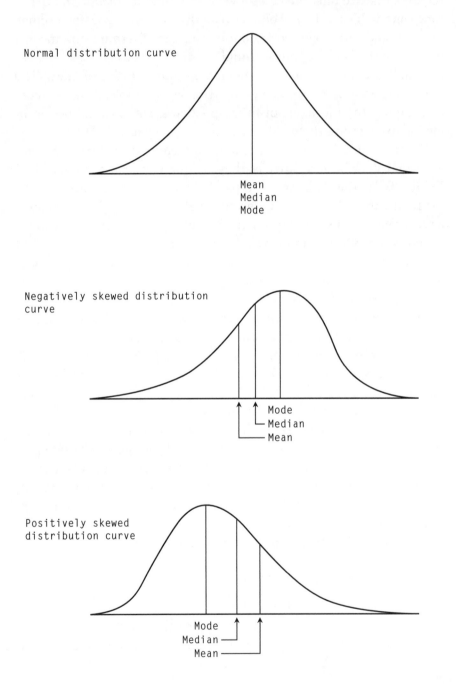

Normal distribution curve

Mean
Median
Mode

Negatively skewed distribution
curve

Mode
Median
Mean

Positively skewed
distribution curve

Mode
Median
Mean

Both have the same mean (X = 16). However, as you can see, the scores in the first set are more spread out than the scores in the second set. Thus it helps to know what the spread was, and for that there are at least three measures: range, variance, and standard deviation.

Range

The **range** is simply the difference between the lowest and highest scores. Although the two sets above have the same mean, the range for set A is 15 (25 –10), and for set B it is 8 (20 –12). If all we knew was that the two sets had the same mean and that the range was smaller in set B, we might be inclined to see the mean of set B as more reflective of the scores in that set than is the mean of the scores in set A. But the range gives only a rough sense of the spread of the values. Although the range is simple to calculate, its main disadvantage is that it only takes into account the two extreme scores. For the earlier example of money spent on CDs (10, 15, 20, 20, 10, 10, 15, 300) the range of $290 gives us an impression of enormous differences in expenditure. Yet in all but one case the range is only $10.

Variance and Standard Deviation

As we noted earlier, the mean is commonly used in everyday situations. One such situation is when we want to know the class mean (average) on an exam, usually because we want to know how our personal mark varies from the class mean. If the class mean is 70 and our mark is 78, we proudly say that we scored 8 points higher than the class mean. But does this imply we have scored higher than most students in the class? Recall that the mean is influenced by extreme scores. A few very extreme scores may account for a class mean of 70 even if most students scored either higher or lower than 70. Is there a way of taking into account the difference from the mean of every score in the distribution and coming up with a measure that is reflective of the variability of the scores?

We can obtain such a measure by calculating the **variance.** It is quite simple to calculate. Take the deviation (the difference) of each score from the mean, square each one, add them up, and divide the sum by the number of scores. Let's illustrate. Suppose you had the following distribution of scores: 8, 9, 11, 5, 2. Here is how to calculate the variance:

1. Calculate the overall mean.

$$\frac{8 + 9 + 11 + 5 + 2}{5} = 7 \quad \text{Or} \quad \overline{X} = \frac{\sum X}{N} = \frac{35}{5} = 7$$

2. Subtract the mean from each score (that is, determine the deviation of each score from the mean). Square the deviation by multiplying it by itself (2 squared is written as 2^2, which is $2 \times 2 = 4$). Note that squared numbers are always positive (e.g. -2^2 is $-2 \times -2 = 4$, the same as 2^2).

$$
\begin{array}{ccc}
X - \bar{X} & & (X - \bar{X})^2 \\
8 - 7 = +1 & & 1 \\
9 - 7 = +2 & & 4 \\
11 - 7 = +4 & & 16 \\
5 - 7 = -2 & & 4 \\
2 - 7 = -5 & & 25 \\
\end{array}
$$

3. Then add the squared deviations and calculate their mean.

$$\frac{1 + 4 + 16 + 4 + 25}{5} = \frac{50}{5} = 10$$

What you have calculated is the variance, symbolized as s^2.

In our example above the variance (s^2) is 10. But there is a problem with this number: it is not expressed in the original unit of measurement. Consider if our scores represented the monthly amount of money spent on CDs, the variance we have calculated is expressed in squared amount of money spent. This makes it quite difficult to interpret. Therefore, we do another calculation to return the measure of variability into its original unit of measurement. We simply take the square root of the variance and have what is called the **standard deviation.**

4. Calculate the square root ($\sqrt{}$) of the variance to determine the standard deviation.

$$\sqrt{10} = 3.2$$

The standard deviation is symbolized by s or SD and the formula is

$$SD = \sqrt{\frac{\sum (X - \bar{X})^2}{N}}$$

In other words, the standard deviation (SD, or 3.2) is equal to the square root of the sum of ( ) squared deviations from the mean, $(X_1 - X)^2 + (X_2 - X)^2$ and so on, or $(8 - 7)^2 + (9 - 7)^2$, and so on, divided by the total number of scores (N, or 5). Computer spreadsheet programs, such as Excel, Lotus 1-2-3, or QuattroPro, and statistical computing programs such as SPSS, SAS, or Minitab will compute the mean and standard deviation. Certain calculators also have keys that can calculate the mean and standard deviation.

The Meaning of the Standard Deviation

Both variance and standard deviation are measures of the distribution of scores (or values of variables such as IQ, income, amount spent on CDs, etc.) around a mean. An advantage of the standard deviation over the variance is that it is in the appropriate unit of measurement. But what is its usefulness? How does it help us to know the standard deviation of a set of scores? Recall that we wanted to measure the spread of scores, for example the various grades on an exam, or the number of hours a person listens to the radio, or the amount spent on CDs. Thus we are basically asking, "How spread out are the scores?" To better understand the usefulness of the standard deviation let us suppose that we have two sets of marks on a similar exam given to two sections of a course.

	Section A	Section B
	10	11
	16	12
	16	13
	16	15
	16	19
	16	21
	22	21
Mean	16	16
Range	12	10
Standard Deviation	3.2	4.0

Now assume all you knew about the two sets of marks were their means. Can you say anything about the spread of the marks knowing only the mean? The mean summarizes the data, but it does not tell us about the spread of the scores. Assume you were also told the ranges. The ranges suggest a smaller spread in section B, and we might be tempted to conclude that more scores are clustered around the mean in section B than in section A. But now consider the standard deviation, which is lower for section A than section B. This tells us there is less of a spread in section A than in section B, as is evident from a quick look at the raw scores. In other words, the scores in section A are closer to the mean than are the scores in section B. Clearly, the standard deviation is a more useful measure of the distribution of the scores. (As you may have realized it is insufficient to judge the overall performance of a class on the basis of the mean; it is best also to know the standard deviation.)

The standard deviation is especially useful when the sample is representative of a population and the sample data are normally distributed. In a normal distribution the mode, median, and mean coincide with 50 percent of the scores above and 50 percent below (see Exhibit 9.2). Consequently, if the class grades are normally distributed and you know the mean is 65 percent, then you know that half the scores are (or half the class scored) below 65 percent and the other half above 65 percent. The standard deviation is a measure of the distribution of scores around the mean. If the standard deviation is large then the scores are widely distributed and most scores are away from the mean, if it is small many scores are close to the mean (see Exhibit 9.3). Mathematicians have established that by knowing the mean and the standard deviation of normally distributed scores we are able to tell the proportion of the scores that are within certain limits.

Let's assume you administered an IQ test to a large sample of college students and the scores were normally distributed with a mean of 100 and a standard deviation of 15. Here we would say that *one* standard deviation equals 15. A characteristic of normally distributed scores is that about 34 percent of the scores will fall between the mean and one standard deviation above the mean (see Exhibit 9.3). Thus in our example, the mean is 100 and one standard deviation is 15; therefore, about 34 percent of the scores would be between 100 and 115 (i.e., 100 + 15 = 115). Since the normal distribution is symmetrical, it holds that about 34 percent of the scores will fall one standard deviation below the mean, or rather between 100 and 85 (i.e., 100 − 15 = 85). Hence, we can also say that about 68 percent of the IQ scores fall between 85 and 115. Stated differently, about 68 percent of the scores lie between one standard deviation above the mean and one standard deviation below the mean, or rather between +1 and −1 standard deviation from the mean. As the normal distribution in Exhibit 9.3 shows, about 95 percent of the scores would lie between +2 and −2 standard deviation from the mean. Therefore, about 95 percent of the IQ scores in your study would fall between 70 (i.e., 100 − 30 = 70) and 130 (i.e., 100 + 30 = 130). You could also state that only about 5 percent have IQ scores that are either below 70 or above 130. Again, this only holds if the scores are normally distributed. To fully grasp the usefulness of the standard deviation and all its implications requires more knowledge of statistics than we can cover here.

Tabular Analysis

Although measures of central tendency and dispersion are useful in understanding particular variables, researchers are usually interested in

EXHIBIT 9.3

Standard Deviation and Normal Distributions

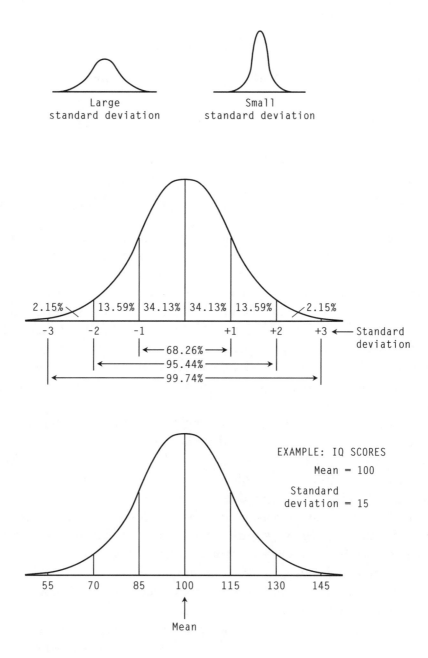

Large
standard deviation

Small
standard deviation

2.15%   13.59% 34.13% 34.13% 13.59%   2.15%

-3   -2   -1   +1   +2   +3   ←— Standard
                                                        deviation

|←— 68.26% —→|
|←——— 95.44% ———→|
|←———— 99.74% ————→|

EXAMPLE: IQ SCORES
Mean = 100
Standard
deviation = 15

55   70   85   100   115   130   145

↑
Mean

understanding the relationship between at least two variables. Let us assume that your research asserts that males enjoy different types of music from females. You would then want to present the data in such a way that it shows the relationship between the independent variable (sex of respondent) and the dependent variable (type of music enjoyed). Thus, you want to split the data according to sex. The skeleton of the table would look like this:

Sex of Respondent

Type of Music	Male	Female
Rock		
Jazz		
Classical		
Country		
Other		
No answer		

For each respondent on your data summary sheet place a tick in the blank cell that corresponds to the sex of the respondent and the type of music enjoyed. Earlier we noted that respondent number 01 is female and enjoys rock music. Therefore you would place a tick in the top row of the right-hand column. Continue to do the same for the other respondents, then add up the ticks in each cell and put the total in the cell. The result is a special type of table known as a **cross-tabulation** (or crosstab). In effect, you are setting up more than one frequency distribution, in this case two of them, one for males and another for females.

Suppose you added up the ticks and have constructed the cross-tabulation (see Table 9.3). Note that the total in the last column of Table 9.3 is similar to the frequency distribution of raw data on the music respondents enjoy in Table 9.1. We have expanded it to include another variable, sex of respondent. In using two variables we are carrying out a **bivariate analysis**. From Table 9.3 you can tell that thirty-one respondents enjoy rock music and of these twelve are males and nineteen are females. Or, you can tell that of the forty-one males, twelve enjoy rock music, six jazz, and so on.

The logic of data summarization is to select categories, code the data, and then present the results in a manner that allows you to interpret the data. However, as with one-variable frequency distributions, it is generally better to express the results of cross-tabulations in percentages.

There are three ways of presenting percentages; the method selected will depend on what is being interpreted. For example, the three tabular percentages in Table 9.4 are all based on the data in Table 9.3.

TABLE 9.3

Cross-tabulation of Type of Music Enjoyed, by Sex of Respondent

	Sex of Respondent		
Type of Music	Male	Female	Total
Rock	12	19	31
Jazz	6	4	10
Classical	5	4	9
Country	5	3	8
Other	11	9	20
No answer	2	3	5
Total	41	42	83

TABLE 9.4

CROSS-TABULATION PERCENTAGES

A. Cross-tabulations of Type of Music Enjoyed and Sex of Respondent with Total Percentages

	Sex of Respondent		
Type of Music	Male	Female	Total
	%	%	%
Rock	14.5	22.9	37.3
Jazz	7.2	4.8	12.0
Classical	6.0	4.8	10.8
Country	6.0	3.6	9.6
Other	13.3	10.8	24.1
No answer	2.4	3.6	6.0
Total	49.4	50.6	100
Number of respondents			(83)

B. Cross-tabulations of Type of Music Enjoyed and Sex of Respondent with Total Column Percentages

Sex of Respondent

Type of Music	Male	Female	Total
	%	%	%
Rock	29.3	45.2	37.3
Jazz	14.6	9.5	12.0
Classical	12.2	9.5	10.8
Country	12.2	7.1	9.6
Other	26.8	21.4	24.1
No answer	4.9	7.1	6.0
Total	100	100	100
Number of respondents	(41)	(42)	(83)

C. Cross-tabulations of Type of Music Enjoyed and Sex of Respondents with Total Row Percentages

Sex of Respondent

Type of Music	Male	Female	Total	Number of
	%	%	%	Respondents
Rock	38.7	61.3	100	(31)
Jazz	60.0	40.0	100	(10)
Classical	55.6	44.4	100	(9)
Country	62.5	37.5	100	(8)
Other	55.0	45.0	100	(20)
No answer	40.0	60.0	100	(5)
Total	49.4	50.6	100	(83)

Take a while to examine each of the tables. Carefully read the titles and note the direction in which the percentages are calculated. In Table 9.4 (A) the percentages are obtained by dividing the frequency in each cell by the total number of respondents, as in the case of males who enjoy rock music ($12/83 \times 100 = 14.5$ percent.). In Table 9.4 (B) the percentages are obtained by dividing each frequency by the total number of respondents in that *column*. For example, the frequency in each cell under males was divided by the total number of male respondents, as in the case of males who enjoy rock music

(12/41 × 100 = 29.3 percent). In Table 9.4 (C) the percentages are obtained by dividing each frequency by the total number of respondents in that *row*. For example, the frequency in each cell of the row for rock music was divided by the total number of respondents in that row, as in the case of males who enjoy rock music (12/31 × 100 = 38.7 percent). Attempt to interpret the figures for males who enjoy rock music in each table.

Each table has a slightly different story to tell. Which one is appropriate? Recall that you expected that the type of music enjoyed (the dependent variable) depended on the sex of the respondent (the independent variable). You want to know, for example, what percentage of females enjoy country music as compared to males. Therefore, Table 9.4 (B), the cross-tabulation with total column percents, would serve your purpose. The table shows that 12.2 percent of males enjoy country music compared to 7.1 percent of females. Take note that since the comparison was between males and females (the independent variable) and these were in columns, you calculated column percents. If the independent variable had been placed instead in the rows then you would have carried out row percents. In addition, a general rule in reading and interpreting tables is to compare the percentages in the direction opposite to that in which they were calculated. For example, you wanted to compare males and females (independent variable) and placed the variable in columns to determine the percentage of total males and percentage of total females that like the different types of music. Therefore, you calculated column percents, but you compare across rows (percentage of males that like a particular music compared to percentage of females).

Correlation

Organizing data in a table on the basis of two variables at the same time, as in Table 9.4, is common practice in social analysis. Cross-tabulation can become very elaborate, as you will discover if you pursue social research further. At this point we shall take up one key idea in cross-tabulation. The key idea is that of a statistical relationship between variables.

Look at Table 9.4 (B). How could you describe what you see? You might answer: "A greater proportion of females than males preferred rock as opposed to each of the other types of music." In other words there is a relationship between sex of respondent and musical preference. This is a *statistical* relationship simply because it shows up as a result of our grouping the data as percentages. Careful examination of percentage tables allows us to discover any statistical relationships that may be present, but other techniques can also be used, such as visual presentations and statistical measures.

For a visual impression of the relationship between the variables we can produce a **scattergram** (also known as a scattergraph or scatter-plot)—a diagram with each point representing a score on two variables. It gives us an indication of the kind of relationship that exists between the two variables.

For example, let us assume that your research asserts that there is a relationship between the number of hours a student spends studying for an exam and his grade on the exam. Suppose we plotted the results, with each point representing a student's time spent studying and his grade. Let us say we did this for three classes and got the following figures.

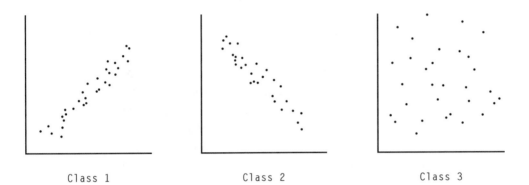

Class 1   Class 2   Class 3

What can you say about how close the relationship is between time spent studying and grades received for each of the three classes? In other words, what is the **correlation** between study time and grades? The figure for class 1 shows a strong **positive correlation:** the grade increases with an increase in the time spent studying. A strong relationship also exists in class 2, but the grade increases with a decrease in the time spent studying! This is a **negative correlation.** By looking at the figure for class 3 it is quite clear that no relationship exists between the time spent studying and the grade; there is a **zero correlation.**

For classes 1 and 2, or situations in which the points are roughly on a straight line, researchers may calculate a numerical value of the correlation. The measure is sometimes called the "Pearson's product moment correlation coefficient" or simply "correlation coefficient" and the symbol is usually the small letter *r.*

Again note that the correlation coefficient is a measure of a linear relationship. The closer the points are to a straight line, the higher the correlation (whether positive or negative). The more scattered the points, and the more difficult it is to imagine a line around which the points cluster, the smaller the correlation. A correlation coefficient ranges from −1.0 to +1.0, with −1.0 indicating a perfect linear negative correlation, and +1.0 a perfect linear positive correlation. Suppose a study tests the association between respondents' years of schooling and their fathers' levels of schooling. The relationship can be summarized with a correlation coefficient. If the result was r = 0.75, we would say that there was a strong positive correlation. In other words people whose fathers were more educated were themselves more likely to be more educated. Be careful in how you understand this: correlation is not the same as causation, but is a relationship that has to be explained. Many factors will influence the level of someone's schooling other than the father's level of schooling.

Pearson's correlation coefficient is only one of several **measures of association**—a single number that summarizes the strength and sometimes the direction (positive or negative) of a relationship between variables. Look again at Table 9.4. Knowing the sex of the respondents, would you have some chance at correctly guessing their musical taste? Which taste(s) are you more likely to be able to guess? Which musical taste would most likely lead to a lot of wrong guesses? The ability to guess at or predict some variable based on your knowledge on another variable is the basis of most of the commonly used measures of association.

These measures of association involve a principle of prediction called *proportionate reduction in error* (PRE). This principle asks: How much does knowledge of one variable reduce the errors that are made when guessing the values of the other variable? If we used sex of respondent to predict a liking for country music we would make many wrong predictions about the respondents, since only one out of eight males and about one out of fifteen females like this kind of music. We would do a bit better using sex of respondent to predict a liking for rock music, but our limited success in both cases suggests that the relationship between sex and musical taste is a weak one. Can you think of other characteristics (i.e., variables, including preferences or tastes) that might be better predicted knowing the sex of the respondent?

If there is a strong association or relationship between the variables, then knowing one variable should enable us to predict well (i.e., most of our guesses will be right). If our guesses are mostly wrong then our variables are not statistically related, they are statistically independent. A measure of association will tell us the *amount* of relationship between the variables. That is, it will tell us how strong or weak the relationship is. If we are dealing with nominal variables such as the relationship between sex and musical taste, or sex and party vote, this is all that the measure can tell us. Analysis of ordinal, interval, and ratio level variables (IQ, age, income, years of schooling, for example) can tell us both the strength and the direction of the relationship. For example, students who get As in one course are very likely to get As in another course—a positive relationship between ordinally measured grades. Or the more years of formal schooling they have, the higher the average income of graduates—a positive relationship between ratio measured variables. A negative or inverse relationship might be found when looking at educational background and the experience of unemployment (i.e., the more highly educated one is, the shorter the time spent unemployed).

It is beyond the scope of this book to cover the method of calculating correlation coefficients and the different types of correlation coefficients that exist. However, statistical computing programs will easily calculate the correlation coefficient, and some calculators provide keys that will calculate them for small sets of data.

Visual Summaries

If you had the choice between reading a table and looking at a visual presentation of the same data which would you prefer? A quick perusal of magazines and newspapers indicates that it is far more popular to summarize data using graphic forms than tabular forms.

Computer spreadsheet programs have made it relatively easy to construct graphs. However, be careful to select the appropriate type of graph. The information in the graph is based on information that could be provided in tabular form, but is often simplified to make the data more readable or more "interesting." Make sure the graph you select still conveys the information efficiently. In other words graphs are useful in summarizing the data and helping others grasp the significance of the information, but only if they present the data accurately.

For example, take the frequency distribution of type of music in Table 9.1. An appropriate graph for such data is the **pie chart,** whose pieces add up to 100 percent (see Exhibit 9.4). However, the pie chart should contain a limited number of sections or else its usefulness is lost. (Software packages generally allow for only a few sections.) In certain instances you want to stress a particular category, such as rock music. You can highlight that section by moving it outward, or "exploding" the section (see Exhibit 9.5).

The same data can also be presented in a **bar graph** (see Exhibit 9.6). But unlike the pie chart, the bar graph can be used for many different types of data. As with the pie chart we have an understanding of the relative preferences of the different types of music. For example, we can tell that the most popular music among the respondents is rock music. Note that the widths of the different bars are the same in order to make an appropriate comparison. Further, there are fixed gaps between each bar to demonstrate that we are referring to different types of music, which are listed below the horizontal axis (or x axis.) The vertical axis (or y axis) on the left side indicates that we are referring to the percentage of respondents. (In this example the bars run vertically. Horizontal bar graphs are generally used when there are many different categories.)

An advantage of the bar graph is that it allows for comparisons, such as the difference in music preferences between males and females. But should we use frequency or percentages? Since the numbers of males and females are not the same, frequency would give a distorted picture. Therefore, we need to graph the percentages. Furthermore, since the comparison is between males and females, we need the information on the percentage breakdown of preference for the different types of music among males and the percentage breakdown of preference for the different types of music among females. Therefore we would use the data in Table 9.4 (B). This gives us the bar graph in Exhibit 9.7, which provides two bars for each category: the percentage of total males and the percentage of total females. The distinction between male and female is clearly shown by using different shades and is stated in the *legend*, which in our example is placed at the bottom of the bar graph.

Probably one of the most widely used visual illustrations is the **line graph,** which displays values that change across time. It allows us to look for trends and to make comparisons. A simple line graph has information on some factor over time, such as the number of rock music records sold in the last ten years. It is also useful in making comparisons by plotting information on more than one factor, such as the number of rock records and the number of jazz records sold over the past ten years.

Suppose we have information on the average amount of money that males and females spent on CDs each month in the last twelve months. We could plot the information on a bar graph, or we could select a line chart. Compare the two graphs in Exhibit 9.8. Which would you prefer? Both graphs are correct. In many respects, your choice will depend on what you want to express visually about your data. The bar graph gives us a clearer perspective of the difference

EXHIBIT 9.4

Pie Chart of Preferred Type of Music

EXHIBIT 9.5

Pie Chart with Exploded Section

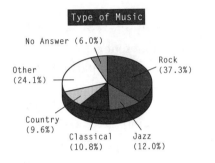

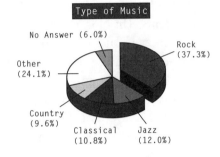

EXHIBIT 9.6

Bar Graph of Type of Music

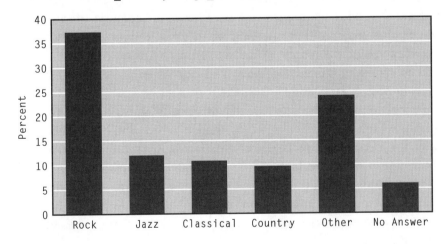

between the average spent by males and females each month. The line graph provides a better perspective on the trend in the average spent on CDs over the twelve months.

What does the line graph tell us about the trend in the amount of money males spent on CDs over the last twelve months? What does it tell us about the trend in the amount of money females spent on CDs? The line graph helps us to visualize the trends in spending for males and females and it allows us to make a comparison between their spending trends.

Thus, when using a graph to summarize the data, it is important to have a clear understanding of the purpose of the graph. For example, the information plotted in the pie charts (Exhibits 9.4 and 9.5) could also be presented as a bar graph, but not as a line graph. The information plotted as bar and line graphs in Exhibit 9.8 would lose its meaning if plotted in a pie chart.

What Are Statistics?

Statistics is a branch of applied mathematics that is concerned with two areas of application. **Descriptive statistics** deals with the collection and classification of information as numbers. **Inferential statistics** applies mathematical ideas to the organization of numerical data in order to draw conclusions or to draw inferences from it.

More simply, statistics can be seen as a language or way of thinking with or about information. As a way of thinking and expression it allows us to say complicated things briefly and with *precision*. Can you express the following statements without using numbers and still be as brief and precise?

> My car's gas consumption seems to be 20 percent less per fill up since its last tune up. That's saving me over $15 per week.

> My grade average is 10 percent lower than last term.

EXHIBIT 9.7

Bar Graph of Type of Music by Sex

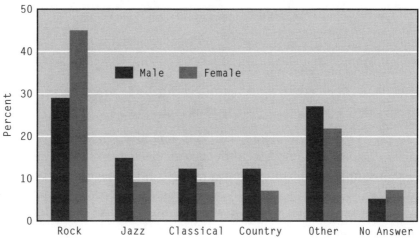

EXHIBIT 9.8

Bar Graph and Line Graph of Average Spent on CDs by Sex

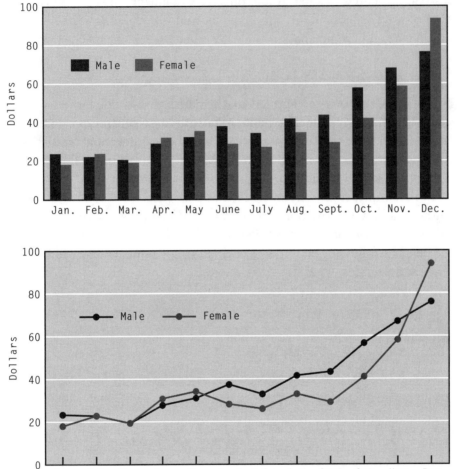

Government revenues from alcohol and tobacco taxes are 8 percent higher this year, while income tax revenues are 13 percent lower.

Purely verbal restatements will lose something in terms of pinpointing *how much* something differs or changes from something else. There is simply no substitute for a "numerical language" for precision and clarity. This is not to say that everything has to be statistically presented, but simply that where it makes sense to do so, statistics have considerable advantages.

The three statements above are examples of descriptive statistics. They use numbers to describe and compare situations. As the first two statements showed, whether we are aware of it or not, we often think in descriptive statistical terms. We are also surrounded by statistical information that is often very important for us as citizens, as consumers, and in almost every other aspect of our lives. Public opinion surveys are often used by political parties competing for our votes. Economic statistics may be useful in helping us decide which areas of job training are likely to have the greatest benefit for our future earnings. Medical statistics are constantly in the news and some of us may even be persuaded to abandon our bad habits as a result of seeing or hearing such reports. Many of us actually enjoy reading sports statistics!

We often think in the more complicated inferential statistical manner as well. What are the chances of my passing the next test if I postpone cramming until the night before? Are an outline and the first three lectures of a course enough to conclude that this course is not for you? Inferential statistics involves interpreting data to see what it means in relation to a hypothesis. Does the data show what we would like it to show—i.e., does it back up our hypothesis or not? How do we know our results are not due to pure chance or coincidence?

For social scientists statistics is like a toolbox from which they select the right tool to help them in their data analysis. Therefore, if you have not already done so, and need to be familiar with more statistical tools, you may want to acquire a knowledge of more concepts and applications of statistics than are covered in this chapter. A text in elementary statistics provides most of the knowledge of statistics that social scientists use in their data analysis.

QUALITATIVE DATA ANALYSIS

In Chapter 7 we pointed out that in field research data collection and analysis are less separated than in other research methods. This is just one of several characteristics of qualitative data analysis.

Danny Jorgenson (1989), a sociologist writing on participant observation methods, defines qualitative data analysis in the following way:

> Qualitative data analysis ... is a breaking up, separating, or disassembling of research materials into pieces, parts, elements, or units. With facts broken down into manageable pieces, the researcher sorts and sifts them, searching for types, classes, sequences, processes, patterns, or wholes. The aim of this process is to assemble or reconstruct the data in a meaningful or comprehensible fashion. (p. 107)

Two things should be noted about this definition. First, the idea of causality; what factor or factors are responsible for the existence, appearance, or change of other factors is underemphasized. Instead stress is placed on the meaning, comprehension, or interpretation of facts and their interconnections.

Second, qualitative data analysis is presented as a two-stage process: first facts are broken down in the search for "types," "classes," etc.; then the resulting patterns are reorganized onto larger units of meaning. In reality, this process is often more like a repeated cycle than two distinct stages. Analysis of qualitative data might be compared to a dialogue or conversation between the researchers and their data, with constant "questioning" of the data through which patterns gradually emerge.

Research based on qualitative data tends to proceed in a more exploratory fashion than quantitative data analysis. For social science researchers who use fieldwork, the main task is often to *describe* what they are studying. These researchers also argue that describing past historical eras, tribal or peasant communities, or contemporary subcultures should be done in terms of the people's own language and outlook—how the participants view their own way of life. Imposing an outsider's view of their lives on them will distort our understanding rather than aid it.

In addition, qualitative researchers often argue that social causation properly refers to the intentions and understandings that motivate human actions. Consequently, even exploratory research must first create a reasonably complete picture of a way of life so that the context of actions and relations can be understood and used in explaining social action and social organization.

This concern with understanding and interpreting the **subjective meaning** of social situations, groups, and ways of life involves a complex process of reading and rereading qualitative data. In the early stages of exploring historical archives or working in the field, attention is focused on two things. First the researcher has to locate sources of data, or gain access to and acceptance by a group. Second, the researcher has to develop a clear, basic understanding of the source or social group.

As the researchers become more at ease with their subjects, they can focus on specific issues of study and a new and deeper understanding of complexities and depths of meaning. As materials are collected in greater number and become familiar and understood, the collection of more documentation or additional observation becomes less important. There is an increasing need to integrate the material into a coherent pattern. Bringing the observations and interpretations together into a coherent picture that combines the "basic sense" of the era or group with its depths and complexities is a very tricky process of moving back and forth between the original documents or field notes and the various interpretations that emerge from successive analyses of the notes or documents.

Filing and Coding

Consider for a moment if you had done field research on a classroom. Think of the many things you would have to observe and carefully take notes on. The different types of classes (large/small, lectures, discussions, presentations, guests, video/films), the different types of teachers (male/female, young/old, strict/informal, humorous/serious), different types of students (male/female, groups/isolates, nerds/goof-offs), various types of behaviour, important or different incidents, and so on. All these items would have to be carefully observed and documented in detailed field notes.

As you can see the primary data of qualitative research involves an enormous mass of notes. The analysis of such data creates more notes, notes on notes, and further notes! In addition to the primary data you would also note down your interpretations, queries, hunches, maybe even associations. All this generates a great amount of material, which has to be organized, filed, and cross-referenced. The success of qualitative research, then, depends on the quality of the primary data and on the researcher's ability to analyze it and to organize it through an appropriate, regularly reviewed, flexible filing system. There are three types of files.

Data files contain primary data in the form of field notes or copies of archival or documentary material along with notes identifying their location, sources, dates, and any other identifying matter.

Analytic files contain the data in broken up and reassembled form— i.e., coded and interpreted. For example, classroom fieldwork analytic files might be broken down into subsections on large versus small classes, male versus female teachers, and types of student roles. Such files might also contain discussions and ideas about the coding (see the next section) and interpretation principles involved, the ideas on which they are based, and so on.

Special purpose files are needed for such materials as bibliography and references, literature review material, correspondence with other researchers in the field, and notes on the history and development of the research project as it shifts perspectives.

Managing these files as they expand requires regular reviews, identifying each file's purpose, labelling emerging new issues, and so on. As you work through your data, trying alternative interpretations, finding new patterns, sequences, or classes, you need to modify your filing system. But do not simply throw out the discarded interpretations! You may well want to return to them later on. Register the changes of your interpretations in a special purpose file and date them so that you can keep track of these changes and clarify the grounds for your views as your interpretations shift and develop.

Sorting and Sifting

It is no simple task to interpret qualitative data so that it emerges as a comprehensible whole combining overall patterns of meaning with underlying complexities. It involves repeatedly coding the data, then breaking it down, recoding, and comparing alternative results.

Coding data is a process of reorganizing raw data into groups or classes according to some research question, issue, or theme. For example, if you are interested in how teachers cope with "class clowns," you would look through and copy all your notes on clowning incidents into a special file or section of a file. Another concern may be differences in the behaviour of male and female students, so you sift through your field notes in search of observations on this aspect of the classroom. These observations are then copied and placed in a separate, appropriately labelled file.

Sometimes the process of sorting and reorganizing involves insights or hunches; sometimes it is suggested by other research that you have read. At other times a theme is clearly suggested by the data itself. Usually, however, the principles of coding emerge from sheer hard work, trying first one scheme and then another until patterns, sequences, repeated processes, cases, or relationships begin to emerge.

The first stage of data analysis involves **open coding.** Here the researcher slowly reads through historical documents or field notes looking for critical terms, key themes, or important events. These are noted and become a basic framework for initial analysis.

A second reading uses this framework in order to explore connections, classifications, sequences, and cases. Are the critical terms, themes, or events systematically connected with others, or found in association with other terms, events, and themes? Are there variations or subtypes of the initial terms, themes, or events or their connections and associations? Are there exceptions, deviations, or situations where parts exist without others?

In reading the data and asking these questions the researcher moves towards a more selective coding approach. The researcher begins to focus, to track down cases that illustrate patterns and themes, and makes comparisons and contrasts to refine and elaborate these patterns.

For example, as you review your material on how teachers cope with class clowns, you may discover different patterns of responses by teachers. These patterns may relate to other aspects of their teaching styles, so you begin to shift your focus onto the latter, pulling in other observations unrelated to class clowns. On the basis of these observations you may begin to develop a classification of types of teachers, or teaching strategies. You may then see that some teachers are very clear examples of these teaching types; you write down a "portrait" or profile of these individuals and add them to your analysis. Such profiles are perhaps no longer just summaries of your observations but are "ideal types"—that is, descriptions that are exaggerated for the sake of clarity.

The coding process, then, moves from a situation where the codes are determined largely by the primary data, to one where concepts increasingly determine the coding categories. These concepts may be partly built from the data and partly developed from ideas and theories drawn from other research. Coding becomes more elaborate as the issues in the study are defined and focused. Isolated concepts become part of a general framework, subthemes are developed, and commentaries on the data move away from pure description to analysis and explanation.

Analytical Strategies

This movement away from description towards analysis and explanation is helped by using certain **analytical strategies.**

Look for Essential Components

When you identify an idea or pattern in a group of historical documents or in your field notes, try to break it down into a cluster of essential subcomponents. Mentally experiment with these subcomponents. If you were to take away any of them, would this change the overall character significantly or not?

If changes are likely, what changes might there be? For example, how would a class operate without a class clown? Without a lecture from the teacher? Would things be different if lectures were preprinted and distributed for reading, and classes turned into question-and-answer sessions or discussion sessions? Suppose the teacher brought in "guest lecturers," would there be a different dynamic?

Look for Relationships

Are there any detectable relationships among particular pieces of information or observations? Is there some larger sequence of events or processes at work? Are there repeated connections or combinations associated with specific actions or situations? For example, do some kinds of teachers seem to provoke or invite some kinds of students? Do some kinds of subjects open up opportunities for talking back, being rowdy, or clowning around? Do things happen in classes more at the beginning of term than at the end, or vice versa?

Compare and Contrast

Is what you see in one case the same or similar to others? Is it different? If it is different, how is it different? Identifying similarities and differences among phenomena enables you to arrange facts into classes or types. For example, how do college classes differ from high-school classes? How do older teachers differ from younger ones? Male teachers from female? Large classes from small classes?

Consider Negative Evidence

Are there exceptions or deviant cases—events, actions, or ideas which seem not to fit into the emerging patterns? What do they mean? Why are they there? How do they challenge the positive evidence or its interpretation? What is hidden or overlooked in the documents or field notes? What is taken for granted or assumed in any explanations by participants?

Ask Alternative Questions

Questions can be asked negatively or positively. Why did something happen? Why this event and not something else?

By constantly taking apart and reanalyzing data through the use of these conceptual strategies, the researcher gradually moves towards a **synthesis.** This is a coherent picture of a past period or event in history, or a way of life of a particular social group or subculture. The picture simultaneously shows life as it is lived from the perspective of the historical society or the particular social group, and as it is interpreted and classified by the researcher.

WHAT YOU HAVE LEARNED

- Data needs organization, summarizing, and interpretation in order for patterns and relationships to be clearly seen or demonstrated.

- The first step is to change the raw data into a more manageable form by coding it; this takes different forms that depend on whether the study is quantitative or qualitative.

- In the case of quantitative data, coding allows the data to be organized into percentaged frequency tables.

- The resulting data will vary in terms of its levels of measurement and this will affect the kinds of statistical organization and analysis you may be able to do.

- Different kinds of tables, graphs, and measures have specific advantages and limitations, which have to be taken into account when searching for the best ways to organize and interpret data.

- The coding process for qualitative data is complex and involves a cycle of progressively more focused filing of the data in relation to particular analytical concerns.

- This interpretative process involves several analytical strategies, which aid the researcher in moving towards a synthesis of the data.

KEY WORDS

1. Quantitative Analysis

raw data	true zero
precode	ratio level of measurement
postcode	central tendency
univariate analysis	mode
frequency distribution	median
spreadsheet	mean
cell	normal distribution
grouped frequency distribution	negative skew
cumulative frequency distribution	positive skew
nominal level of measurement	range
ordinal level of measurement	variance

standard deviation   measures of association

cross-tabulation   bivariate analysis

scattergram   pie chart

correlation   bar graph

positive correlation   line graph

negative correlation   descriptive statistics

zero correlation   inferential statistics

2. Qualitative Analysis

subjective meaning   open coding

data files   analytical strategies

analytic files   synthesis

special purpose files

REVIEW QUESTIONS

1. What is coding? What are the basic rules of coding?
2. What are the different levels of measurement? Find two examples of social science variables for each level.
3. What is a measure of central tendency? Why is it useful?
4. What are the differences between the mode, the median, and the mean?
5. What is a measure of dispersion? Why is it useful?
6. Why is it necessary to calculate the standard deviation from the variance?
7. What is the purpose of cross-tabulation?
8. What kinds of data are produced by qualitative research?
9. What is the "two-stage process" of qualitative data analysis?
10. What are the different kinds of files used in qualitative data analysis?
11. What different kinds of coding are used in qualitative data analysis?
12. What are the analytical strategies used in qualitative data analysis? At what stage in the analysis are they used?

RECOMMENDED READINGS

Bowen, R. W. (1992). *Graph it! How to make, read, and interpret graphs.* Englewood Cliffs, NJ: Prentice-Hall.

A complete but brief survey of the major types of graphs used in scientific research in all fields. It is clearly written and assumes no statistical knowledge.

Huff, D. (1954). *How to lie with statistics.* New York: Norton.

A humorous survey of the pitfalls and tricks associated with the use of statistics by politicians, advertisers, and others who use statistics to communicate their ideas to the public.

Paulos, J. A. (1988). *Innumeracy: Mathematical illiteracy and its consequences.* New York: Hill & Wang.

If you suffer from math phobia, read this book. It is clearly written and may actually get you hooked on math.

Zeisel, H. (1985). *Say it with figures* (6th ed.). New York: Harper & Row.

Originally published in 1947, this is a nontechnical introduction to tables and elementary statistical analysis.

CHAPTER 10

The Research Report: The End and the Beginning

WHAT YOU WILL LEARN

- suggestions for how to review and conclude
- the basic parts of the research report
- differences between qualitative and quantitative reports
- the APA and MLA styles of documentation

INTRODUCTION

The journey started some time ago when you puzzled over some aspect of the social world. You began by collecting background information, which made you more aware of various facets of the issue and helped refine the focus of your investigation. Next you clarified the variables, chose a sample, and selected the research method(s). Then you began the task of collecting the data. Once completed you had what seemed to be a mountain of evidence. Painstakingly, you summarized and organized the data. Throughout the research process there was a good feeling of accomplishment as you became increasingly more knowledgeable about the issue. But probably the greatest excitement came at the stage when you summarized and organized the data. You finally had the information you had been looking for. You now had an answer to the research question or hypothesis that first launched you on this journey of discovery.

At this stage you will want to crown this achievement by writing up a report to let others know what you found. You may be tempted to rush immediately into writing the research report. But before doing so, consider this: What are your interpretations of the data? What can you conclude? What else needs to be examined? What should others be told about the research? How should the research report be organized? Thus before drafting the report it is well worth spending some time reviewing your work. It also helps to write down notes for yourself as you answer these questions; they may be useful in writing the draft copy of the report. In this chapter we will suggest ways to clarify your ideas, bring the research to a close for now, discuss the preparation and organization of the research report, and consider what to do next.

REVIEWING AND CONCLUDING

What Did I Want to Find Out?

In the process of collecting and organizing the data it is easy to get bogged down in detail and lose sight of the original research question or hypothesis. Thus, before we draw conclusions, we need to take note of the initial research objective, the findings, the interpretations of the findings, and the limitations of the study.

In Chapter 3 we suggested that you write down the research issue that you were interested in and then ask a series of clarifying questions. The purpose was to arrive at a research question or hypothesis about the issue that would be the focus of your research. Here we suggest you keep the focus on the general issue and the specific research question or hypothesis. Suppose your initial interest was about the relationship between gender and academic aspirations. Your interest was sparked by a media report that implied that males were more likely to drop out of school than females. This prompted you to ask various questions, which helped isolate a particular aspect of the issue for your research. After further consideration and a literature review, let's say you settled on a specific issue to research:

> Among university students, are females more likely than males to express an interest in pursuing graduate studies?

BOX 10.1

Checklist: Reviewing the Research

The aim of the review is to bring the entire research process into focus. Write down notes for yourself; they will be useful when you write the draft copy of the report. Below are suggestions of questions to consider.

REFLECTION AND REVIEW

[ ]   What was the general issue?

[ ]   What was the specific issue (research question/ hypothesis)?

[ ]   Was the research exploratory, descriptive, or explanatory?

[ ]   What was the research design and why?

[ ]   What was the population and sample?

[ ]   What were the findings?

[ ]   What do the findings say about the issue or hypothesis?

[ ]   What were the limitations of the research?

[ ]   What can be concluded?

[ ]   What are the implications for future research or analysis?

PLANNING THE REPORT

[ ]   Who will be the readers of the report?

[ ]   What language, style, and presentation are appropriate?

[ ]   Is there a specified length for the report?

[ ]   Is there a specified style of documentation (e.g., parenthetical, footnote, or endnote)?

[ ]   How much space should be given to the different sections of the report?

Thus, the general issue was the relationship between gender and academic aspirations. But your research focused on a particular aspect of the issue, that of male and female university students and their future interest in doing graduate studies. Moreover, what was the population of your study? How did you select your sample? Suppose your study was a social survey of a randomly selected group of university students in their last year, and the results showed that more females than males planned on doing graduate studies. Could you claim on the basis of the results of your study that females are less likely than males to drop out of university? The answer is no. The question is quite broad and asks about the relationship between gender and academic aspirations. Your study did not concern the possibility of dropping out of university. Again, it is important to take into account the larger issue, but you will want to remain especially focused on the research question or hypothesis.

What Did I Find?

After you decided on a particular research question or hypothesis that related to the general issue, you clarified the variables and selected a research method. Why? You decided to compare the academic aspirations of female and male university students. Why? You decided to measure academic aspirations in terms of whether a respondent intended on doing graduate studies. Why? In other words, you had reasons for concentrating on a particular aspect of the general issue, and your main findings should reflect that focus.

What do the data tell you? For example, say your survey found that females were more likely than males to continue their studies after completing their undergraduate degree. You could of course simply state what you found. But that is not enough.

While the information is interesting, you need to interpret what you found. How do the data relate to your research question or hypothesis? For example, in examining academic aspirations among university students you need to do more than simply state the proportion of females that intended on doing graduate studies; you need to give information on the male students and then contrast the academic aspirations of the female and male students. Or, suppose you wanted to compare the social behaviour of boys and girls in a daycare. To say that boys push and shout at other children does not fully relate to your research objective. You will want to describe the behaviour of girls and then compare the behaviour of boys and girls in the day care. Likewise, in interpreting the results of an experiment using an experimental and a control group, the analysis would focus on both groups. The results of the experimental group only partly relate to your research objective—you also need to take into account the findings on the control group. You will also want to relate the findings to the research question or hypothesis. Thus, you need to interpret the data by comparing the results of the control and experimental groups.

Did you answer the research question or find support for the hypothesis? If your findings did not provide a definite answer or support, then that in itself is important information. However, it is essential not to interpret vague and confusing data as providing a clear answer to the research question or support for the hypothesis. Recall that you focused on a specific aspect of a larger issue. Your research is a small part of many research journeys around that larger issue. Once you have considered what you found, it is time to take note of the limitations of your research.

What Were the Limitations of My Research?

Early in the research process you made several decisions about the operationalization of the variables, the population and sample, the research method, and so on. Possibly there were constraints that affected your decision, such as time and resources. You would have liked to carry out a social survey on a random sample of university students, but lacked the resources and therefore used a nonrandom sample of students at only one university. You wanted to compare how women were portrayed in advertisements in two magazines from 1939 to 1946, but only had access to the copies published from 1943 to 1946. You would have preferred to do an experiment, but were unable to get the necessary permission and so did an observational study of children in a day care. Clearly, as with virtually all research, your research had certain **limitations.**

In addition, you are likely to note some limitations when the research is in progress or is completed. Again, this is true of most studies. For example, after completing the data collection you realized that you neglected to ask the respondents a particular question. Or, you realized too late that the control group was in a room next to a noisy class, which may have distracted their attention. Or, there were certain variables you were unable to control but believe could have an influence on the results. The limitations of your research do not necessarily make your study less worthy. On the contrary, recognizing the limitations of the study allows you to arrive at a more appropriate conclusion and to make suggestions for future research.

What Can I Conclude?

Recognizing the limitations of your research will help you to arrive at a proper **conclusion.** You did not carry out a social survey on a random sample of all university students, but only on a nonrandom sample of students in one university. You only compared the advertisements of two magazines from 1943 to 1946, and not the copies from 1939 to 1946. You observed children in a day care; you did not do an experiment. You neglected to ask respondents for their age. And so on. Whatever the limitations, they need to be taken into account as you consider the conclusion of the study. For example, if you selected a nonrandom sample for your survey then you cannot claim that the results are representative. In this case you have to argue that your findings are suggestive, indicating directions for further inquiry in subsequent research.

There are two main facets to a conclusion, the specific and the general. First, note the main results and relate them to your research question or hypothesis. What are the main results? What do they say about the research question? Do they clearly support or reject the hypothesis? Next, note how the main results relate to the larger issue you were interested in. Suppose the general issue was the relationship between gender and academic aspirations. You limited the study to finding out whether female university students are more likely than male university students to express an interest in doing graduate studies. What do the results say about the relationship between gender and academic aspirations? The principal purpose of the conclusion is to connect your main findings back to the research question or hypothesis and to the larger issue. (We have more to say about the conclusion later in the chapter.)

THE RESEARCH REPORT

You put a lot of effort and energy into carrying out the research; its accomplishment will have given you great satisfaction. In some small way you came to better understand our social world. But others need to be informed about your research if it is going to contribute to the further development of knowledge on the issue. The widely accepted way of informing others is through a **research report.** The research report tells others what you found, allows them to evaluate your work, and suggests directions for future research. Before discussing the writing and formatting of the research report, let us briefly consider some guidelines.

Who Are Your Readers?

As with all pieces of writing, the research report has to clearly communicate the information to the relevant **audience.** A report directed to a general audience will differ in language, style, and presentation from one intended for an audience of experts on the topic. Suppose you carried out an experiment on cognitive development among grade schoolers. If your report is intended for a nonspecialist audience, say the parents of grade schoolers, then you will want to tailor your report for them. However, you will want to adopt a different approach if your readers are child psychologists. If the report is for a course, you may want to discuss the intended audience with your professor. Thus, before drafting the report, consider who will read it and adopt the language and style that is appropriate for that audience.

What Is the Aim of the Report?

We noted in Chapter 2 that your research could be exploratory, descriptive, or explanatory. The aim of the research led you to select a particular method and search for certain data. It will, therefore, have an impact on what you tell the reader about the research.

The principal aim of exploratory research is to find out more about an issue on which there is little firm information and to point the way to more research. Suppose there was a lack of research on what happens to high-school dropouts in small towns. Perhaps your research was to find out more about the topic, including whether it is a serious problem or not. Key aims of your research report would be to provide more information about the issue and to indicate the direction more detailed research should take.

A descriptive study would usually follow an exploratory study. Assuming research has shown that there is indeed a problem with high-school dropout rates in small rural towns, the aim of your descriptive research could have been to describe the variations of the problem. You may have described the difference between males and females who are high-school dropouts, or compared the high-school dropout rates of rural towns and metropolitan areas, and so on. Thus, be especially careful to tell the reader what applies to a sample and what applies to the population.

An explanatory study goes beyond description and instead attempts to find out why the variations exist. For example, the aim of your research could have been to explain why the high-school dropout rate was higher among males than females in certain types of rural towns. Explanatory research tends to be quantitative in approach and

How Long Should the Report Be?

The length of reports varies and usually depends on their purpose and audience. Some reports are brief research notes of about one to five pages. In such a report you mainly highlight the findings and only briefly state the method. However, the most popular research report is the one whose intent is to tell readers the research question or hypothesis, discuss earlier studies that formed the basis of the research, explain how the data were collected, present and analyze the data, answer the research question or hypothesis, and suggest future research. Although the length will vary, it will have to be sufficient to provide the necessary information. Such a report is basically modelled on the articles found in academic journals, discussed in Chapter 3. They are generally equivalent to between twenty and thirty double-spaced typed pages. If the report is for a course, you may want to discuss the length of your report with your professor.

therefore the results are often expressed in the form of statistics. Consequently your report is likely to be organized around tables and figures that will clarify your conclusions. You will want to be especially concerned with the level of knowledge your readers have about the statistics used in the report. A nonspecialist audience, particularly one that is not comfortable with statistical analysis, may need more verbal explanation of the results than a specialist audience.

PRESENTING THE RESEARCH REPORT

Now that you spent some time reviewing why you did the research, what you found, what you concluded, and for whom you want to, or have to, write the report, let us turn to the organization and writing of the report. In most research reports, the information is provided in the order of the basic steps of the research, although how much importance is given to the various sections may vary. The following parts are usually included in all research reports:

1. Title

2. Introduction - Literature Review
3. Research Design
4. Data Analysis
5. Discussion and Conclusion
6. References or Works Cited

Other parts may also be included, such as acknowledgments, the abstract (which is usually found in research reports of academic journals; see Chapter 3), notes if necessary, and an appendix. We will discuss the research report in the order of the parts presented above. (If the report is for a course you may want to discuss with your professor what additional elements are required). The parts can also help you to think through the information you need for the report. However, you will not necessarily write the report in order. For example, you may decide on a title only after you have finished the draft of the entire report. But whatever order you find easiest, the final report should include the various parts in their logical sequence.

Title

Deciding on a **title** for the report might seem relatively easy. But a title must not be simply catchy; it must provide enough information to give the reader a sense of the general and specific issues of the research. All of this should be expressed in as few words as possible. What would you understand was the subject of the study based on the following title?

Academic Aspirations

This title gives no sense of what the study was about except to assume it had something to do with academic aspirations. Now consider the following title:

Academic Aspirations of University Students

This version is an improvement in that we now know it concerns academic aspirations among university students. But if the study focused on students in their final year of university you may want to convey that information in the title:

The Academic Aspirations of Students in the Final Year of University

Can we still improve on the above title? Certainly. What is important to remember in deciding on a title is that you want to convey enough information to give the reader a good sense of what the research is about.

BOX 10.3

Appearance

While much effort goes into the content of the report, its appearance is also important. Consider how willing you would be to read a report that looked disorganized. Your audience will respond to your report based partly on how it looks. The key to an acceptable report is clear language and a text that is easy for the readers to follow. Here are some suggestions.

TITLE

In addition to the title of your report, the title page should include your name and other relevant information. If it is written for a course, include the name and number of the course, your professor's name, and the date. Do not number the title page.

INTRODUCTION AND LITERATURE REVIEW

This follows the title page. From this page on a number is allotted to each page of the report. There is no need for a major heading for this part, but you may want to use subheadings that reflect its organization. Suppose your literature review first concentrated on Canadian works and then on American works. Subheadings could be used to distinguish the sections. You will have to be the judge of whether subheadings are needed. But make sure they are appropriate and enhance the appearance of the report.

How many pages you dedicate to the introduction will depend on various factors; there is no standard length. If there are no restrictions on the length of the introduction keep in mind the overall length of the report. Moreover, consider the expertise of the readers and how much information they need. If the readers are nonspecialists, more clarification is usually needed.

RESEARCH DESIGN

This part has a major heading. Again, there is no standard length for this part of the report. But take note that much effort went into the research design and gathering of the data. While you want to tell the readers only what is necessary, it is important they clearly understand the various steps you went through. Subheadings may be useful to emphasize the importance of each topic. For examples, glance through one of the leading journals in your discipline (see Box 1.3 for names of such journals).

DATA ANALYSIS

A major heading clearly identifies this section, which is the heart of the paper. Although there is no standard length, this section deserves much importance. If you have no restrictions on the length of this section, we suggest at least one-third of the report be on the data analysis. Subheadings are especially helpful in this part of the report. Again for examples, we suggest you refer to one of the leading journals in your discipline.

DISCUSSION AND CONCLUSION

This part is clearly noted by a heading. There are usually no subheadings. Although this is the last section in the report, it may be the first that some readers will turn to. It should give them a quick sense of what the research is about and the main conclusions, so they can decide whether to read the rest. Thus, its appearance can be critical.

REFERENCES OR WORKS CITED

This section provides the complete bibliographic citation of the sources mentioned in your report. The information on the sources begins on a separate page after the text of the report and before any appendices that you may have included. The section is clearly titled as "References," if you use the APA style, and "Works Cited" if you use the MLA style. (See Box 10.5.)

Introduction and Literature Review

In some reports the introduction and the literature review are treated as separate sections. Here we treat them as one section.

The introduction leads the reader into the paper. The opening paragraphs should give the reader a general understanding of what the research is about, including an understanding of the research question or hypothesis.

Your report is a small contribution to the larger body of knowledge about an area and you will want to tell the reader where your research fits in. Thus, much of the introduction is a review of the literature, whereby you assess previous research that is especially relevant to your research question or hypothesis. In Chapter 3 we provided some advice on preparing the literature review. However, here the literature review needs to be incorporated in the research report and there will probably be limited space available. In deciding which ones to concentrate on, keep in mind that you want to tell the reader what is already known, and that it has to be relevant to your research question or hypothesis.

The introduction closes by building on the literature review. State your research question or hypothesis clearly and connect it back to what you determined to be an important gap in the previous research you reviewed. After reading the introduction the reader should have a clear sense of why you decided to focus on a certain research question or hypothesis.

It is your responsibility to make certain that readers clearly understand what you wanted to find out. Suppose you specifically focused on the relationship between the kind of magazines people read and their voting behaviour. Your readers need to know more about this relationship; that is, they need to be able to distinguish the dependent and independent variables. Are you expecting that people's voting behaviour is dependent on the magazines they read? Or do the magazines people read depend on the people's voting behaviour? According to your study, which comes first?

Research Design

Now that the readers know *what* the research question or hypothesis is and *why* you selected it, you need to tell them *how* you collected the data. Thus you need to describe the sample, the type of measurement instrument used to gather the data, any ethical issues, and any other information regarding the context of the research. Keep in mind that you should provide enough detailed information for readers to be able

In-Text Citations

APA STYLE

The APA style of **in-text citations** places the information on the author(s) and the date of the publication directly in the text. The following example provides the date of publication of the source after the author(s):

> Bibby and Posterski (1992) show that Quebec teens have a different attitude towards premarital sex than teens in other parts of the country.

The next example credits a source by giving the family name(s) of the author(s), followed by a comma, a space, and the date of publication.

> According to at least one study, Quebec teens have a different attitude towards premarital sex than teens in other parts of the country (Bibby and Posterski, 1992).

If you include a direct quotation, then provide the page on which the quote is found after the date. For example:

> "Quebec teens, be they francophones or anglophones, are far more open than teens elsewhere in the country to premarital sex and homosexuality" (Bibby and Posterski, 1992, p. 116).

If the author's name is part of the phrase then place the date of publication in parentheses after the name and put the page number in parentheses at the end of the quotation. For example:

> As Bibby and Posterski (1992) found, "Quebec teens, be they francophones or anglophones, are far more open than teens elsewhere in the country to premarital sex and homosexuality" (p. 116).

MLA STYLE

The following are examples of in-text citations using the MLA style of citation. Most documentation, according to the MLA style, includes the author and page number in parentheses, or just the page number if the author has been mentioned in the phrase. Since the citation provides little information, whatever is cited must refer to a source in the Works Cited list at the end of the report (see Box 10.5).

Give the last name of the author(s) in the text and place the relevant page number(s) in parentheses at the end of the paraphrased material.

> Bibby and Posterski show that Quebec teens have a different attitude towards premarital sex than teens in other parts of the country (116).

When no mention is made of the author(s), place the name of the author(s) and the relevant page number(s) in parentheses (with no comma) directly after the quoted material.

> One study found that "Quebec teens, be they francophones or anglophones, are far more open than teens elsewhere in the country to premarital sex and homosexuality" (Bibby and Posterski 116).

to replicate the study. To help you in writing this section we suggest different questions to ask yourself about the research. They do not necessarily have to be presented in the order noted here. However, all these points should be covered.

How Was the Data Collected?

It is important that readers are clearly told the type of instrument selected to gather the data. Do not simply state the research method used. What instruments did you use? How did you conduct the experiment, the nonparticipant observation research, the content analysis, and so on? If all you told your readers was that you conducted a social survey, they would be unable to replicate the study. You will want to briefly tell the readers how the questionnaire was prepared and pretested; how you administered the questionnaire; whether it was administered to individuals or groups; whether you sent it by mail or handed it to individuals and waited until they completed it; and where the questionnaires were administered and under what conditions.

When in doubt about including some information, we suggest including it, especially in your draft of the report. Suppose while you were carrying out your experiment the tape recorder broke and had to be replaced. This fact may be important to readers, in properly appraising the procedure and evidence.

The readers also need to know how the key variables were measured. In most cases these involve the dependent and independent variables. Take the earlier example of the magazines people read and their voting behaviour. How did you measure what magazines people read? How did you measure their voting behaviour? Assume you measured voting behaviour by means of a questionnaire that included a question asking respondents which political party they would vote for if an election were held. Respondents were then categorized according to the political party they supported. Assume you measured magazines people read by asking respondents which magazines they subscribe to and which magazines they bought in the last month. All this information is of interest to your audience, because it gives them a clear understanding of what you mean by your variables and how you measured them. They can also better judge your research and appraise the validity and reliability of the research.

What Was the Sample and How Was It Selected?

Recall that all research is based on some sort of sample. The readers need to know what was the sample of your study, and in turn what was the target population. Further, they need to be told how you selected the sample. Try not to leave out necessary information. For example, if you carried out an experiment in which you used control and experimental groups, state how you selected the participants and how they were assigned to the groups. Do not embellish your sample to make it seem more perfect than it really was. If you had difficulties with selecting the sample, inform your readers. Suppose you carried out a survey and initially planned to select a random sample but had difficulty obtaining the necessary list of the population from which to select the sample. Inform the reader why you were unable to select a random sample.

Nor is it enough simply to state the type of sample used. Suppose you selected a simple random sample of 100 students from the population of second-year students at your college or university. Telling your audience that it was a simple random sample is insufficient. How was the sample selected from the population? Did you have a list of all the second-year students? What kind of list was it and were there flaws with the list? Why did you choose the particular sampling procedure?

How many people did you have to select from the list to arrive at the actual number of persons who agreed to take part in the study?

What Were the Ethical Considerations?

As we noted in various sections of this book, social scientists have responsibilities to the people they research. You will now want to tell the readers what ethical issues your research faced. Did the people you studied volunteer to take part in your research? What did you tell them your research was about? Did you deceive them? Were people told their responses would be kept confidential? How did you assure confidentiality? Did you infringe on people's privacy? Did your study have any psychological consequences on the participants? Did you seek out proper professional consultation before carrying out the study? And so on. Do not easily dismiss the ethical considerations; consider how you would feel if you were the respondent of the questionnaire, the participant in the experiment, or the subject of covert observation.

Data Analysis

This is the main section of your paper. Your readers know the research question or hypothesis, the reasons for carrying out the research, and how you gathered the data. Now tell them the findings and your interpretations of the findings. In the process you will also be building up a response to your research question or hypothesis.

The method used in the research will largely determine how you present and interpret the data. As noted in other chapters, social science research can be broadly divided into quantitative studies and qualitative studies. The two approaches may greatly differ in their presentation and interpretation of data. For the sake of clarity, we discuss the two separately.

Quantitative Data

Your aim in analyzing quantitative data is to inform the reader. As noted in Chapter 9, tables and figures are helpful in summarizing and organizing this type of information. Make sure they are properly labelled, have a title that clearly describes the content, and are numbered consecutively. For example:

```
Table 4: Earnings of Part-Time Working University
Students
```

Since it is labelled as "Table 4" it is the fourth table in the report. But is the title clear? Is there room for improvement? What "earnings?" Do you mean weekly wages, hourly wages, or what? And which university students? For example, if the data are restricted to university students registered as full time, then say so. Now consider the following title:

Table 4: Average Hourly Earnings of Full-Time University Students Who Work Part Time

The improved title tells more about the data in the table. Remember that the title of the table has to make sense to your readers.

The data in the table should be arranged in an appropriate format. Keep in mind what interpretations you want to make of the data, and pass these on to the readers. Always ask yourself what information you are trying to convey.

Suppose you want to create a percentage table on sex and support for candidates running for president of the student government. Should you do row percentages or column percentages? The choice will depend on what information you want to get across. Tables need to be formatted in such a way that they convey the kind of information you want the readers to consider. For example, is the aim of your table to tell the readers the breakdown of support among males and females for each candidate? If so, your table might look like this:

TABLE 1

BREAKDOWN OF CANDIDATES' SUPPORT BY SEX

Sex	Candidates		
	Lee	**Santoni**	**Marshall**
	%	%	%
Females	25	50	70
Males	75	50	30
Total	100	100	100
(Number of respondents)	(88)	(64)	(80)

Here you are telling the readers, for example, that among the supporters of the candidate Lee, 25 percent are females and 75 percent are males. In addition, the total number of respondents that support Lee is 88.

But what if you want to describe the support for the various candidates among females and males? Then your table would be quite different.

TABLE 2

BREAKDOWN OF SUPPORT FOR CANDIDATES BY SEX

Sex	Candidates				
	Lee	Santoni	Marshall	Total	(Number of Respondents)
	%	%	%	%	
Females	20	29	51	100	(110)
Males	54	26	20	100	(122)

This table shows the readers that among females 20 percent support Lee, 29 percent Santoni, and 51 percent Marshall. In addition, there were 110 female respondents.

Clearly, which tables you choose to include in the report depend on the interpretations you want to make of the data. The above examples also illustrate the importance of identifying the variables and the type of data in the table. If you do use percentage tables, also remember to indicate the base ("Number of Respondents" in the above examples) on which you computed the percentages (see Chapter 9). This allows readers to recalculate the data. For example, knowing that in the second table 20 percent of the 110 females supported Lee, the reader can reconstruct the raw numbers from the percentages and possibly arrive at a different interpretation.

Whatever tables or figures you include in the report, make certain to discuss them in the text. But try to avoid simply repeating the data that is in the table. For example, do not simply repeat what support each candidate has; instead guide the readers in interpreting the data. Which candidate is more popular among females? Which candidate is more popular among males? Which candidate is more likely to win? Your tables serve as evidence to support your claims.

Qualitative Data

Unlike quantitative data analysis, which presents findings numerically, qualitative data analysis describes and interprets a social phenomenon. The basic findings are not numerical, but are instead details about an aspect of the social world that occurred in a real-life situation. This is not to say that there will be no tables or figures. But in large part you describe and interpret what you observed and communicate the information to the reader by means of the written word. Be careful, do not turn the report into a mere reportage of what you observed.

Suppose you carried out a one-month nonparticipant observational study on the social behaviour of a class of "gifted" high-school students. You would not only *describe* what you saw, but also *discuss* what you saw. Let's say you gradually noted a different pattern in the behaviour of the teachers that seemed to be connected to which students they were interacting with. What did you observe? What was the behaviour of the teachers when they interacted with male students and with female students? If there were definite differences, what were they? Based on what you observed, why do you think there were differences in their behaviour? The reader has to understand what you observed, and how you interpret your observations.

The organization of this section will partly depend on the particular type of qualitative study you are describing. For example, say your study was on how one becomes accepted into a group of gifted high-school students. You might choose to give a chronological account of the process of becoming accepted by the group. You may also want to break down the description of the process into stages and describe and discuss what occurs at each stage.

Qualitative research involves keeping extensive field notes, which may also include direct quotations. You may find that in some instances you want to include direct quotations, either from your field notes or from participants. In either case, make sure it is clear to the readers that these are separate from your discussion of them. One suggestion is to indent and single space quotations that are lengthy.

In describing a place or people make sure that you do not identify them. In the study on the gifted high-school students, you might choose simply to refer to it as a high school in a large metropolitan city, which in your study is called City High. Similarly, do not identify the people in the study by name.

Discussion and Conclusion

Now that the readers have been told all they need to know about your research, you need to tell them what your main conclusion is. And since there is undoubtedly more to learn about the issue, you may suggest directions for future research.

What have you concluded about the research question or hypothesis? Should the hypothesis be accepted or rejected, or is there no clear evidence? What is your answer to the research question? What do the results say about the larger issue of which your research was a small part?

Suppose the research question or objective was to find out whether there was enough support among students to justify setting up a new student club. The conclusion would state whether students were for or against setting up the club. But perhaps the results showed that social science students expressed more interest than pure and applied science students. You may want to also mention this in your conclusion. Finally, is there enough overall support to justify setting up the new club?

Suppose the study was to test a hypothesis derived from a theory on child development. Assume the hypothesis was that four-year-olds who have siblings are more cooperative than those who have no siblings. The conclusion would state whether or not you found support for the hypothesis. It is also possible that from the data collected you are unable to arrive at a clear decision. That in itself is a conclusion. Next, ask yourself what your conclusion about the hypothesis says about the theory of child development. Does it lend support to the theory? Should the theory be modified?

After you have drawn conclusions about your findings, you will want to briefly consider suggestions for future research. The conclusion was restricted by the limitations of your research. How could future research overcome some of these limitations? Ask yourself how you would do the study all over again, if you had the time and resources. Would you focus on the same hypothesis? Would you operationalize the variables differently? Would you take into account other variables, such as age, ethnic background, or marital status? Would you select the same research method? Your suggestions are helpful, since no study is the final word on an issue. Your work contributes to the accumulation of knowledge about the issue. It becomes part of the existing research, which guides future research.

References or Works Cited

Although the research process follows the same basic steps, the various disciplines use different documentation styles. If the report is for a course, you may want to discuss with your professor which is the preferred style for the course. You can also find out what is the more widely used approach in your discipline by looking at a leading journal in your discipline (see Box 1.3 for names of such journals). Whatever style you use, be consistent throughout your report.

There exist two commonly used documentation styles, one recommended by the **American Psychological Association (APA)** and the other by the **Modern Languages Association (MLA)**. The more widely used in the social sciences is the APA style. Examples of in-text citations for the APA and MLA styles are provided in Box 10.4.

Although the APA and the MLA recommend different bibliographic styles, the essential information on the sources is virtually the same. For example, both require the name of the author, title, place and date of publication, and publisher. Further, both list the sources alphabetically by the author's last name and place the information on a separate page after the text of the report and before any appendices. The APA entitles the section **"References"** and the MLA entitles it **"Works Cited."** Examples of both styles are provided in Box 10.5.

BOX 10.5

References and Works Cited

Both the APA and MLA styles list the sources in alphabetical order by the last name of the author and if there is no author by the first word of the title (other than "The," "An," or "A"). The list appears at the end of the report and starts a new page with the appropriate heading. The list of works is titled "References" in the APA style and "Works Cited" in the MLA style. The following models show the forms of the APA and MLA styles.

SINGLE AUTHOR

APA Style
The information usually includes the author's last name, the initials of the author's other names, the year of publication in parentheses, the title of the book, the place (in most cases the city) of publication, and the publisher.

> Newman, P. C. (1995). *The Canadian revolution, 1985–1995: From deference to defiance.* Toronto: Penguin Books.

MLA Style
The information given is the author's last name followed by the first name, the title and subtitle, the place of publication, the publisher, and the date.

> Newman, Peter C. *The Canadian Revolution, 1985–1995: From Deference to Defiance.* Toronto: Penguin Books, 1995.

For both the APA and MLA styles the place of publication is usually the city of publication followed by a colon. But more information is provided if the city is not well known or if its name can be confused with another one elsewhere, such as London, Ontario, with London, England. You would then write the name of the city followed by a comma, the name of the province or country, and a colon (e.g., London, ON:).

TWO OR MORE AUTHORS

Present the names of the authors in the order in which they appear on the title page.

APA Style
The initials only are used for the first names. The names of the authors are joined by "&". For example:

> Gagnon, A., & Montcalm, M. B. (1989). *Quebec: Beyond the quiet revolution.* Scarborough, ON: Nelson Canada.

MLA Style
For the first author only, provide the last name followed by the first name. Separate the names of the authors by commas.

> Gagnon, Alain, and Mary Beth Montcalm. *Quebec: Beyond the Quiet Revolution.* Scarborough, ON: Nelson Canada, 1989.

AN EDITED BOOK

If you refer to an edited book (e.g., a book that contains articles by various authors), but not to a specific author in the book, then the book is listed according to the name of the editor.

APA Style

> Hinch, R. (Ed.). (1992). *Debates in Canadian society.* Scarborough, ON: Nelson Canada.

MLA Style

Hinch, Ronald, ed., *Debates in Canadian Society*. Scarborough, ON: Nelson Canada, 1992.

AN ARTICLE IN AN EDITED BOOK

If you refer to an article that is in an edited book, then list the article by its author's name.

APA Style

Darroch, G. A. Another look at ethnicity, stratification and social mobility in Canada. (1992). In R. Hinch (Ed.), *Debates in Canadian society* (pp. 60-70). Scarborough, ON: Nelson Canada.

MLA Style

Darroch, Gordon A. "Another Look at Ethnicity, Stratification, and Social Mobility in Canada." *Debates in Canadian Society*. Ed. Ronald Hinch. Scarborough, ON: Nelson Canada, 1992. 60-70.

AN ARTICLE IN AN ACADEMIC JOURNAL

An article in an academic journal is listed by the author's last name. The name of the journal is underlined and followed by a comma.

APA Style
The volume of the journal is underlined and the number of the journal is placed in parentheses followed by a comma and the pages of the article. For example:

Evans, P. M. (1993). From workfare to the social contract: Implications for Canada of recent U.S. welfare reforms. *Canadian Public Policy, 19* (1), 54-67.

MLA Style
The volume of the journal is followed by a period and the number of the journal.

Evans, Patricia M. "From Workfare to the Social Contract: Implications for Canada of Recent U.S. Welfare Reforms." *Canadian Public Policy 19*.1 (1993): 54-67.

AN ARTICLE IN A POPULAR MAGAZINE

APA Style

Cook, P. (1996, January). Brave new worlds. *Report on Business Magazine,* pp. 28-31.

MLA style

Cook, Peter. "Brave New Worlds." *Report on Business Magazine* January 1996: 28-31.

REFERENCES OR WORK CITED

The alphabetical list of the sources is entitled "References" in the APA style and "Works Cited" in the MLA style.

APA Style

References

Cook, P. (1996, January). Brave new worlds. *Report on Business Magazine,* pp. 28-31.

Darroch, G. A. Another look at ethnicity, stratification, and social mobility in Canada. (1992). In R. Hinch (Ed.), *Debates in Canadian society.* (pp. 60-70). Scarborough, ON: Nelson Canada.

Evans, P. M. (1993). From workfare to the social contract: Implications for Canada of recent U.S. welfare reforms. *Canadian Public Policy, 19,* (1), 54-67.

Gagnon, A., & Montcalm, M. B. (1989). *Quebec: Beyond the quiet revolution.* Scarborough, ON: Nelson Canada.

Hinch, R. (Ed.). (1992). *Debates in Canadian society.* Scarborough, ON: Nelson Canada.

Newman, P. C. (1995). *The Canadian revolution, 1985-1995: From deference to defiance.* Toronto: Penguin Books.

MLA Style

Works Cited

Cook, Peter. "Brave New Worlds." *Report on Business Magazine* January 1996: 28-31.

Darroch, Gordon A. "Another Look at Ethnicity, Stratification, and Social Mobility in Canada." *Debates in Canadian Society.* Ed. Ronald Hinch. Scarborough, ON: Nelson Canada, 1992. 60-70.

Evans, Patricia M. "From Workfare to the Social Contract: Implications for Canada of Recent U.S. Welfare Reforms." *Canadian Public Policy* 19.1 (1993): 54-67.

Gagnon, Alain, and Mary Beth Montcalm. *Quebec: Beyond the Quiet Revolution.* Scarborough, ON: Nelson Canada, 1989.

Hinch, Ronald, ed., *Debates in Canadian Society.* Scarborough, ON: Nelson Canada, 1992.

Newman, Peter C. *The Canadian Revolution, 1985-1995: From Deference to Defiance.* Toronto: Penguin Books, 1995.

BOX 10.6

Checklist: Research Report

[ ] TITLE

[ ] Title is short, precise, and appropriate for the readers of my report

[ ] Title page includes my name and other relevant information, such as the number of the course and professor's name

[ ] INTRODUCTION AND LITERATURE REVIEW

[ ] Clearly states the aim, issue, or hypothesis

[ ] Places the research in the context of other research and ideas

[ ] Points out any ethical issues that arose and explains how they were resolved

[ ] RESEARCH DESIGN

[ ] States the design selected and explains why it was selected

[ ] Discusses how the data was collected

Quantitative Study

[ ] Explains how the variables were measured

[ ] Describes the population and type of sample and explains how the sample was selected.

Qualitative Study

[ ] Clearly explains how I gained access to the information (data)

[ ] Points out the factors that influenced the selection of the individuals, groups, documents, events, etc., that were studied

[ ] DATA ANALYSIS

Quantitative Data

[ ] Tables and graphs are properly labelled; in appropriate formats; and discussed in the text

[ ] Provides appropriate statistical analysis

[ ] Interprets the findings

Qualitative Data

[ ] Tables and graphs (if included) are properly labelled and discussed in the text

[ ] Describes the social organization or social process (e.g., roles, stages in the process of becoming part of a group, relationships among the people observed, etc.)

[ ] Interprets the findings

[ ] DISCUSSION AND CONCLUSION

[ ] Highlights the main findings

[ ] Indicates the strengths and weaknesses of the research

[ ] Draws out the practical implications or implications for further study

[ ] REFERENCES AND CITATIONS

[ ] Uses a proper and consistent form of documenting sources

[ ] Reference section is placed immediately after the text

[ ] Sources in reference section are listed in alphabetical order according to author's last name

[ ] Provides complete bibliographic citations of the sources cited in the report

WHAT NEXT?

Recall that when you thought of an interesting researchable issue, your first step was to explore what other research existed on the issue. You then clarified your initial issue and built on the research of others, thereby making a contribution to our understanding of the social world. But your quest to better understand the issue does not end there. As you noted in the conclusion of the report, there is more to know. Many other research journeys will be undertaken to help us better understand the social world.

We hope that this book has given you a sense of the serious effort and thrill that goes into social science research. The information you have gained has, we hope, made you more critical of what is acceptable as social science research. More importantly, we hope you will be able to carry out your own research and experience for yourself the challenge and exhilaration of doing social research. Research is the very foundation of the social sciences; as one research project ends, another begins. Enjoy!

WHAT YOU HAVE LEARNED

- Before we draw conclusions, we need to take note of the initial research objective, the findings, the interpretations of the findings, and the limitations of the study.

- Before drafting the report, we need to consider who will read it and adapt the language and style to that audience.

- All research reports include the following parts: Title, Introduction and Literature Review, Research Design, Data Analysis, Discussion and Conclusion, and References (or Works Cited).

- Although different types of research reports exist, the main difference is how much importance is given to the various sections.

- It is essential to use a proper form of documenting sources and to provide a complete bibliographic citation of the sources mentioned in the report.

KEY WORDS

limitations

conclusion

research report

audience

title

in-text citations

APA style

MLA style

references

works cited

REVIEW QUESTIONS

1. What is the aim and purpose of writing a research report?
2. Why should you take into account the audience of your report?
3. What are the main sections of a research report?
4. Why is it important to properly document the sources and provide a reference list at the end of the report?
5. Why should you take into account the limitations of your research?
6. What are some differences between writing a quantitative data analysis and a qualitative data analysis?
7. What should you include in the conclusion of the report?

RECOMMENDED READINGS

Hult, C. A. (1996). *Researching and writing in the social sciences*. Needham Heights, MA: Allyn and Bacon.

An interdisciplinary text that includes information on library resources, briefly discusses various research methods, and mainly focuses on planning and writing research papers in different disciplines. It also provides samples of research papers.

Seyler, D. U. (1993). *Doing research: The complete research paper guide*. New York: McGraw-Hill.

The text provides an extensive overview of carrying out library research and writing the research paper. It includes various sample student papers illustrating the documentation styles of the APA and the MLA.

References

Becker, H. S. (1958). Problems of inference and proof in participation observation. *American Sociological Review, 23*, 652–660.

Bibby, R. W., & Posterski, D. C. (1992). *Teen trends: A nation in motion.* Toronto: Stoddart.

Cantril, H. (1940). *The invasion from Mars.* Princeton, NJ: Princeton University Press.

Freeman, D. (1983). *Margaret Mead and Samoa: The making and unmaking of an anthropological myth.* Cambridge, MA: Harvard University Press.

Geertz, C. (1973). *The Interpretation of Cultures.* New York: Basic Books.

Ginzberg, E., & Henry, F. (1984/1985, Winter). Confirming discrimination in the Toronto labour market. *Current Reading in Race Relations, 2*, 23–28.

Goffman, E. (1962). *Asylums: Essays on the social situation of mental patients and other inmates.* Chicago: Aldine.

Griffin, J. H. (1976). *Black like me.* New York: New American Library.

Hall, E. T. (1959). *The silent language.* Garden City, NY: Doubleday.

Jorgenson, D. L. (1989). *Participant observation: A methodology for human studies.* Beverly Hills, CA: Sage.

Lewis, O. (1951). *Life in a Mexican village: Tepoztlan restudied.* Urbana, IL: University of Illinois Press.

Milgram, S. (1974). *Obedience to authority.* New York: Harper and Row.

Millar, W. A trend to a healthier lifestyle. (1994). In *Canadian social trends: A Canadian studies reader* (Vol. 2, pp. 91–93). Toronto: Thompson Educational Publishing.

Parliament, J. B. Labour force trends: Two decades in review. (1994). In *Canadian social trends: A Canadian studies reader* (Vol. 2, pp. 255–258). Toronto: Thompson Educational Publishing.

Perrow, C. (1984). *Normal accidents: Living with high risk technologies.* New York: Basic Books.

Sacco, V., & Johnson, H. Household property crime. (1994). In *Canadian social trends: A Canadian studies reader* (Vol. 2, pp. 393–395). Toronto: Thompson Educational Publishing.

Schachter, S. (1959). *The psychology of affiliation: Experimental studies of the sources of gregariousness.* Stanford, CA: Stanford University Press.

Statistics Canada (1992). *Guide to labour force survey* (Catalogue No. 71–528). Ottawa: Minister of Industry, Science and Technology.

Strike, C. Aids in Canada. (1990). In C. Makie and K. Thompson (Eds.), *Canadian social trends* (pp. 83–85). Toronto: Thompson Educational Publishing.

Thompson, E. P. (1963). *The making of the English working class.* New York: Vintage.

Weber, M. (1958). *The Protestant ethic and the spirit of capitalism* (T. Parsons, Trans.). New York: Charles Scribner's Sons. (Original work published 1904–1905)

Young, P. (1994, July). Sex survey: Canadian women tell all! *Flare,* pp. 34–40.

Bibliography

Agnew, N. M., & Pyke, S. W. (1994). The science game: An introduction to research in the social sciences (6th ed.). Englewood Cliffs, NJ: Prentice-Hall.

Alonso, W., & Starr, P. (1987). *The politics of numbers.* New York: Russell Sage Foundation.

Anderson, B. F. (1966). *The psychology experiment: An introduction to the scientific method.* Belmont, CA: Brooks/Cole.

Aries, P. (1962). *Centuries of childhood: A social history of family life* (R. Baldick, Trans.). New York: Vintage.

Babbie, E. R. (1986). *Observing ourselves: Essays in social research.* Belmont, CA: Wadsworth.

Babbie, E. R. (1990). *Survey research methods* (2nd ed.). Belmont, CA: Wadsworth.

Babbie, E. R. (1995). *The practice of social research* (7th ed.). Belmont, CA: Wadsworth.

Baker, T. L. (1994). *Doing social research* (2nd ed.). New York: McGraw-Hill.

Barnes, J. A. (1979). *Who should know what? Social science, privacy and ethics.* New York: Cambridge University Press.

Bart, P., & Frankel, L. (1986). *The student sociologist's handbook* (4th ed.). New York: Random House.

Baxter-Moore, N., Terrance, C., & Church, R. (1994). *Studying politics: An introduction to argument and analysis.* Toronto: Copp-Clark.

Becker, H. S. (1986). *Writing for social scientists: How to start and finish your thesis, book, or article.* Chicago: Chicago University Press.

Benjafield, J. G. (1994). *Thinking critically about research methods.* Boston: Allyn and Bacon.

Berger, J. (1973). *Ways of seeing.* New York: Viking.

Berry, J. W., & Ponce, J. A. (Eds.). (1994). *Ethnicity and culture in Canada: The research landscape.* Toronto: University of Toronto Press.

Bertaux, D. (Ed.). (1981). *Biography and society: The life history approach in the social sciences.* Newbury Park, CA: Sage.

Blalock, H. M. (1960). *Social statistics.* New York: McGraw-Hill.

Bloch, M. (1953). *The historian's craft* (P. Putnam, Trans.). New York: Vintage.

Bowen, R. W. (1992). *Graph it! How to make, read, and interpret graphs.* Englewood Cliffs, NJ: Prentice-Hall.

Bowers, J. W., & Courtright, J. A. (1984). *Communication research methods.* Glenview, IL: Scott, Freeman and Company.

Bulmer, M. (Ed.). (1982). *Social research ethics*. London: Macmillan.

Burgess, R. G. (Ed.). (1982). *Field research*. Boston: George Allen and Unwin.

Burman, P. (1988). *Killing time, losing ground: Experiences of unemployment*. Toronto: Wall and Thompson.

Busha, C. H., & Harter, S. P. (1980). *Research methods in librarianship: Techniques and interpretation*. New York: Academic Press.

Campbell, D. T., & Stanley, J. C. (1963). *Experimental and quasi-experimental designs for research*. Chicago: Rand McNally.

Chadwick, B. A., Bahr, H. M., & Albrecht, S. L. (1984). *Social science research methods*. Englewood Cliffs, NJ: Prentice-Hall.

Cole, R. L. (1980). *Introduction to political inquiry*. New York: Collier Macmillan.

Cole, S. (1980). *The sociological method: An introduction to the science of sociology*. Boston: Houghton Mifflin.

Converse, J. M., & Schuman, H. (1974). *Conversations at random: Survey research as interviewers see it*. New York: Wiley.

Cook, T. D., & Campbell, D. T. (1979). *Quasi-experimentation: Design and analysis issues for field settings*. Chicago: Rand McNally.

Cooper, H. M. (1989). *Integrating research: A guide for literature reviews*. Newbury Park, CA: Sage.

Cozby, P. C. (1993). *Methods in behavioral research* (5th ed.). Mountain View, CA: Mayfield.

Cuba, L. (1993). *A short guide to writing about social science* (2nd ed.). New York: HarperCollins.

Curry, T. J., & Clarke, A. C. (1977). *Introducing visual sociology*. Dubuque, IA: Kendall/Hunt.

Dale, A., Arber, S., & Procter, M. (1988). *Doing secondary analysis*. Boston: Unwin Hymen.

Davenport, P. (1988). Economics. In *The Canadian encyclopedia* (2nd ed., pp. 648–650). Edmonton: Hurtig.

Davis, J. (1971). *Elementary survey analysis*. Englewood Cliffs, NJ: Prentice-Hall.

Denzin, N. K. (1989). *The research act: A theoretical introduction to sociological methods* (3rd ed.). Englewood Cliffs, NJ: Prentice-Hall.

Dey, I. (1993). *Qualitative data analysis: A user friendly guide for social scientists*. New York: Routledge.

Dixon, B. R., Bouma, G. D., & Atkinson, G. B. J. (1987). *A handbook of social science research: A comprehensive and practical guide for students*. New York: Oxford University Press.

Douglas, J. (1985). *Creative interviewing*. Beverly Hills, CA: Sage.

Eichler, M. (1988). *Nonsexist research methods: A practical guide*. Boston: George Allen and Unwin.

Emerson, R. M. (Ed.). (1983). *Contemporary field research*. Boston: Little, Brown.

Festinger, L., Reicken, H. W., & Schachter, S. (1956). *When prophecy fails*. New York: Harper and Row.

Fetterman, D. M. (1989). *Ethnography step by step*. Newbury Park, CA: Sage.

Filstead, W. J. (Ed.). (1970). *Qualitative methodology*. Chicago: Markham.

Freedman, D., Pisani, R., Purves, R., & Adhikari, A. (1991). *Statistics* (2nd ed.). New York: W.W. Norton.

Giere, R. N. (1991). *Understanding scientific reasoning* (3rd ed.). Fort Worth, TX: Holt, Reinhart and Winston.

Giffen, P. J., Official rates of crime and delinquency. (1976). In W. T. McGrath (Ed.), *Crime and its treatment in Canada* (2nd ed.). Toronto: Macmillan.

Golde, P. (Ed.). (1992). *Women in the field: Anthropological experiences* (2nd ed.). Berkeley, CA: University of California Press.

Goldman, R. (1992). *Reading ads socially*. New York: Routledge.

Gordon, R. L. (1980). *Interviewing: Strategy, techniques, and tactics* (3rd ed.). Homewood, IL: Dorsey.

Grabb, E. G. (1990). *Theories of social inequality: Classical and contemporary theorists* (2nd ed.). Toronto: Holt, Rinehart and Winston.

Graham, A. (1994). *Teach yourself statistics*. London: NTC Publishing.

Granger, L. (1988). Psychology. In *The Canadian encyclopedia* (2nd ed., pp. 1778–1779). Edmonton: Hurtig.

Gray, G., & Guppy, N. (1994). *Successful surveys: Research methods and practice*. Toronto: Harcourt Brace.

Grimes, M. D. (1991). *Class in twentieth-century American sociology: An analysis of theories and measurement strategies*. New York: Praeger.

Gubrium, J. F. (Ed.). (1989). *The politics of field research: Beyond enlightenment*. Newbury Park, CA: Sage.

Harvey, L., & MacDonald, M. (1993). *Doing sociology: A practical introduction*. London: Macmillan.

Heller, F. (Ed.). *The use and abuse of social science*. Beverly Hills, CA: Sage.

Hollander, A. (1978). *Seeing through clothes*. New York: Viking.

Holsti, O. R. (1969). *Content analysis for the social sciences and humanities*. Reading, MA: Addison-Wesley.

Homan, R. (1980). The ethics of covert methods. *British Journal of Sociology, 31*, 46–57.

Hoover, K. R. (1992). *The elements of social scientific thinking* (5th ed.). New York: St. Martin's Press.

Hoy, C. (1989). *Margin of error: Pollsters and the manipulation of Canadian politics.* Toronto: Key Porter.

Huff, D. (1954). *How to lie with statistics.* New York: W.W. Norton.

Hult, C. A. (1996). *Researching and writing in the social sciences.* Needham Heights, MA: Allyn and Bacon.

Humphreys, Laud. (1975). *Tearoom trade: Impersonal sex in public places* (Enlarged ed.). Chicago: Aldine.

Hunt, L. (Ed.). (1989). *The new cultural history.* Berkeley, CA: University of California Press.

Hunt, M. (1985). *Profiles of social research: The scientific study of human interactions.* New York: Russell Sage Foundation.

Hyman, H. H. (Ed.). (1991). *Taking society's measure: A personal history of survey research.* New York: Russell Sage Foundation.

Jackson, W. (1995). *Methods: Doing social research.* Scarborough, ON: Prentice Hall.

Katz, J. (1972). *Experimentation with human beings.* New York: Russell Sage.

Katzer, J., Cook, K. H., & Crouch, W. W. (1982). *Evaluating information: A guide for users of social science research* (2nd ed.). Reading, MA: Addison-Wesley.

Keegan, J. (1995). *The battle for history: Re-fighting World War Two.* Toronto: Vintage Books.

Kirby, S., & McKenna, K. (1989). *Experience research social change: Methods from the margins.* Toronto: Garamond Press.

Kranzler, G., & Moursund, J. (1996). *Statistics for the terrified.* Englewood Cliffs, NJ: Prentice-Hall.

Krippendorf, K. (1980). *Content analysis: An introduction to its methodology.* Beverly Hills, CA: Sage.

Levin, J., & Fox, J. A. (1991). *Elementary statistics in social research* (5th ed.). New York: HarperCollins.

Lewis, G. H. (Ed.). (1975). *Fist-fights in the kitchen: Manners and methods in social research.* Pacific Palisades, CA: Goodyear.

Liebow, E. (1993). *Tell them who I am: The lives of homeless women.* New York: Free Press.

Light, R. J., & Pillemer, D. B. (1984). *Summing up: The science of reviewing research.* Cambridge, MA: Harvard University Press.

Lofland, J., & Lofland, L. (1984). *Analyzing social settings* (2nd ed.). Belmont, CA: Wadsworth.

Lowenthal, D. (1985). *The past is a foreign country.* New York: Cambridge University Press.

Marsh, C. (1982). *The survey method: The contribution of surveys to sociological explanation*. Boston: George Allen and Unwin.

Marsh, L. (1993). *Canadians in and out of work: A survey of economic classes and their relation to the labour market*. Toronto: Canadian Scholars' Press.

Martin, D. W. (1991). *Doing psychology experiments*. Monterey, CA: Brooks/Cole.

McCall, G., & Simmons, J. L. (Eds.). (1969). *Issues in participant observation research*. Reading, MA: Addison-Wesley.

McDiarmid, G. (1971). *Teaching prejudice: A content analysis of social studies textbooks authorized for use in Ontario*. Toronto: Ontario Institute for Studies in Education.

McGuigan, F. J. (1990). *Experimental psychology: Methods of research* (5th ed.). Englewood Cliffs, NJ: Prentice-Hall.

McKie, C., & Thompson, K. (Eds.). (1990). *Canadian Social Trends*. Toronto: Thompson Educational Publishing.

McKillop, A. B. (1988). Historiography in English. In *The Canadian encyclopedia* (2nd ed., pp. 993–994). Edmonton: Hurtig.

Miles, M. B., & Huberman, A. M. (1984). *Qualitative data analysis*. Beverly Hills, CA: Sage.

Miller, D. C. (1991). *Handbook of research design and social measurement*. Newbury Park, CA: Sage.

Mills, C. W. (1959). *The sociological imagination*. New York: Oxford University Press.

Monette, D. R., Sullivan, T. J., & DeJong, C. R. (1994). *Applied social research: Tool for the human services* (3rd ed.). Fort Worth, TX: Harcourt Brace.

Moore, D. S. (1991). *Statistics: Concepts and Controversies* (3rd ed.). New York: W. H. Freeman and Company.

Neale, J. M. (1973). *Science and behavior: An introduction to methods of research*. Englewood Cliffs, NJ: Prentice-Hall.

Neuman, W. L. (1994). *Social research methods: Qualitative and quantitative approaches* (2nd ed.). Boston: Allyn and Bacon.

Newman, O. (1972). *Defensible space: People and design in the violent city*. London: Architectural Press.

Northey, M., & Tepperman, L. (1986). *Making sense in the social sciences: A student's guide to research, writing, and style*. Toronto: Oxford University Press.

Outhwaite, W., & Bottomore, T. (Eds.). (1993). *The Blackwell dictionary of twentieth-century social thought*. Oxford: Blackwell Publishers.

Palys, T. (1992). *Research decisions: Quantitative and qualitative perspectives*. Toronto: Harcourt Brace Jovanovich.

Paulos, J. A. (1988). *Innumeracy: Mathematical illiteracy and its consequences.* New York: Hill and Wang.

Platek, R., Pierre, F. K., & Stevens, P. (1985). *Development and design of survey questionnaires* (Catalogue No. 12-519). Ottawa: Statistics Canada.

Porter, T. M. (1986). *The rise of statistical thinking: 1820–1900.* Princeton, NJ: Princeton University Press.

Preston, R. J., & Tremblay, M. A. (1988). Anthropology. In *The Canadian encyclopedia* (2nd ed., pp. 82–83). Edmonton: Hurtig.

Rabinow, P., & Sullivan, W. (Eds.). (1979). *Interpretative social science.* Berkeley, CA: University of California Press.

Rathje, W. L. (1989). The three faces of garbage: Measurements, perceptions, behaviours. *Journal of Resource Management and Technology, 17,* 14–71.

Reeves, C. C. (1992). *Quantitative research for the behavioural sciences.* New York: Wiley.

Rehner, J. (1994). *Strategies for critical thinking.* Boston: Houghton Mifflin.

Reinharz, S. (1992). *Feminist methods in social research.* New York: Oxford University Press.

Reiter, E. (1991). *Making fast food: From the frying pan into the fryer.* Montreal: McGill-Queens University Press.

Rosenberg, K. M., & Daly, H. B. (1993). *Foundations of behavioral research: A basic question approach.* Fort Worth, TX: Harcourt Brace.

Rosenthal, R. (1976). *Experimenter effects in behavioural research.* New York: Irvington.

Rowntree, D. (1981). *Statistics without tears: A primer for non-mathematicians.* New York: Charles Scribner's Sons.

Roy, F. (1988). Historiography in French. In *The Canadian encyclopedia* (2nd ed., pp. 992–993). Edmonton: Hurtig.

Rutman, L. (Ed.). (1984). *Evaluation research methods: A basic guide* (2nd ed.). Beverly Hills, CA: Sage Publications.

Sanders, W. B. (1983). *The conduct of social research.* New York: CBS College Publishing.

Satin, A., & Shastry, W. (1993). *Survey sampling: A non-mathematical guide* (2nd ed., Catalogue No. 12-602). Ottawa: Statistics Canada.

Saxe, L., & Fine, M. (1981). *Social experiments: Methods for design and evaluation.* Beverly Hills, CA: Sage.

Schachter, S. (1959). *The psychology of affiliation: Experimental studies of the sources of gregariousness.* Stanford, CA: Stanford University Press.

Sechrest, L. (Ed.). (1979). *Unobtrusive measurement today.* San Francisco: Jossey-Bass.

Seyler, D. U. (1993). *Doing research: The complete research paper guide*. New York: McGraw-Hill.

Shaffir, W. B., & Stebbins, R. A. (Eds.). (1991). *Experiencing fieldwork: An inside view of qualitative research*. Newbury Park, CA: Sage.

Shaffir, W. B., Stebbins, R., & Turowetz, A. (Eds.). (1980). *Fieldwork experience*. New York: St. Martin's Press.

Shively, W. P. (1990). *The craft of political research*. Englewood Cliffs, NJ: Prentice-Hall.

Sicher, J. E. (1992). *Planning ethically responsible research: A guide for social science students*. Newbury Park, CA: Sage.

Silverman, D. (1993). *Interpreting Qualitative Data*. Newbury Park, CA: Sage.

Sitton, T., Mehaffy, G., & Davis, Jr., O. L. (1983). *Oral history*. Austin: University of Texas Press.

Slonim, M. J. (1966). *Sampling*. New York: Simon and Schuster.

Sommer, B., & Sommer, R. (1991). *A practical guide to behavioural research: Tools and techniques*. New York: Oxford University Press.

Stern, P. C. (1979). *Evaluating social science research*. New York: Oxford University Press.

Stewart, D. W. (1984). *Secondary research: Information sources and methods*. Beverly Hills, CA: Sage.

Strauss, A. (1987). *Qualitative analysis for social scientists*. New York: Cambridge University Press.

Sudman, S., & Bradburn, N. M. (1983). *Asking questions: A practical guide to questionnaire design*. San Francisco: Jossey-Bass.

Sullivan, T. (1991). *Applied sociology: Research and critical thinking*. New York: Macmillan.

Survey Research Center, Institute for Social Research. (1976). *Interviewer's manual* (Rev. ed.). Ann Arbor: University of Michigan.

Taylor, K. W. (1990). *Social science research: Theory and practice*. Scarborough, ON: Nelson Canada.

Thompson, P. (1978). *The voice of the past: Oral history*. New York: Oxford University Press.

Thomsett, M. C. (1990). *The little black book of business statistics*. New York: American Management Association.

True, J. A. (1989). *Finding out: Conducting and evaluating social research* (2nd ed.). Belmont, CA: Wadsworth.

Tufte, E. R. (1983). *The visual display of quantitative information*. Cheshire, CT: Graphics Press.

Tutty, L. M., Rothery, M. A., & Grinnell, Jr., R. M. (1996). *Qualitative research for social workers*. Boston: Allyn and Bacon.

U. S. Department of Health and Human Services (1992). *Survey measurement of drug use.* Washington, DC: Government Printing Office.

Vallee, F. G. (1988). Social science. In *The Canadian encyclopedia* (2nd ed., p. 2031). Edmonton: Hurtig.

Van Maanen, J. (1988). *Tales of the field: On writing ethnography.* Chicago: University of Chicago Press.

Wagner, J. (Ed.). (1979). *Images of information: Still photography in the social sciences.* Beverly Hills, CA: Sage.

Wargon, S. (1986). Using census data for research on the family in Canada. *Journal of Comparative Family Studies, 3,* 150–158.

Webb, E. T., Campbell, D. T., Schwartz, R. D., Sechrest, L., & Grove, J. B. (1981). *Nonreactive measures in the social sciences.* Boston: Houghton Mifflin.

Weber, R. P. (1985). *Basic content analysis.* Beverly Hills, CA: Sage.

Whitaker, R. (1988). Political science. In *The Canadian encyclopedia* (2nd ed., pp. 1711–1712). Edmonton: Hurtig.

Whyte, D. R., & Vallee, F. G. (1988). Sociology. In *The Canadian encyclopedia* (2nd ed., pp. 2035–2037). Edmonton: Hurtig.

Whyte, W. F., & Whyte, K. K. (1984). *Learning from the field: A guide from experience.* Beverly Hills, CA: Sage.

Williams, B. (1978). *A sampler on sampling.* New York: Wiley.

Williams, F. (1992). *Reasoning with statistics: How to read quantitative research* (4th ed.). Fort Worth, TX: Harcourt Brace Jovanovich.

Williams, G. (1989). Enticing viewers: Sex and violence in *TV Guide* Program Advertisements. *Journalism Quarterly, 66,* 970–973.

Wolf, D. (1991). *The rebels: A brotherhood of outlaw bikers.* Toronto: University of Toronto Press.

Yegidis, B. L., & Weinbach, R. W. (1996). *Research methods for social workers.* Boston: Allyn and Bacon.

Yin, R. K. (1989). *Case study research* (Rev. ed.). Beverly Hills, CA: Sage.

Zeisel, H. (1985). *Say it with figures* (6th ed.). New York: Harper and Row.

Zeller, R., & Carmines, E. G. (1980). *Measurement in the social sciences: The link between theory and data.* New York: Cambridge University Press.

Zimbardo, P. G. (1972). Pathology of imprisonment. *Society, 9,* 4–6.

Zuckerman, H. (1978). Interviewing an ultra-elite. *Public Opinion Quarterly, 36,* 159–175.

Index

To the owner of this book

We hope that you have enjoyed *First Steps: A Guide to Social Research,* and we would like to know as much about your experiences with this text as you would care to offer. Only through your comments and those of others can we learn how to make this a better text for future readers.

School _____ Your instructor's name _____

Course _____ Was the text required? _____ Recommended? _____

1. What did you like the most about *First Steps?*

_____

_____

_____

2. How useful was this text for your course?

_____

_____

_____

3. Do you have any recommendations for ways to improve the next edition of this text?

_____

_____

_____

4. In the space below or in a separate letter, please write any other comments you have about the book. (For example, please feel free to comment on reading level, writing style, terminology, design features, and learning aids.)

_____

_____

_____

Optional

Your name _____ Date _____

May ITP Nelson quote you, either in promotion for *First Steps* or in future publishing ventures?

Yes _____ No _____

Thanks!

You can also send your comments to us via e-mail at
college_arts_hum@nelson.com

PLEASE TAPE SHUT. DO NOT STAPLE.

TAPE SHUT

TAPE SHUT

- - - - - - - - - - FOLD HERE - - - - - - - - - -

I(T)P® Nelson

an International Thomson Publishing company

MAIL ▶ POSTE

Canada Post Corporation
Société canadienne des postes

Postage paid   Port payé
if mailed in Canada   si posté au Canada
Business Reply   Réponse d'affairess

0066102399   01

TAPE SHUT

TAPE SHUT

0066102399-M1K5G4-BR01

ITP NELSON
MARKET AND PRODUCT DEVELOPMENT
P.O. BOX 60223 STN BRN 8
TORONTO ON M7Y 2H1